Strange Eventful Histories

HARVARD-YENCHING INSTITUTE MONOGRAPH SERIES 80

Strange Eventful Histories

Identity, Performance, and Xu Wei's *Four Cries of a Gibbon*

SHIAMIN KWA

Published by the Harvard University Asia Center
Distributed by Harvard University Press
Cambridge (Massachusetts) and London 2012

Printed in the United States of America

The Harvard-Yenching Institute, founded in 1928 and headquartered at Harvard University, is a foundation dedicated to the advancement of higher education in the humanities and social sciences in East and Southeast Asia. The Institute supports advanced research at Harvard by faculty members of certain Asian universities and doctoral studies at Harvard and other universities by junior faculty at the same universities. It also supports East Asian studies at Harvard through contributions to the Harvard-Yenching Library and publication of the *Harvard Journal of Asiatic Studies* and books on premodern East Asian history and literature.

Library of Congress Cataloging-in-Publication Data

Kwa, Shiamin.
Strange eventful histories: identity, performance, and Xu Wei's Four cries of a gibbon / Shiamin Kwa.
p. cm.
Includes bibliographical references and index.
ISBN 978-0-674-06685-4 (acid-free paper) 1. Xu, Wei, 1521-1593. Si sheng yuan. 2. Identity (Philosophical concept) in literature. I. Xu, Wei, 1521-1593. Si sheng yuan. II. Title.
PL2698.H775S735 2012
895.1'24--dc23

2012031801

Index by the author

♾ Printed on acid-free paper

Last figure below indicates year of this printing
21 20 19 18 17 16 15 14 13 12

For Benno and Roo

So when our mortal frame shall be disjoined
The lifeless lump uncoupled from the mind
From sense of grief and pain we shall be free
We shall not feel, because we shall not be.
—Lucretius, "Against the Fear of Death"

The puppets performing before the curtains
are already an illusion.
A painting of puppets moves still further
from reality.
But just consider that the sky
is also a vast curtain:
then which of us is not an actor on this stage?
—Xu Wei, "Painting Inscription for Hangzhou Visitors"

Contents

Acknowledgments xi

Introduction 1

1 Undressing for Success: *The Mad Drummer Plays the Yuyang Triple Rolls (Mi Heng)* 15

2 The Shape of Things: *Zen Master Yu Has a Dream of Cuixiang* 37

3 The Namesake: Costumes of Words in *Mulan* 63

4 The Woman Who Took Herself for Himself: Truth, Evidence, and Identity in *The Girl Graduate* 84

Conclusion 105

Appendixes

I *The Mad Drummer Plays the Yuyang Triple Rolls* 117

II *Zen Master Yu Has a Dream of Cuixiang* 139

III *The Female Mulan Joins the Army in Place of Her Father* 169

IV *The Girl Graduate Rejects the Female Phoenix and Gains the Male Phoenix* 189

Reference Matter

Notes 243

Bibliography 259

Index 269

Acknowledgments

I owe a debt of gratitude to Wai-yee Li for first introducing me to *Zen Master Yu*, and then reading subsequent drafts of the manuscript many times over, explaining fine details that I could never have caught. There could be no finer advisor than Wilt Idema, who survived my nervous emails of despair and tolerated my abject ignorance while teaching me how to read vernacular fiction and drama. When I moved away from Cambridge, he cleared his schedule for my day-long visits and patiently went through my translations with me line by line, and then treated me to french fries at Charlie's Kitchen for sustenance during breaks.

I would like to thank others who contributed comments at different stages of this manuscript's production. I thank Rick Todhunter at Hackett Publishing for editing an earlier version of the *Mulan* chapter and translation. Maghiel van Crevel, Michel Hockx, and Tian Yuan Tan edited and commented on an earlier version of the chapter on *Zen Master Yu*. I would like to thank this book's editors: Will Hammell, who shepherded the book through the submissions process, and Kristen Wanner, who oversaw every stage of the editing. I would also like to thank the two anonymous reviewers of this book, whose questions, criticism, and suggestions answered many of the lingering questions I had about tricky lines in the plays and inspired me to think more carefully about what I was trying to argue. Though at this point it feels like this book is more the product of crowd-sourcing, the one area where I gladly take full responsibility is in the errors and faults that remain in these pages.

Additionally, I would like to thank Diana Abouali, Sarah Allan, Shar'-Lin Anderson, Deborah Barrett, Susan Blader, Bob Dostal, Tom

Gauld, Hank Glassman, Paul Goldin, Lisa Johnston, Martin Kern, Nadine Knight, Julia Lee, Victor Mair, Steve Owen, Sharrona Pearl, Lino Pertile, Michael Puett, David Rosen, Atsuko Sakaki, Emi Shimokawa, Paul Smith, Karen Thornber, and Bill Todd for their help along the way. Special thanks go as well to the staff and librarians at Baker Library, Fondren Library, Widener Library, Van Pelt Library, and, especially, Yenching Library.

Finally, I thank my family: Shialing Kwa, Stephen Powell, and Helene and Daniel Roses. Most of all, I know that I could not have started, written, nor finished this book without the constant support of Robert Roses.

John Adams wrote in a letter to his wife Abigail, "I must study politics and war, that my sons may have the liberty to study mathematics and philosophy, natural history and naval architecture, in order to give their children a right to study painting, poetry, music, architecture, tapestry, and porcelain." Many thanks go to my parents, Lucy and Boo Hoe Kwa, and their parents, Fanny and Tchan-Wing Tze, and Seok Hui and Eng Bee Kwa: they all did the hard work, so that I could study poetry and music.

S.K., June 2012

Strange Eventful Histories

Introduction

I CELEBRATE myself, and sing myself,
And what I assume you shall assume,
For every atom belonging to me as good belongs to you.
—*Walt Whitman "Song of Myself"*

If you want to know the heartbreaking cry of the gibbon,
You must make yourself into a gibbon.[1]
—*Xu Wei*

Even if I could by gradual degrees be transformed into a bat, nothing in my present constitution enables me to imagine what the experiences of such a future stage of myself thus metamorphosed would be like. The best evidence would come from the experiences of bats, if we only knew what they were like. So if extrapolation from our own case is involved in the idea of what it is like to be a bat, the extrapolation must be incompletable. We cannot form more than a schematic conception of what it is like.

—*Thomas Nagel*

Spontaneous. Unbridled. Direct. Such adjectives describe the work of Ming dynasty artist Xu Wei 徐渭 (1521–93). The paintings and calligraphy he left arrest our attention. Grapes bend boughs with their pregnant weight. Spiky bamboo leaves and paddles of lotus pads bloom outward in ink washes of the darkest of blacks and the most transparent of grays. One cannot help but imagine his hand at work: the brush strokes are simultaneously so specific and individual, yet they project an image both immediate and familiar. The artist transmits what is in his mind through spontaneous expression (*xieyi* 寫意). His pseudonyms and sobriquets—Xu Wenchang (需文長), Mountain Man of the Heavenly Pond (Tianchi shanren 天池山人), Heaven Water Moon (Tianshuiyue

天水月), and the Mountain Man of the Green Vines (Qingteng shanren 清藤山人) are among the variations—although not uncommonly numerous for a Ming dynasty (1368–1644) man of letters, carry great significance because of the way that they reflect his incredibly productive and varied life. Not only was he an artist, but he was also a poet, an essayist, a dramatist, a drama critic, and a calligrapher. In a historical period replete with exceptional figures and iconoclasts, Xu Wei stood out among them all.[2]

Xu Wei's influence has been so lasting that by the early decades of the twentieth century, he had become identified as one of three popular archetypes in folklore. Known by his style, "Xu Wenchang" became interchangeable with the "clever male," even as the other two archetypes, "foolish son-in-law" and "clever-tongued wife," were represented solely by their generic descriptions.[3] This cleverness and demonstrations of quick wit separate the man of letters, Xu Wei, from the legendary figure "Xu Wenchang" in the popular imagination.[4] Upheld as a sort of patron saint of the unbridled eccentric in the late imperial period, he asserted a near-supernatural anxiety of influence on successive generations of Chinese would-be iconoclasts. Because they sought to emulate his individualism and freedom from style constraints, they were also haunted by the possibility that this emulation might become yet another form of imitation. One of Zhang Dai's 張岱 (1597?–1684) early literary efforts was to publish an edition of Xu Wei's uncollected works. Later, however, he ruefully burned poems of his that he thought too similar to Xu's.[5] Yuan Hongdao 袁宏道 (1568–1610) jubilantly champions Xu Wei's work in a preface that reveals his personal, very physical, discovery of and engagement with Xu Wei's text. Although the subject is literary, Xu Wei's poems, Yuan Hongdao evokes the theater with his description in the preface of the actual scene of reading that attracts a crowd of servants.[6] Yuan thus stages his joyous scene of discovery:

> One evening, while sitting upstairs at Grand Scribe T'ao's, I randomly pulled out something from his bookshelves and found it to be a portfolio of several volumes of poetry entitled *A Collection of Scraps*. The paper was of poor quality, the calligraphy was slipshod, and soot had dimmed the printing, so the text was barely legible. I had to get closer to the lamp to read it. But after reading a few poems, I jumped up in surprise and cried out to Wang-ling, "Who's the author of this *Collection of Scraps*? Is he dead or alive?" Wang-ling replied, "This book was by Mr. [Xu Wei], a fellow townsman of mine." We both bounced up and down. We read and yelled, yelled and read in the lamplight, and all the servant boys who had fallen asleep were roused from their sleep.[7]

Yuan's compulsion to uncover the name of the man responsible for the kinds of poems that could cause one to jump up and down and shout is palpable.[8]

A woodcut portrait printed in Zhang Dai's own *Xu Wenchang yigao* shows a world-weary whiskered man with heavily rimmed eyes.[9] Another likeness is the anonymous painting, now in the collection of the Nanjing museum, showing a somewhat younger, slightly fuller-cheeked, thinner-browed version of the artist. They are a reminder of the corporeal presence of Xu, of a man who made things, of the hands that put intent into words and shape. And yet that body, that physical person, is quite remote from the words and shapes we see now. As Xu Wei himself observes, he was already distant from his own physical representation even then. Observing his own portrait, he once remarked:

> At birth I was fat. When I was twenty, I was so skinny that my clothes overwhelmed me. By the time I was thirty, I had gradually fattened up again. Now we have this idiotic fellow pictured here: the years have rushed me along to fifty. Now how can we know that this idiot of today will not become skinny again, just like the mountain marshes that dry up? Trying to grasp me through this picture would be like notching the side of your boat where the sword is dropped, or watching the tree stump for another hare to dash against it. Is he a dragon? Is he a crane? Is he a flitting butterfly? Is he a weighty Zhuang Zhou? Who can know his beginnings?[10]

This is a sentiment that most can readily understand. Carving a mark on the outside of a boat is like capturing a likeness. The mark remains on the side of the boat, but the boat has moved on in the water: the sword is no longer there. The passage of time, the gradual shifting of an object's shape, makes retrieval impossible. The obverse argument is that while the mark may only indicate a fixed and irretrievable moment, the very act of indicating is important, too. It does not gesture merely *at* emptiness. It gestures *to* memory.

Xu Wei's biographies are in many ways like fixed portraits of him: each represents a version of the artist at a specific moment in time. In Xu Wei's case, those specific moments are distinct and indelible. He was a military strategist. Yet he was a lifelong failed scholar. When he was a boy, his family became so impoverished that they sold his biological mother.[11] Xu Wei attempted to commit suicide in particularly gruesome ways; according to various biographies, there were awls in ears and crushed testicles. He beat his wife to death in a murderous rage, and he would have met with execution if not for the intercession of Zhang Dai's great-grandfather, Zhang Yuanbian 張元忭 (1525–90), on his behalf. These few wildly disparate examples alone suggest the impossibility of fully capturing a complete picture of a person.

Xu Wei's prose and poetry reflect these preoccupations. He muses on the blurred space between reality and non-reality, maintaining that to get to the authentic, one has to be able to inhabit another reality. That claim is less a statement about the impossibility of knowing others than it is a statement about the manipulation of one's perspective. In a poem, he refers to the mournful lament of the gibbon cry, saying that the only way to know why the gibbon cries as it does is to become a gibbon oneself. This is the same argument that he makes in his "Foreword to Ye Zisu's Poetry" ("Ye Zisu shixu" 葉子肅詩序). He describes the sound of birds trying to mimic humans, and that of humans trying to mimic bird calls. Though each may perfectly imitate the sounds made by the other, they can never become the other:

> There are people who study how to make bird sounds; their sound is that of a bird, but their nature is still human. There are birds that study how to make human sounds; their sound is that of a human, but their nature is still bird. From this can we take the measure of bird and man? Now, this is no different from writing poetry. If it does not come from one's own self and is instead stolen from what others have already said, if we ask whether a particular text is in a certain style, that particular text is not the poet's own; if we ask whether a particular sentence is like a certain person's, that sentence is not the poet's own. Thus, though one may work to excess to near a likeness, one's self cannot help but be like a bird making human sounds.[12]

Xu Wei's preface was written in response to the kind of poetry that measured its success by imitation of earlier styles, a strategy that someone who subscribes to an authentic (*bense* 本色) way of writing would naturally decry. An imitation can never fully convey another being, nor can it truly convey one's self. A human ear hearing the gibbon cry will not understand its despair; a human voice imitating the sound of a bird will not truly be a bird's. The only true way that one can have access to another is to become the other, and to speak directly from that experience. One must inhabit rather than imitate. The emphasis here, however, is not so much on achieving an internal, static self, but on the sincerity of one's outward show.

Duncan Campbell, comparing Yuan Hongdao's biography of Xu Wei to an act of autobiographical writing, notes that Yuan took care to limit his discussion of Xu Wei's literary works to his poetry and prose. Even though in his biography Yuan mentions that his earlier encounter with Xu Wei's work was with the four-play cycle, collectively known as *Four Cries of a Gibbon* (*Si sheng yuan* 四聲猿), he goes on to rhapsodize about the singularity of Xu Wei's efforts in what were considered the worthier form of literary expression of Yuan's time: poetry.[13] Xu Wei was an important figure in the field of drama, generally considered the author of the play *Singing in Place of Screaming* (*Ge dai xiao* 歌代嘯) and of the treatise on southern drama entitled *Nanci xulu* (南詞敘錄).[14] *Four Cries of a Gibbon* is Xu Wei's most famous dramatic masterpiece, deliberately taking up the same themes introduced in his essays and verse in each of its plays: *The Mad Drummer Plays the Yuyang Triple Rolls (Mi Heng)* (*Kuang guli yuyang sannong* 狂鼓史漁陽三弄), *Zen Master Yu Has a Dream of Cuixiang* (*Yü chanshi cuixiang yimeng* 玉禪師翠鄉一夢), *The Female Mulan Joins the Army in Place of Her Father* (*Ci Mulan tifu congjun* 雌木蘭替父從軍), and *The Girl Graduate Rejects the Female Phoenix and Gains the Male Phoenix* (*Nü zhuangyuan cihuang defeng* 女狀元辭凰得鳳). Discussions of inhabiting instead of imitating are of course already somewhat accessible in poetry and prose, but they find their fullest expression in drama. On stage, the bodies of actors and actresses are, quite literally, occupied by characters. Even when it is only read silently, drama proceeds within this logical frame of the expectations created by outward show. *Four Cries of a Gibbon*, especially, exploits this aspect of the staged world, repeatedly drawing attention to moments where one person transforms into another "self" right before our eyes. In Yuan Hongdao's time, drama was too unorthodox a genre to be taken seriously as a literary form. This is a pity, because *Four Cries of a Gibbon*, as Yuan Hongdao most surely must have observed, overflows with these questions: What are our authentic and true selves? How can they be accessed? This book returns the focus to *Four Cries of a Gibbon*.

Four Cries of a Gibbon comprises four distinct *zaju* (雜劇), or short plays. Drama reached its "golden age" in the Yuan in the form of *zaju*, the short plays that were typically four acts long, although they occasionally stretched to five acts. The Yuan *zaju* was characteristically marked by the use of rigid rhyme and song tune schemes, and the restriction of one singing role per act.[15] The *zaju* form lost its dominance with the emergence of a second golden age of drama, flowering in the late imperial period of the sixteenth and early seventeenth centuries, of the much longer and elegant southern-style *chuanqi* (傳奇) plays that were not only distinguished by their length (often consisting of fifty or more acts), but by their use of southern song tunes, languorous and filigreed singing style, and a greater flexibility regarding the distribution of singing roles and rhymes.[16] By the end of the Ming dynasty, distinctions between *zaju* and *chuanqi* could sometimes be reduced to a shorthand for describing length or musical style. Certainly Xu Wei did not himself abide by the strict rules of the Yuan *zaju* style, although the more workman-like *zaju* form over the sophisticated and embellished *chuanqi* form allowed him to explore the fantastic situations available to drama in a more immediate manner.

The efflorescence of playwriting in late imperial China dovetailed with discussions of questions of identity that typified this period of China's history and were encapsulated in masterpieces of the form, like Tang Xianzu's 湯顯祖 (1550–1616) masterpiece *Peony Pavilion* (*Mudan ting* 牡丹亭), first performed in 1598, a few years after Xu Wei's death. Tina Lu notes how two *chuanqi* plays, the late Ming dynasty *Peony Pavilion* and the early Qing dynasty (1644–1911) *Peach Blossom Fan* (*Taohua shan* 桃花扇) by Kong Shangren 孔尚任 (1648–1718), highlighted late imperial questions of how a person was defined:

> Late Ming China was colored by a concern with the theatre, fascinated by the possibilities of costume and disguise both on and offstage. Theatre, a space that legitimated disguise, informed ostensibly non-theatrical spaces with its concerns. For costume and design were central to late Ming culture, not least in the realm of fashion.... Early Qing China had a distinctly political stake in the question of disguise. The Manchu conquerors mandated that all male subjects shave their pates, plait the hair at the back of their heads into a queue, and wear a style of clothing based on Manchu riding gear. [The state would read its citizens' outward appearances as a direct confrontation of the new regime to the extent that] appearances matter and promise access to a person's state of mind. But what about the many who obediently shaved their pates while secretly harboring sentiments of Ming loyalism? They surely felt that appearances—even a shaved head and the clothes to be worn every single day—were nothing but a disguise; but, of course, a fascination with disguise is another way of expressing interest in what a person might truly be.[17]

The performative aspect of theater—that of roles being played—happens to parallel exactly the issues of representation raised when a new regime claims its legitimacy and power over a reluctant populace. The transition was a period that curiously highlighted the tropes of drama through real experience; the dynastic struggle seen during the early Qing, marked by attempts to resurrect the Ming in the south, underscored the significance of playing a role, even offstage. The cultural milieu of the Ming, in which the personal was defined by accumulations of commodity or displays of connoisseurship, also suggested new ways of thinking about what could constitute a person's life story.[18] This period indeed marked a rising concern with issues of subjectivity, a concern insistently reflected in its fiction and drama.

Although Xu Wei's historical circumstances may well have influenced the topics he chose to explore in his plays,[19] the kinds of questions these plays ask are more generally universal ones that transcend the borders of their historical moment. How does a person know another? How can what one says affect how one is understood? How does clothing, or the removal of clothing, reveal who one is? Does it reveal the true person, or is the unclothed person distinct from the clothed one? A reader of this book might object that I am imposing my own modern preoccupations on to a five-hundred-year-old text, but the plays speak for themselves. Each of them transmits a quality of timelessness and universality that reflects less a cultural or historical anxiety than a certain kind of temperament. Xu Wei's is an artistic temperament that insistently challenges the viewer to ask himself how he can be as he is, and yet be mistaken for someone else completely. Actors invest their roles with meaning, but their outer appearances dominate the audience's perception of them. In other words, plays make the question of actual, physical, palpable bodies unavoidable. Xu Wei's plays, in particular, focus the argument to specifically engage plots about characters wrestling with how they are perceived. *Mi Heng* restages a famous episode from *Three Kingdoms* lore, allowing Mi Heng to posthumously redeem himself and upbraid the warlord Cao Cao. *Zen Master Yu* depicts a monk who is seduced and ruined before he can reach Nirvana, is reborn as a prostitute in the second act, and is restored to his original identity by the end of the play. *Mulan* is the story of a young girl who goes to fight the invading barbarians in place of her elderly father, returning as a war hero and trading in the emoluments for a happy wedding. Finally, *Girl Graduate* shows in five acts how an impoverished orphan girl, through wisdom and hard work, disguises herself as a man to take part in the official examinations and earns the place of top graduate. Stretching the conventions of northern and southern drama, these four plays forecast the way that drama would flourish and develop in the century that followed, serving unofficially as a treatise on the possibilities of drama. With their self-reflexive themes and motifs, they directly confront the kinds of questions that would become highly fashionable in the late Ming and early Qing periods and that are being asked again in twentieth- and twenty-first-century scholarship.

Four Cries of a Gibbon giddily stages multiplicities with such magical qualities that they would be impossible in its audience's world. Souls transmigrate, spirits fight back, girls elude detection in exclusively masculine trials. As a form of entertainment that explicitly challenges the viewer to accept a person as who she says she is simply because she says so, and then to accept her again as a different person because she has changed her clothes and taken on a different name, drama holds up a mirror to our world. This is, after all, the nature of drama: we witness pretend actions in a pretend world, but that world contains its own categories of true and false. The performers know that they are performing. The audience knows that it is viewing. Roles are played by people who are not actually who they are.

The reader of *Four Cries of a Gibbon* will see moments in the text suggesting that these plays were written to be performed: physical acts such as costume changes and pantomime are integral to the plots, and action is interrupted with interludes of singing or courtroom trials that are inserted for entertainment. Such scenes are not crucial to the movement of the plot, although it can be argued, as I do in the following chapters, that they are crucial to the meaning of the play. Stage directions that directly affect the plot—and sometimes, more notably, don't affect the plot at all—abound in Xu Wei's plays. The literary merit of the plays is not the reason for their popularity; indeed, their lack of refinement is often mentioned, and sometimes even criticized.[20] Wilt Idema has suggested that their great popularity in sixteenth-century Jiangnan was due to the performative aspects, especially the explicit sexual nature of onstage dressing and undressing that naturally accompanied the plays featuring female characters cross-dressing as men: *Mulan* and *Girl Graduate*.[21] Xu Wei's plays are typically studied for their historical significance, whether as evidence of a historical moment or of the author's allegorical protest of social or personal conditions, or for their literary qualities. This book suggests a different way of looking at his works that is neither dependent on their historical significance nor limited to a critique of their literary merits. The philosophical question of identity is incidental not to *Four Cries of a Gibbon*, but to its subject. This book explores the seeming paradox of reaching direct, spontaneous authenticity by engaging in an art form that is by nature false. By looking carefully at the way that each play presents a variation on the theme of one character's revealing his or her true identity to another, in front of an audience that witnesses multiple roles played by one actor, *Four Cries of a Gibbon* demonstrates the theatrical nature of human interaction and proposes a way to live in a world that is governed by perceptions and necessary concealments. The characters in *Four Cries of a Gibbon* are contextually defined; they exist as a sum result of the version that they present and the version that the one who perceives them expects. The unifying theme of this quartet of plays is their exploration of the vigorous calibration required to reveal an authentic self: that is to say, revelation is itself a kind of presentation.

A characteristic shared by all four of these plays, incongruent with readings of the plays as forms of social protest or cries of grief, is simple "play" itself. *Four Cries of a Gibbon* capitalizes on the visual and aural aspects of theater; all of the plays make use of costume changes, some more risqué than others, as crucial plot devices. The emphasis is on how roles are played. Characters are called up to recreate favorite scenes for a viewing audience made up of underworld gods, or a character's deceit results in another character's becoming another person who can, in turn, only be redeemed through the motions of watching a play. Stage work is employed in such a way that would be irrelevant if the play had been written only as reading matter. *Mi Heng* finds a pretext to have two singing girls perform doltish songs; the monk in *Zen Master Yu* performs elaborate pantomimes that allow for comic misunderstandings; *Mulan* stages a woman turning herself into a man, and then effortlessly returning, many years later, as a woman; and *Girl Graduate* has an interlude of courtroom scenes where the heroine metes out justice in three cases unrelated to the play itself except to illustrate her wisdom. If these plays have been typically construed as Xu Wei's allegories of social protest, they must also be much more than that. The plays are particularly significant because, through these expressions of play, they directly address the difficulty of depicting one's real and true self.

In a preface to the great Yuan dynasty play *The Story of the Western Wing* (*Xixiang ji* 西廂記), Xu Wei complained:

> In the affairs of the world there is the authentic and there is the imitative. In plain words, authentic is the real self; imitative is the substitute self. The substitute self is what is meant in the commentary "The maid acting as mistress ultimately feels embarrassed." This means that the maid acting as mistress wants to make herself up to become the mistress and adds on more ornaments, but just covers up her simplicity. This is why in this book I think little of the imitative, and value the authentic; what everyone "oohs and aahs" about, I "ho-hum" about. How is it that among dramatists and writers not one of them is like this? Alas, who can I talk to? What everyone neglects, I alone savor; what everyone prioritizes, I alone spit out. Alas, who can I talk to?[22]

This complaint gives voice to one of the most intriguing questions about drama. Xu Wei is speaking about the authentic self, using characters of a play to explain what it is. In his conceptual vision, the staged world is a real one, where distinctions exist to separate the authentic from the imitative, all within a form that is entirely imitative. Yet, the genre of drama, which ostensibly depends upon play-acting, substitution, and imitation, still manages to depict the authentic. The process of watching drama and contemplating how it works demonstrates that what we know is derived nearly exclusively from what we are told and shown as viewers of a staged work and, similarly, as participants in life.

The parallels of our "real" world with the world of the theater are apparent. "Dramatic irony" describes the state of an audience's awareness of information unknown to characters onstage, as when Oedipus pronounces a death sentence on the person who has caused the plague in Thebes in Sophocles' fifth-century BCE play. Although Oedipus is unaware that he is the one who has brought on the curse by killing his father and marrying his mother, the audience knows the facts, and their experience of the play is enhanced by their possession of this privileged knowledge. This sensation of being granted access to some shared privilege plays a large part in making the experience of theater so compelling. The theater audience, with its privileged access to authenticity, can witness a character realizing something that it already knows, an experience that is rare in our own world. Audiences thus rely on the knowledge they receive from the characters onstage to shape their understanding of events as they occur. In life, too, we glean information from what we are told, but our sources are not uniformly reliable; in drama, what we are told is our most reliable source of information—far more reliable, sometimes, than what we see with our eyes. A stage may contain a bedroom, or it may contain a whole world; a few men in battle may represent armies of thousands; an old male actor may really be a young girl; a man appearing on stage may actually be a ghost. In all of these cases, we the audience accept these scenarios because that is how the players describe them to us; the lines of the play help us decide whether the puppet on the stage is meant to be seen as a puppet or whether it is meant to be seen as a real boy.

Another particularity of drama is the unavoidable presence of the performing body. Questions about selfhood and subjectivity, expressed in contemplation of the interplay between one's body and the self residing within it, were routinely raised in the poetry and prose of Xu Wei's time. These questions find their best expression in drama, where they become directly accessible through the limitations of the actors' bodies. John Hay, writing about the body in Chinese art, notes that even in the sexually explicit novel *Plum in the Golden Vase* (*Jinpingmei* 金瓶梅) "there is no image of a body as a whole object, least of all as a solid and well-shaped entity whose shapeliness is supported by the structure of a skeleton and defined in the exteriority of swelling muscle and enclosing flesh."[23] Garments or other inanimate objects may stand in for bodies quite easily in Chinese literary descriptions and even pictorial work, but drama requires an unmistakably physical presence, even as costume plays a crucial part.[24] Mark Elvin draws the distinction between the corporeal body (*shen* 身), which includes the sartorial in its definition, and the heart-mind (*xin* 心), and demonstrates how the two are intertwined. He writes of how "defects of character could lead to bodily deformity," calling to mind the fluidity of boundaries and the way that the body, *shen*, does not simply contain but *is* the self.[25] The interesting balance between what we see and what we are told is highlighted by this disparity, especially given the fact that Chinese drama lays special emphasis on what the costume tells us about the character because of his or her role type. From its inception in the Song dynasty through its dizzyingly varied and obsessively catalogued subdivisions by the time of Peking Opera (*jingju* 京劇), characters were played by role types that each already had its own constellation of referents. A character made up as a *dan* (旦 young female lead) could never be anything but what was expected of a *dan*, never to be confused with a clown (*chou* 丑), for example.[26] The physical appearance, whether marked by makeup on the face, costume, or a combination, told the audience essential qualities about the character. Xu Wei's plays complicate the relationship between clothing and the self-body in these plays, which all have a variation on a stripping scene, challenging the viewer's assumptions about believing what he sees. Mi Heng, Liu Cui, and Auntie Huang (in *Mi Heng, Zen Master Yu*, and *Girl Graduate*, respectively) all remove their clothes to make a point: Mi Heng does it to express his outrage toward Cao Cao, Liu Cui does it to demonstrate her enlightenment as she changes to monks' garb, and Auntie Huang does it to demonstrate that she is a woman. Mulan and Huang Chonggu (in *Mulan* and *Girl Graduate*, respectively) change into male clothes and back into female clothes again as the central subjects of each play. Eric Henry, shedding light on the emphasis on clothing and its relation to the characters' expressions of self, suggests that clothing is tied to the very construction of humanity in China.[27]

Three chapters consider how gender is implicated within these negotiations of showing and telling. As the actual roles are more important than the gender of the actor or actress who plays them, costume and makeup stand in as gender markers. This is so much a part of the conventions of drama of the time that it should be unremarkable, and yet *Zen Master Yu, Mulan*, and *Girl Graduate* stand out because they specifically take up gender changing as their subject. Charlotte Furth, writing about cases of gender overlap in the late Ming, notes that "late Ming gender identity was not easily compromised by the sexually 'strange.' Social role normally overshadowed the sexual in gender construction, and the result for males was that mutability of bodies and diversity of objects of desire need not render male gender problematic."[28] Nor does it imply a change in the assessment of the role of women in society. In this book I consider how these plays instead use gender changes to emphasize how the sartorial can underscore the importance of maintaining a true, unaffected self.

The four chapters that follow provide a critical reading of each short play within *Four Cries of a Gibbon*. Although the plays do not share characters or specific plot elements, they are indisputably connected to each other by a shared preoccupation with the complications of defining oneself. Each play can be seen as a variation on the same model: a character sees clearly how he or she wishes to be, and then sets out to ensure that others will see things the same way. This is especially underscored in chapter 2's reading of *Zen Master Yu*, as the Zen Master himself ends up reincarnated as a woman and unable to recognize himself; s/he needs to rely on evidence planted by his former self to establish and accept his true identity. Yet, as I demonstrate in the three other chapters, the primary concern of the protagonist in each play is first to define him or herself, and then to secure agreement from everyone else of that identity. Although Mulan, Mi Heng, and Chonggu do not need a monk to awaken them to their true identity, they, too, spend a great deal of time onstage displaying themselves to others and musing aloud about it. The plays are appended at the end of this book in fully annotated English translation; the reader unfamiliar with these plays may wish to read the appendixes first, before turning to the critical analysis found within the four chapters. The shared themes of play and dress, of voicing sincerity in regard to one's identity and seeking evidence to affirm that identity, recur insistently throughout the plays. When read together as a set, the variations on these themes harmonize and find greater resonance, demonstrating the cohesiveness of *Four Cries of a Gibbon*. By drawing our attention to the extreme measures taken by these characters to establish something so basic as their sense of self, Xu Wei brings to light the complex negotiations involved in our worldly interactions.

Drama has first and foremost always referred us to how we comprehend the world. It questions how we understand ourselves with respect to others, and how we understand others with respect to ourselves, a concern that enters into every social transaction, and cultural construct. These transactions, both in life and in entertainment, are made through the simultaneously crucial and untrustworthy medium of language. If language is important in the drama of Shakespeare or Sophocles, for example, then how much more so in Chinese theater, where characters are filled by set role types, known to every audience member through the tradition of symbolic gestures, costume, and face makeup. The stock characters necessitate the actor's self-introductory speech upon entering the stage, as the audience would have no other way of knowing who a *dan*, a *sheng*, or any other familiar role type is playing without this statement of self. Each time a new play is performed, the same familiar faces and costumes take on new personalities, once again emphasizing how we depend on what we are told to make sense of what we see.

In spite of the peculiarities of Chinese drama performance that draw attention to the dominance of type and self-identification, this book's argument extends beyond the drama of the Ming dynasty, beyond the drama of China even, to make a claim about the workings of a play itself. Whether or not it explicitly depicts a scene of acting on stage, which is so often a feature in dramatic works of every period and culture, drama is grounded in assumptions about acting: the audience knows what is expected of it and complies by believing what is presented. Meaning is formulated situationally, alongside the narrative progression of the drama, and this is a pattern that we are enjoined to recognize in the world of our own experience. Each play resolutely focuses on situations where one entity encounters another, and the ways that the viewer's perspective and the subject's choices shift, sometimes sharply and sometimes subtly. It almost always requires modulations that disorient, sometimes even quite violently, and yet they are modulations from which, in the world of these plays, all parties recover a mutually acceptable understanding. This push and pull, this assuming one thing only to quickly assume quite the opposite, these plays reveal, is after all just a fact of everyday life. For all of its fascinating layers and bold and profound strokes, *Four Cries of a Gibbon*, like Xu Wei's inky scrolls, projects a lightness of spirit both buoyant and refulgent. It is this buoyancy and refulgence that cause us to look closer, to learn a little bit more about the hand that crafted it. In the end, in our examination of the plays themselves, we find this to be patently clear: those strokes of wit, those plays of dark and light, are both the question and the answer. *Four Cries of a Gibbon* helps us to understand something of the nature of drama; this contemplation of the nature of drama challenges us to understand something of the nature of our world.

I

Undressing for Success: The Mad Drummer Plays the Yuyang Triple Rolls (Mi Heng)

> The speech we hear is an indication of that which we don't hear. It is a necessary avoidance, a violent, sly, and anguished or mocking smoke screen which keeps the other in its true place. When true silence falls we are left with echo but are nearer nakedness. One way of looking at speech is to say that it is a constant stratagem to cover nakedness.
>
> —*Harold Pinter*

The Mad Drummer Plays the Yuyang Triple Rolls (*Kuang guli yuyang sannong* 狂鼓史漁陽三弄), or *Mi Heng* (禰衡), after the name of the lead character, is the first play in *Four Cries of a Gibbon*. Thought to be the first of the plays to have been written, it is thus printed first in all published editions of the collection. It is also generally regarded as the best written of the plays and has been singled out by critics from Xu Wei's time to the present.[1] *Mi Heng* sets the tone for the rest of the plays in the set, establishing all of the distinctive qualities and introducing themes, innovations, and variations seen in the other three plays.

Although it is the shortest of the plays, consisting of only one act, it represents Xu Wei's original contributions in the evolution of Ming drama, and displays the shared qualities of *Four Cries of a Gibbon* that are at the heart of this study. All of the plays in the cycle, beginning with this one, toy with the typical conventions of *zaju*. The characteristics that established *zaju* as a northern genre, which typically reserved songs to specifically northern modes and melodies, are overturned in these plays, as Xu Wei allows for a mixing of northern and southern tunes. Whereas the bulk of *Mi Heng* proceeds in the standard *zaju* form—a single actor in the play (in this case, the one playing Mi Heng) lays claim to all the songs and sings them in the northern mode—Xu Wei inserts an interruption in the form of two singing girls who perform a bawdy popular song and, later, allows even further deviance from the traditional *zaju* form when the play gives way to a duet, multiple singers, and southern tunes.[2]

The play's dramatic construction has been discussed most recently in terms of its musical emphases;[3] here, I will consider *Mi Heng* from the perspective of how it elucidates concerns about the body and the way those concerns relate to play-acting. *Mi Heng* encapsulates themes elaborated throughout *Four Cries of a Gibbon*. Its preoccupations with body and how we are defined by dress (or, in this case, undress), its concerns about the way speech defines our understanding of ourselves and other people, its use of a literal trial as an opportunity for metaphorical self-definition, its desire to be understood by an audience (whether an audience of one or many), and its emphasis on witnessing things with one's own eyes are all distilled here in one act. In fact, the play wastes no time in presenting the questions that will be repeatedly asked throughout the rest of the collection: Are we who we say we are? Can we represent ourselves through language? What part does seeing things happen before one's eyes play in how we make sense of our world—how we are understood and how we understand others? These questions will become increasingly complex with the introduction of gender and transmigration in successive plays, adding new levels of nuance around the question of identity.

All of these themes reverberate in the plays that follow, and the fact that the bulk of *Mi Heng* is taken up by a literal performance should not be lost on us. This is, after all, a play celebrating a character whose actions are so memorable that he is asked to produce a repeat performance. Mi Heng bares himself again for an internal audience, and consequently for the reading (or literal) audience, thus revealing a "genuine" self in contrast to the figure of the wicked and false conniver Cao Cao. That this is a *performance* of an authentic moment should not be lost on us, either. For all its claims of authenticity, as the venting of one's honest grievances indeed are, Mi Heng's original drum scene also enfolded another performance within it: a performance of madness.[4] Here the specter of authentic rant lies beneath the pretense of madness, which in itself is under cover of the performance of a drum song, and which now is resurrected in the Underworld as a new performance.[5] How authenticity can be performed, or how authenticity does not have to be ruled out simply because it is performed, is another theme common to all four plays in the quartet.

Repetition and Performance

The play begins with the typical self-introduction, made by a judge of the Underworld, Judge Searcher, who quickly announces that Mi Heng has been demonstrating his talents in literature down in the Underworld and is set to be promoted outside of the Underworld to serve the "Lord on High." The prospect of Mi Heng's imminent departure makes the judge consider those daring acts of being "wild-eyed and naked, beating out a rhythm, banging the paddle, reinventing that ancient tune "Yuyang Triple Rolls." Feigning madness to vent his spleen, acting deaf and playing dumb, he exposed Cao's every fault so that he had nowhere to hide."[6] The judge muses further:

> Now wasn't that something to shake up Heaven and Earth? Wasn't it a wonderful sight [*yi chang qiguan* 一場奇觀] like some grand wooden puppet show? Now he is about to ascend to Heaven, and I intend to summon him here, and at the same time release Cao Man, and have them reenact the age-old scenario of cursing the host.[7] Having the two of them give such a performance will make for a good amount of conversation for those of us in the Underworld Offices. I will also let them see that bad and good deeds, ultimately, are just like debts that must be repaid: how can they not be![8]

The reenactment as a premise for a retrial is made clear in the judge's statement about no debt going unpaid; not only does Mi Heng have the opportunity to accuse Cao Cao of the specific crimes Cao Cao committed against him, he also accuses him of every crime that he has ever committed, including those that occurred even after Mi Heng had been dismissed from Cao Cao's court.

The bulk of the play consists of Mi Heng's thirteen songs of accusation, sung in the northern style and accompanied on the drum with "Yuyang" triple roll drumbeats. This is interrupted briefly by an absurd doggerel duet insulting Cao Cao, performed as a song (*ci* 詞) by two of his own singing girls. Finally, Mi Heng is summoned to serve the Jade Emperor, and a pair of messengers performs a duet to southern tunes praising Mi Heng. After asking for leniency for Cao Cao, Mi Heng sings a parting duet with the judge. The play ends with the judge remarking how satisfied he is to have witnessed Mi Heng's performance, emphasizing again how it redresses the imbalance of justice that he suffered in his lifetime.

Literal Resurrection

Mi Heng is a minor character relative to the huge historical cast of the final decades of the Eastern Han (25–220 CE) period. What distinguishes him is his consistent brashness toward everyone, including the intimidating warlord Cao Cao. Finally meeting his early end after making a nuisance of himself in more than one principality, he is best remembered for two things. The first is his talent as a poet, evident in his poem "Rhapsody on a Parrot."[9] The second is the story that tells of how, when commanded by Cao Cao to demonstrate his skill on the drum, he insults Cao Cao by refusing to appear in the required uniform and then stripping naked in front of him to change into the uniform. Cao Cao is enraged by this flaunting of propriety but does not want to show the extent of his anger by punishing such a widely admired character. He simply sends Mi Heng off to offend someone else who will be willing to punish him. The image of Mi Heng and this peculiar form of insult are indelible: it is an insult that marries subtlety with vulgarity. The vulgarity is obvious in his defiant nudity followed by loud cursing; the subtlety is in the fact that the insult begins with a seemingly mundane request: that Mi Heng should wear a certain kind of clothing for a performance.

Xu Wei's play features a cast of Underworld characters already very familiar with the entire story, but they are eager to see it performed for the enactment of its two most visual aspects: that of Mi Heng stripping, and that of his insulting Cao Cao to the beat of his drum. The conflation of the two is Xu Wei's innovation, and he uses the device of a demanding Underworld audience to incorporate the two scenes into a single performance. Xu Wei's *Mi Heng* takes liberties with the chronology of the story by retelling it long after all parties have died and setting it in the Underworld. The premise of a performance allows for the stripping and a drum song accompanied by a list of grievances within the one-act play.

The first historical mention of Mi Heng comes in the *Records of the Later Han* (*Hou Hanshu* 後漢書). The story reads as follows:

> As Kong Rong[10] admired Mi Heng's talent, he spoke of him to Cao Cao several times. Cao Cao wanted to see him, but Mi Heng treated it carelessly, and said he was ill with madness and would not go. After several more of these sorts of responses, Cao Cao was upset but did not wish to kill him due to his famed talent. Hearing that Mi Heng was an accomplished drummer, he summoned him to perform and held a large party with many guests to serve as an audience. The other drummers all took off their regular clothes and changed to regulation drummers' hats and garments. When it came to Mi Heng, he marched forward, beating out the "Yuyang" drum roll thrice. His expression looked strange, and the sound and rhythm of the drum were melancholy and vigorous. All of the listeners were moved. Mi Heng advanced towards Cao Cao and then stood before him. An official scolded him, "How can an official drummer not change clothes and dare to enter so flippantly?" Mi Heng said, "Fine," and at that, he first threw off his outer garments, then doffed the rest of his clothes, and stood there naked. In a leisurely manner he took the plain official garment and put it on, and having done that, he beat the drums thrice and left, his facial expression unmoved. Cao Cao laughed and said, "I meant to shame Heng, but instead he shamed me." Kong Rong withdrew and scolded, "Zhengping [Mi Heng] is so upright, so why would you do that?" Because of Kong Rong's multiple assurances of Cao Cao's humble feeling, Mi Heng again came forward. Kong Rong went to see Cao Cao again and said that Mi Heng had been taken by madness and would now like to beg forgiveness. Cao Cao happily ordered the doorkeepers to allow guests at the door to enter, and having had a great banquet prepared, he awaited Mi Heng's arrival. Mi Heng then put on the plain garment and simple turban and grasped a three-foot staff in his hand. He sat outside the camp gates, using the staff to pound the ground while cursing loudly. The officer said, "There is a madman sitting outside the camp gates; as his words are treasonous, allow us to brand him guilty!" Cao Cao angrily said to Kong Rong, "That bastard, Mi Heng! I will kill him—he's nothing but a rat or a sparrow to me. But this person, though he and his name mean nothing, would cause everyone from far and near to say that I could not tolerate him. Now I will send him to Liu Biao, and let's see what happens." Then he ordered his men to escort him on horse.[11]

Mi Heng has obviously insulted Cao Cao first by his refusal to wear the proper garments, which he feels would mark him as a menial entertainer. He follows this refusal with an insouciant stripping and changing of clothes. While he does proceed to play the drum, there is no mention of specific insults that accompany his drumming. When he is described later as cursing Cao Cao, there are no details about what he says: the cursing accompanied by drumming are original to Xu Wei's version.

Severe Dressing Downs

The principle of improper dress representing improper conduct would culturally resonate with its audience. Some of the earliest references can be found in several puzzling entries on Confucius' behavior in the *Analects*. In Book 9, in addition to other details about the sage's upright behavior, the reader is treated to the minutiae of proper dress and appropriate response. For example, "When the Master encountered men who were in mourning or in ceremonial cap and robes or were blind, he would, on seeing them, rise to his feet, even though they were younger than he was, and, on passing them, would quicken his step [as a sign of respect]."[12] More tellingly, in Book 10, we learn:

> The gentleman avoided using dark purple and maroon colored silk for lapels and cuffs. Red and violet colored silks were not used for informal dress. When, in the heat of summer, he wore an unlined robe made of either fine or coarse material, he invariably wore it over an under-robe to set it off. Under a black jacket, he wore lambskin; under an un-dyed jacket, he wore fawnskin; under a yellow jacket, he wore fox fur. His informal fox fur coat was long but with a short right sleeve. He invariably had a night robe, which was half as long again as he was tall. Their fur being thick, pelts of the fox and the badger were used as rugs. Once the period of mourning was over, he placed no restriction on the kind of ornament that he wore. Other than skirts for ceremonial occasions, everything else was made up from cut pieces. Lambskin coats and black caps were not used on visits of condolence. On New Year's Day, he invariably went to court in court dress.[13]

The implicit lesson here is that the finest details of even the most superficial gestures and ornaments are never without meaning. Clothes are just as important as behavior; in fact, clothes stand in for behavior. The color, material, and cut of a piece of clothing are part of a vocabulary and grammar that inscribes ritual into everyday life and are meant to communicate intent and feeling. The two examples above represent two halves of a dialogue that is expressed through clothing. When the master saw the mourning or ceremonial attire in the excerpt from Book 9, he knew how to adjust his behavior to show respect; when he dressed according to the situation, in Book 10, he was again demonstrating respectful behavior.

Mi Heng, by flaunting ceremony, insults Cao Cao and disregards Cao Cao's presentation of himself as a leader who deserves to be treated with formality and respect. Indeed, this is the kind of behavior that Kong Rong, in the original story, can only explain away as madness. Madness is an excuse that Mi Heng had previously used to decline invitations to pay court to Cao Cao. Madness, after all, means that a person is not in control of his wits: he is not being himself. Of course, the problem here is that Mi Heng is in possession of himself; he just isn't being who he is expected to be. It is precisely his possession of himself that causes him to behave so outrageously in Cao Cao's presence. In Mi Heng's view, he has been insulted first. He thinks little of anyone at Cao Cao's court besides Kong Rong, and the fact that he has been summoned at all has already been insult enough.[14] Cao Cao compounds the insult when he orders him to change into a regulation costume, reducing him not only to one of many drummers, but confining his identity to outer raiment alone. Up until this point, he had been famed for his reputation and his talent, what we might call "internal" qualities, but when he appears before Cao Cao he is scolded for failing to dress appropriately.

The emphasis on proper attire may explain the virtual absence of such examples of exposing one's naked body in China's literary and cultural history. Clothing and words are accepted as the full definition of the person who fills or produces them, and there is no corollary to the naked, "true" self of the Western cultural imagination. What are we to make, then, of a case where the exposure of this character's commitment to his individual self deliberately gestures to a space between one costume and the next: the blank, naked, self? Mi Heng's case calls to mind another exceptional case: that of the Warring States figure Yu-rang 豫讓, whose biography is included among the "Biographies of the Assassins" (*qike liezhuan* 刺客列傳) (Ch. 86) in Sima Qian's 司馬遷 *Records of the Historian* (*Shiji* 史記). Sima Qian's version quotes largely from the *Schemes of the Warring States* (*Zhanguo ce* 戰國策) from the early Western Han:[15]

> Yu-rang, grandson of Bi Yang of Jin, first entered the service of the houses of the Fan and the Zhong-hang, but he was unhappy there. He quit and went to the Earl of Zhi of Jin, who treated him with great favor. When the three branches of Jin divided up the realm of the house of the Earl of Zhi, it was Lord Xiang of Zhao who felt the greatest ill will toward the Earl of Zhi and took his skull as his drinking vessel. Yu-rang had fled to the hills and said, "A liegeman dies for the man who appreciates him; a woman makes herself beautiful for the man who is pleased with her. May I then take vengeance on this enemy of the house of the Earl of Zhi!"[16] He changed his name and made himself a branded criminal. Thus he got into the palace as a plasterer of the latrines, with the purpose of assassinating Lord Xiang.
>
> Lord Xiang was on his way to the latrine and had a trembling of the heart. He had the plasterer seized and questioned, and it turned out to be Yu-rang, who had put a sharp edge on his trowel. Yu-rang said, "I wanted to take revenge on the enemy of the Earl of Zhi." His entourage wanted to put Yu-rang to death, but Lord Xiang of Zhao said, "This is a liegeman of principle. I will merely keep him away from me. The Earl of Zhi is dead and has no offspring, yet one who served him will go so far as to seek revenge on his enemies. This is one of the most worthy men in the world." And in the end he had Yu-rang set free.

Yu-rang next put lacquer on his body to cover it with sores; he got rid of his whiskers and eyebrows and mutilated himself to alter his appearance. He then went begging.... After this he swallowed ashes to make himself hoarse and changed the sound of his voice. A friend said to him, "The course you are following is one of great hardship, yet one that does not do the deed. If you would be spoken of as a man of powerful will, then it will be so; but you will not be spoken of as a resourceful man. If you used your talents in the skillful service of Lord Xiang, he would certainly draw you close to him and make you his favorite. If you could get close to him, then you could do whatever you wanted. This would be very easy, and the deed could be done." Yu-rang then laughed and answered him, "This would be to take revenge on the second man who appreciated me for the sake of the first man who appreciated me. This would be to turn outlaw against a new lord for the sake of a former lord. Nothing could more violate the principle of the bond between a lord and one who serves him. What I intend in doing as I do is to make clear the bond between a lord and one who serves him—it is not to take the easy way. To give a pledge of fealty and serve a man while seeking to assassinate him is to serve one's lord with duplicity in the heart. This hard thing that I do now may even put to shame all those in the world who in later times serve their lords with duplicity in their hearts."

After some while, Lord Xiang was to go forth, and Yu-rang hid under a bridge across which he would have to pass. But when Lord Xiang reached the bridge, his horse reared, whereupon Lord Xiang said, "Yu-rang must be here." He ordered someone to question the man, and it was indeed Yu-rang. Thereupon Lord Xiang of Zhao faced Yu-rang and said, "Did you not once serve the houses of Fan and Zhong-hang? Yet when the Earl of Zhi destroyed those houses, you did not take revenge on him, but rather pledged him your fealty. The Earl of Zhi is dead now, so why only in this case are you so deeply determined to take revenge on his enemy?" Yu-rang said, "I served the houses of Fan and Zhong-hang, yet they treated me as an ordinary man. The Earl of Zhi treated me like one of the liegemen of the domain. So in return I behave like a liegeman of the domain."

Lord Xiang gave a great sigh and shed tears, saying, "Oh, Yu-rang! You have already become famous for what you have done on the Earl of Zhi's account. And I forgave you then—that too was enough. You make plans on your own behalf now, and I may not forgive you." And he ordered his men to form a ring around him.

Then Yu-rang said, "I have heard it said that a wise ruler does not force a man to conceal his principles and I have heard that one who serves with loyalty, to make his fame complete, does not cling to life. Before you were lenient and forgave me, and for this the whole world praises your virtue. I do indeed accept the punishment that must follow from what has happened today. Still, if I could ask for your coat and stab it, I would feel no resentment in my death. I cannot expect this, but I reveal what is within me."

Thereupon Lord Xiang saw that Yu-rang did indeed have principles, and he ordered one who served him to take his coat and give it to Yu-rang. Yu-rang drew out his sword, leapt around several times, shouted to Heaven, and stabbed the coat, saying, "By this I take vengeance for the Earl of Zhi." Then he fell on his sword and died. On the day he died the liegemen of Zhao heard of it, and they all wept.[17]

This story is quoted in full here because it so effectively crystallizes the issues at stake in Mi Heng's act of protest. Both historical figures are remembered for their acts of a symbolic nature, both use outward appearance to make a statement about their true inner worth, and both pay the ultimate price for their stance. Whatever the true intentions of the actual men, these specific qualities are the ones highlighted and interpreted as demonstrative of worthiness in the histories.

Yu-rang, like Mi Heng, is a dislocated individual whose loyalty is not bound to a specific geographic location, but rather to those who recognize his true talents. The text introduces Yu-rang by disclosing that he has found happiness only at the home of the Earl of Zhi, where his talents were recognized and appreciated. In his quest for vengeance, he compares himself to a woman making herself beautiful to please a man, thus introducing a vocabulary that relates inner value and outward attractiveness. The first outward layer that he sheds is his name; then, he disfigures himself with the brand of a criminal in order to infiltrate Lord Xiang's palace. Interestingly enough, Lord Xiang immediately senses his presence, and Yu-rang is seized in spite of his disguise. Again Yu-rang encounters someone who sees beyond his appearance and recognizes his innate worth. Lord Xiang is lenient and, owing to his admiration of Yu-rang's loyalty, frees him. Yet again, Yu-rang assumes another disguise through self-mutilation: he lacquers his body so that it scabs, he burns off all of his facial hair, and he eats ashes to change his voice. The disfiguration of his physical self—his clothing, his facial hair, his skin, and his voice—is a deliberate statement intended to make an abstract concept clear.

Of course, the story is all the more satisfying because of the structural parallels that occur in Lord Xiang's own display of sensitivity. Lord Xiang first senses Yu-rang's dangerous presence because of a trembling he feels in his heart while he is on his way to the latrine, and so he questions a yet unknown Yu-rang, who admits his desire for vengeance. Later, when a completely disfigured Yu-rang is hiding under a bridge, Lord Xiang's horse, sensing his presence, rears and he responds immediately, "Yu-rang must be here." To put it plainly, Lord Xiang recognizes him, in spite of a thorough stripping of external identification, and, in fact, with his total concealment. There is no signifier, only a sense that he is there. Admire and recognize Yu-rang though he may, Xiang also realizes that Yu-rang cannot be dissuaded from pursuing his plan of vengeance and therefore must be stopped. Understanding that Lord Xiang must punish him, Yu-rang responds with a drastic act.

Previously, in the contest between internal versus external and thought versus attire, the prize for the righteous went to what was not immediately visible: fealty and true feeling were more important than one's outward appearance. Yet when Yu-rang finally accepts his fate, his final request is to have Lord Xiang's coat, through which he seeks to run his sword before falling upon the same sword. He is proposing a symbolic gesture, against a piece of clothing no less, to satisfy his need for vengeance, and he frames this desire with the statement "I reveal what is within me." Why, at this point, is it no longer enough for the thought alone to count? Why must there be a tangible sign, a demonstration to make things real?

The answers extend beyond our reading of Yu-rang's biography. For a true self to be revealed, there needs to be a physical conveyance. Thoughts depend on expression: language, gesture, and symbolic moves are necessary vehicles through which we convey the more abstract concept of self. Although Yu-rang's presence may be sensed by the man who truly recognizes him, he still has to explain aloud what has brought him to these circumstances. Before he falls on his own sword, he asks to make a symbolic gesture of revenge on Xiang's coat, an act that reinforces the fact that material objects do matter.

Although the path I have just traced is by no means a direct one from Confucius to Sima Qian to *Mi Heng*, it represents a real line of continuity, for we find that clothing remained a no less interesting question to intellectuals and commentators during the late Ming than it did to those from centuries before. Later, especially, in the aftermath of the Qing transition, the clothes one wore would become increasingly political in nature, as loyalty to the new regime was enforced by conformity to Manchu customs of dress, and men were required to wear their hair in a queue. This no doubt would have been present in the collective subconscious, if not in the conscious minds of the people, and might have contributed to the continued interest in this play's themes. In any case, the ubiquitous nature of clothing ensures that it is always immediately understood as carrying meaning, and the putting on and taking off of clothing, especially certain articles *required* by an unwelcome ruler, was given special consideration.

Clothing is, after all, the easiest way to quickly assess a person one has just met, whether the clues given are as visually direct as the characteristics of a uniform or appear in a subtler form, as in the quality of fabric. When ordinary clothing takes on the qualities of disguise, when fine clothing is worn by someone who does not belong to the socially designated privileged group, his identity becomes a matter of question, too.[18] Timothy Brook has written that, in much the same way that contemporary cultural critics today dissect the democratization of luxury goods, late Ming commentators bemoaned the blurring of boundaries between classes that previously had been demarcated by one's dress as all kinds of clothes in the marketplace became increasingly accessible. Brooks writes, "late-Ming people felt the sartorial restrictions and simple tastes of an earlier era slip from their grasp as commoners dressed above their station and used clothing to renounce the anonymity of membership in a class community."[19] He quotes the scholar Chen Yao pointing to the Zhengde (1505–21) reign, which ended in the year of Xu Wei's birth, as the turning point in this change, as Chen Yao lamented the inappropriate flaunting of distinctions that had previously guaranteed social norms. When clothing alone was no longer invested with meaning, what could be done to properly distinguish one class from another? One result was the elite's retreating into ever more ambitious efforts toward connoisseurship to establish the real from the false, a kind of parsing out toward truth.[20] At the heart of *Mi Heng* is the issue of clothes; specifically, the removal of clothes, and how this removal creates the audience's idea of the man, Mi Heng. How others assess him is tied to how they weigh the social value of these clothes against the inner values of honor represented by Mi Heng.

Mi Heng engages these questions by demonstrating the way that external mechanisms such as clothing and speech express an authentic inner self, even as those external mechanisms are shed. Meanings find purchase from actions and reactions: by stripping himself bare, Mi Heng exposes Cao Cao. By accompanying a drum song to an inventory of Cao Cao's crimes, Mi Heng justifies his wordless insult of shedding clothes. Movements on the outside result in inward shifts and displacements: the section that follows will examine what is displaced and what is revealed. First I consider the references to play-acting and witnessing, contemplating their relevance in a play that is generally singled out for its literary merits but has to be at least imagined in performance to work completely. I then consider the conceit of the play's theme: that nothing can be hidden forever, and that it is the responsibility of the play—and, specifically, Mi Heng's performance within it—to reveal everything before the stage audience as well as the real audience, both of which serve as witnesses to the truth. Finally, I will look at the methods of exposure. The body and language are employed in the most uncomplicated manner in *Mi Heng*; and, as will be shown in the next three chapters, the compromises of claiming unmediated authenticity become ever more complex in the plotting of the three plays that follow. *Mi Heng* prepares readers for those deeper waters with a primer on the negotiations between outer and inner, seen-self and heard-self, which become further entangled in the other plays with questions of gender and, in the case of *Zen Master Yu*, reincarnation.

Seeing Is Believing

References to play-acting and theater within plays are part and parcel of the genre. Certainly some plays contain more of these references than others, and some, like *Mi Heng*, make performance their central premise. But in the final analysis, plays are uniquely situated to exploit the nature of disguise, self-representation, and witnessing by the very fact that they call upon the audience's willingness to comply with those features every time it watches a play. Practically speaking, the audience enters into an agreement with the players on stage every time it sits down to view a performance: for the audience's part, it accepts that this is a performance, that what the characters say is true within the parameters of the play, that a person is who she says she is, that when the actors step into their roles, the characters they represent have no consciousness of being watched beyond the borders of the stage. The audience knows that it is attending a performance, that it is a scripted performance, and that the performance is presented by actors who are consciously playing a role. This unspoken contract between the play and its audience holds true whether it is realized by actors, or whether it is imagined in the mind of a reader.[21] Plays that draw special attention to those conventions rely on their universal acceptance to make an impact.

Erving Goffman's classic work *The Presentation of Self in Everyday Life* argues that all human interactions are forms of performance. In our everyday exchanges with other people, we are aware of how we are being perceived, and we adjust our behavior to the expectations of the particular situation. Experienced, then, as we are in being both actor and audience in our daily interactions, what interest could the experience of watching (or reading) a work of drama contain? Goffman notes that in social life, people tend to have an intense interest in the disruptions of "projected definitions" of cooperation between two humans to behave in a certain manner.[22] In normal, everyday situations, we know that we are expected to perform in a certain way, and we generally do. When we don't, the disruption, using vulgar language in genteel company, for example, makes for an anecdote that can generate discussion, laughter, or gossip. Theater, then, and especially comedy, entertains by providing relief from the expectations of normal social behavior without any of the consequences of guilt or shame that would occur if one were to violate those expectations. Not social performances but rather real, theatrical performances, these performances rely equally on the audience's understanding of social mores and rules for their success. In Ernest Bauman's words, "performance as a mode of spoken verbal communication consists in the assumption of responsibility to an audience for display of communicative competence. This competence rests on the knowledge and ability to speak in socially appropriate ways. Performance involves the performer's assumption of accountability to an audience for the way in which communication is carried out, above and beyond its referential content."[23] These kinds of performance are precisely the moments that are the focus of this chapter, as they are simultaneously the subject of the drama and the manufacturers of the drama. The audience is engaged by Mi Heng's obvious disruptions, and also by the chaos that *Mi Heng* the play evokes in its very reenactment of such disruptions.

In looking at these moments of drama in *Mi Heng*, we are able to see and appreciate the disjunctions in the play, because we can imagine, with a certain amount of dread, what would happen to us if we ever dared transgress these boundaries. Mi Heng's aberrations are interesting because they capture what would not escape punishment in real life, and, indeed, did not escape punishment in his own lifetime. On stage, Mi Heng can break social rules without censure. Framed by the protective barriers of drama, his actions have meaning in a way that simply cannot be obtained in real life. Here in the stage world we can read his stripping and his insults as metaphors of truth-telling, which is no doubt why the play constantly references acting and audiences.

The conventions of Chinese drama are often cited as the inspiration for modernist playwrights like Bertolt Brecht to break the "fourth wall" of the theater and in turn to raise awareness in Western criticism about performance and audience response. As such, an attempt to read Chinese drama through the lens of Western theater criticism is often a backward effort. One example in which the inadequacies of comparison come to light is the device of addressing the audience. Writing about Shakespeare, Bridget Escolme implicates the actor addressing the audience while in character as an act of creating subjectivity. Her argument asserts that the impact comes because it upsets the conventions of drama in Shakespeare's time, which did not incorporate transgressions between the stage and audience. For the most part, the actor's occasions for direct address had evolved mainly into soliloquies; therefore, the direct address would cause a certain degree of interest as well as, perhaps, sympathy of feeling when it occurred.[24] Although by Shakespeare's time (which was almost exactly contemporaneous with Xu Wei's) drama in the West had shifted away from the ancient conventions of direct address and self-introduction inherited from the Greeks, its song drama never did. In terms of generic considerations, then, *xiqu* (traditional Chinese drama) would be better compared to Western music theater when discussing how onstage "reality" works. By convention, characters in *xiqu* always introduce themselves to the audience when entering; this occurs without any fanfare or hidden meaning or suggestion. The presence of such a convention by no means suggests that the imagination of the audience is somehow less engaged; it still plays a significant role in the interpretation and understanding of the play.

The self-introduction in Chinese drama may not be an anomaly as it is with Escolme's Shakespeare; yet, it is still worthy of our consideration. This is especially the case in Xu Wei's plays, where the roles of actors, playing, and performance are themselves plot features. Although the outcome of his performance differs from the real trajectory of Mi Heng's life, the performance is taken to be a true reenactment of Mi Heng's assault on the usurper, with the added embellishments of a few more of Cao Cao's crimes that postdated Mi Heng's original moment in court. Yu-ming He argues that these moments of performance allow the reading audience to imagine, at least, a performed space in the play; one of the examples that she gives is the switch from northern to southern songs circumscribing the end of the play within the play.[25] Moreover, the switch in musical styles is used to signal a shift in points of view; whereas the northern songs had all addressed Cao Cao's misdeeds, the southern songs celebrate Mi Heng and his accomplishments. Most importantly in this play, the self-introduction is first used to tell the audience not only what they are about to see but how they are meant to see it. Through this introduction, the judge includes the audience in the audience that will gather on stage, to witness the scene with the same attitude. This is natural to the convention, but the use of the convention has lasting implications further along in the play, which is, after all, about contested sides of a story.

At the very outset of the play, when the judge refers to the re-creation of the scene, he does not present it as a formal trial where the audience sits as a jury to sentence him. In fact, he tells the audience that the Underworld has already made its decision, and Mi Heng is soon to be promoted to Heaven as a result of his celebrated actions. The reenactment is merely an entertainment put on for the viewers' enjoyment, albeit an entertainment with a moral message. The judge describes Mi Heng's reputation: "Now wasn't that something to shake up Heaven and Earth? Wasn't it a wonderful sight like some grand wooden puppet show?"[26] The judge has already likened the historical event of Cao Cao's trial to a puppet show, something that was a spectacle or wonderful sight (奇觀 *qiguan*), yet his description is an imagined one; having only heard of what happened, he imagines that it was likely to have been a great performance, and this inspires him to request a reprise.

As Mi Heng is set to leave the Underworld at any moment, the judge hastens to invite him: "Now he is about to ascend to Heaven, and I intend to summon him here, and at the same time release Cao Man, and have them reenact the age-old scenario of 'Cursing the Host.'"[27] This is the premise of Xu Wei's play, boldly stated: the spirits in the Underworld want to see a show. This show is specified, and the characters are explicitly said to be performing the scene that is so often referred to as "Cursing the Host" (*mazuo* 罵座) throughout *Mi Heng* that it takes on the flavor of a title, almost always referred to as "Cursing the Host Back Then" (*jiuri mazuo* 舊日罵座). It is also more explicitly referenced when the judge instructs: "Cao Cao, today we want you to take on your former role of Prime Minister and, with Mister Mi, perform the affair of

'Beating the Drum and Cursing the Host' from back then,"[28] cunningly emphasizing the "role" Cao Cao "played" as Prime Minister in the context of their play-acting.

With the play staged in this way, we are always aware that we are watching a performance and not a retrial. This in no small part mirrors the experience of watching drama in general. Certainly actors can be counted on to embellish some of the details, to improvise around certain standard set scenes, or to perform on "off" or "on" days; but the audience understands that it is more or less watching the same play every time. The judge phrases it this way: "I humbly beseech you, may I be so bold as to trouble you to return to the events of that long-past day?"[29] The repeated references to returning to a moment in the past emphasize drama's ability to recreate that moment for the sole purpose of entertainment.[30] Later in the play, when Cao Cao is told to summon his famous singing girls to entertain the stage audience, he protests, "That was back then, how can we do that now?" to which the judge responds, "Don't worry about it, just call for them and you'll have them."[31] Even within the already impossible parameters of this scene (an Underworld feast), which we would not be able to witness except through a play, the judge proposes what even the phantom Cao Cao considers another impossibility. He asks Cao Cao to summon girls who would not have accompanied him to the Underworld; but in the world of Xu Wei's theater, anything is possible. These experiences can only occur in the world of the theater, making them even more delectable for their audiences. The work for the actors, then, is to set aside their identities and take on the qualities of these imagined characters, in order to transport the audience to an imagined world once the curtain is drawn and the play begins.[32]

The appearance of the singing girls, who are brought out for an interlude in which they criticize Cao Cao first indirectly and then directly, further reminds us of the artificiality of theater. Although this does not add to the plot or to our knowledge about the characters, it allows for yet another reference to an embedded performance: here is a performance (the singing girls) within a performance ("Cursing the Throne") that is already embedded in the play (*Mi Heng*). It is also the strongest evidence in the play that *Mi Heng* was written with performance in mind. A reader of the play can equally imagine and be delighted by the scene, and in fact many of the men who wrote encomia of Xu Wei singled out *Mi Heng* as delightful reading. Yet part of the delight of reading it comes from imagining it as it was performed, just as all of the souls in the Underworld delighted in imagining Mi Heng's deeds performed before they had the chance to actually see it before their eyes, which had been their "long cherished wish."[33]

As one of the girls sings during the song interlude: "Rub in the powder, paint on the rouge, you'll stay flushed for a while."[34] Although the reference to rouge and painted faces is a common convention of *ci* song lyrics, it takes on significance in the context of both "Cursing the Throne" and *Mi Heng*. Already in this play, the judge has called Cao Cao's position as Prime Minister a role and reduced the whole historical moment to a stage entertainment. Mi Heng and Cao Cao are requested to play their parts—or to put on a performance—repeatedly, again drawing attention to the fact that they are acting. Mi Heng is doing double duty as a performer, playing himself as he hurled insults at the throne, and also playing the drum in accompaniment. Not surprisingly, he tires of these tasks and puts an end to the performance by announcing that he can no longer play the drum roll. These references all prepare the audience to contemplate the meaning of truth and authentic intent when performance and pretense are part of how those qualities are expressed. The entertainment is derived from watching this performance while at the same time making commentaries and editorializing as it goes along. The importance of the performance is in the audience's witnessing, but what exactly are they witnessing?

As the judge tells Mi Heng, "That day when you took up the drums and beat them to curse Cao Cao, it amazed the world."[35] This is a moment in history that caught people's attention, so much so that the denizens of the Underworld expressed their desire to view it for themselves. Foremost in the motivation for witnessing this exchange, although later justifications will come, is the potential for pure entertainment. Apparently even travails of the Underworld can become routine and dull; perhaps there are only so many times one can talk about the latest newcomer before longing for new topics of conversation. The judge expresses his wish: "Having the two of them give such a performance will make for a good amount of conversation for those of us in the Underworld offices."[36] It is a highly anticipated night at the theater, fodder for next-day small talk, rather than an opportunity to mete out justice, as that has already been decided.

Even as the audience is alerted to the aspects of formal performance in *Mi Heng*, the play itself draws attention to the audience. A play is, after all, meant to be watched, and *Mi Heng* reminds us of this fact by making explicit references to the stage audience. Cao Cao is doubly implicated, as he is both a member of the audience, seated as a guest as part of the audience, and a participant in the performance. The judge, too, is asked to take part in the performance while watching it. Clearly, there is more at work here than a simple gladdening of everyone's hearts, a happy distraction from the tedium of everyday life; Mi Heng suggests as much when he asks to include anachronous events in his revival of the scene. Witnessing the scene also allows for participation between members of the audience, especially the stage audience, who are not only invited to speak during the performance but who will have something to talk about afterward. The judge often responds after each of Mi Heng's accusations to weigh in on whether the accusations are within the realm of acceptability, exclaiming "the Prime Minister [Cao Cao] is right" (*Chengxiang shuo de shi* 丞相説得是) and then immediately afterward, "this too, that the madman [Mi Heng] says, makes sense. Let's have another cup and hear some more of these silly excuses."[37] It is not difficult to imagine this happening during a real staging of *Mi Heng*, too, where it would have been considered perfectly decorous for an audience member to call out accolades during a scene or to share thoughts or reactions aloud with other members of the audience. It is just as easy to imagine a reader commenting along the margins with notes in a reading copy of the play, and then later to see that accompanying commentary appearing printed in a new edition of the play.

What all this points to is a relationship of exchange between performance and viewer, demonstrating just how much one relies upon the other. Having heard about something from someone else is not the same thing as having seen it firsthand, even though this reenactment of "Cursing the Throne" is not in fact a return to the past. The participants constantly remind us that they are merely putting on a performance. Mi Heng receives permission to introduce events into the scene that occurred long after that day in Cao Cao's court, and Cao Cao protests, bringing up the differences between the present moment in the Underworld and the events that they are presenting. Yet, the judge insists: "Although I, in the time that I conducted my official investigation, got to hear one or two pieces of evidence regarding this incident, I regret that I never had the chance to experience it firsthand."[38] Even within this fantastical framework, the judge does not imagine a time-travel machine that ensures his presence in the actual moment. Acknowledging that he cannot possibly take part in the historic scene, he takes first-hand experience in the form of a simulacrum of this well-known event, not at all unlike what we in the real audience experience. The implication is that something distinct is to be gained from watching the events unfold before one's eyes.

The primary claim of entertainment notwithstanding, the judge's final comments in the play point to further ramifications:

> Having seen this Mi Zhengping's "The Yuyang Triple Rolls,"
> I laughed until my all-seeing eyes could barely see.
> Were it not for the thousand statutes of criminal law in Fierce Yama's Hell,
> All would say "Prime Minister Cao is a divine immortal in the Eight Grottoes."[39]

The judge refers to the play within the play not as "Cursing the Throne," but as "The Yuyang Triple Rolls," which is one of the alternate titles of Xu Wei's play.[40] Within the context of Xu Wei's play, the judge notes that Mi Heng's performance has been a success because it has made him laugh: it is good entertainment. Then he addresses the legacy of this performance, and not just of the historical performance, but also of the one they have just witnessed. Because Mi Heng was allowed to take the drum up again to curse Cao Cao, he has managed to change how Cao Cao is viewed. To anyone who might have thought that Cao Cao was enjoying the afterlife in grand style, the play stands as evidence that he is punished forevermore in the Underworld for this inventory of misdeeds. This calls to mind the judge's opening quatrain:

> Our judgments here are very clear indeed,
> Bad and good deeds, ultimately, cannot be denied.
> As for those debtors, though they may hide, it's not for long,
> Never does a debt go unpaid.[41]

In referring to Mi Heng's performance not as "Cursing the Throne" but rather as "The Yuyang Triple Rolls," the judge extends the view farther outward, conflating the stage audience and the real audience. The only difference between the audience experience of the play and that of the stage audience's is that they are, unknown to them, also part of a performance; otherwise, we have all shared an experience. Here a trivial performance made for entertainment and resulting in laughter claims to have also altered history, for it presents drama as a force powerful enough to change the way real historical personages are seen and remembered. This play could also be a celebration of the absolutely superficial. Viewed in this way, it is a mere entertainment, written off the cuff, to titillate a few friends in private company with a bit of vulgar undressing and rude language. This may well be the case, yet its artful legacy lies beneath the surface: all kinds of performances are, by default, revelatory. When Cao Cao criticizes one of the singing girls for her use of cliché (*jiuhua* 舊話), she retorts that clichés and metaphors work because they are true:

> Second Girl (sings): Obscured by the snow, the egret is seen only when it flies.
> (*Ya-yi-ge-qiao-xi, ya-yi-ge-qiao-xi*)
> Hidden among the willows, the parrot (*Qiao-da-xi, da-qiao-xi*)
> is known only when it speaks.
> (*Ya-yi-ge-qiao-xi, ya-yi-ge-qiao-xi*)
>
> Cao: Those last two lines are clichés.
> Second Girl: Though clichés, they stick.[42]

The lines, which echo the belief that the truth will always come out, "stick" because they contain an element of truth. As the judge said in his preamble to inviting Mi Heng to perform, "he exposed Cao's every fault so that he had nowhere to hide."[43] *Mi Heng* is about revealing truths, and it reveals them to an audience onstage as well as to the people who have gathered to watch the play. The accusations that Mi Heng levies against Cao Cao are all part of the historical evidence surrounding Cao Cao's many exploits, but here they have been inventoried to make a picture of the man. What was hidden is now exposed, and this exposure makes all of the members of the audience complicit in their knowledge of Cao Cao's misdeeds. Now they share an open secret, a secret that is accessed only through the play itself, and expressed through external, surface elements. The secrets that they have taken into their confidence are the knowledge of Cao Cao's true nature. Any rumors of his adversary's accomplishments or acts of heroism notwithstanding, Mi Heng has finally set the record straight. Intriguingly, the elements in service of revealing the truth are the elements that become increasingly problematized over the course of the next three plays. For now they are presented with little ambivalence. It is not a case of word made flesh, but simply a case of word and flesh, equal in meaning, both employed in the act of making meaning and defining oneself.

Mi Heng explains what he is going to do before he begins to berate Cao Cao through his song and his drumming:

> He held a banquet and reclined on the couch,
> Told me to grasp my mallets, clack the clapperboards, and beat the drum,
> And, in time with the drumbeat, I attacked him.
> My insults, sentence by sentence, were sharp points like flying daggers and spears,
> My drumming, beat by beat, were crashing thunder churning up wind and sand.

He tells the audience directly that the music is going to be the instrument that reveals Cao Cao's crimes, as if the actual movement of the mallets is going to beat out some abstract form of Cao Cao that will let out the truth: a version of word made flesh. Here musical instruments, song, and sentences collude not just to attack, but to reveal. He emphasizes:

> Cao Cao! This drumskin is your body's own husk.
> This mallet is your own rib from elbow's height,
> This nail hole is like your empty heart,
> These clappers are those monstrous fangs in your mouth.
> With these two sticks I'll beat your roguishness through your skin,
> And in that space of time, I still won't be able to give your wicked heart its due honors.[44]

The conceit gets more complicated when the instruments take on symbolic meaning to represent the actual parts of the body. When the song began, Mi Heng was beating instruments as if against Cao Cao's body to strike out the facts. As he progresses, the instruments begin to symbolize various body parts. This depiction of the body as truth is especially remarkable in contrast to what the audience witnessed several moments before: the momentous scene of Mi Heng's stripping on stage. He takes off his clothes and stands naked while exchanging insults with Cao Cao for several lines before putting on the regulation garments. The scene sets the precedent for our understanding of what clothing and the body mean in this play. Wordless actions, like stripping or drumming, are significant and carry great visual meaning. We learn about what these actions signify through language; the words of Mi Heng's songs accompanying the "Yuyang Triple Rolls" are what justify these actions. After the judge comments, "Prime Minister, you really can't outtalk him on this," Cao Cao concedes: "If I could, I wouldn't be in this state now."[45]

Mi Heng offers a simple presentation of the tropes central to the remainder of the plays. The play introduces questions of the body and what covers it, but the act of removing layers is unidirectional: Mi Heng strips in service of the truth. *Mulan* and *Girl Graduate* introduce the necessity of clothes for a person to reveal her true talents, even as she protests that the internal self has always been the only essential self. *Zen Master Yu* complicates things further, with selves actually exchanging one body for another. *Mi Heng* is not the only play within *Four Cries of a Gibbon* to feature stripping of some form or another, but it is the last time that we will see it displayed so bare of ambiguity.

2

The Shape of Things: Zen Master Yu Has a Dream of Cuixiang

Zen Master Yu Has a Dream of Cuixiang (*Yu Chanshi cuixiang yimeng* 玉禪師翠鄉一夢), or *Zen Master Yu*, is a two-act *zaju* with a symmetrical plot structure.[1] Indeed, it is almost hyper-symmetrical: the way that the text mirrors itself echoes the very tropes of mirroring and repetition that are at the heart of the play. Wang Jide cited this play and not *Mi Heng* as the first play that Xu Wei wrote for the collection *Four Cries of a Gibbon.*[2] This may be because, when considered in the context of the other three plays, *Zen Master Yu* is the play that best articulates, and complicates, the themes within the entire collection. Dress and costume play a crucial role in all of the *Four Cries of a Gibbon.* Here, however, costume changes are not used simply to titillate or amuse the audience, as with the characters Hua Mulan, Mi Heng, and Huang Chonggu in the other plays; instead, costume changes constitute the main action and predicaments of *Zen Master Yu.*

Of the four plays, this one most emphasizes the power costume can impart and the act of putting on an identity by changing one's clothes. Above and beyond drama's implicit ability to do so, it addresses the symbolic nature of clothing by employing actors in costume, by having a character like the Moonlight Monk (*Yueming heshang* 月明和尚) use masks as he acts out a story to a bewildered Liu Cui, who doesn't yet know she is the reincarnation of Master Yu, or Yu Tong. To make things more complicated, he acts out a truth profound enough to cause her to cast off her own clothes and to put on a monk's robes; yet, the pat turn of events and the absolute lightness of spirit never let us forget that this is, after all, a folly. Even more fascinating, the play not only shows how bodies can be inscribed with meaning, as when one "reads" the clothed body as text, but it delightfully illustrates how meaning can be inscribed by bodies, as when the Moonlight Monk literally spells out the characters for "reincarnation," making his body resemble the actual word.

Like *Mulan* and *Girl Graduate*, which will be discussed in the following two chapters, *Zen Master Yu* exploits the comic potential of gender transgressions. Those two plays, with their female cross-dressers, seem practically tame in this context. After all, Mulan and Huang Chonggu only assume male dress out of necessity; their physical bodies are not affected by any transformation; and each remains aware of her true female identity, returning to it at play's end. *Zen Master Yu*, on the other hand, does not have such a simple solution; for in this play, physical bodies are abandoned or occupied, and the main character's original gender is not restored at the end. Yutong, a male monk, deliberately seeks to be reborn as a woman. Having achieved this goal between the first and the second act, he loses awareness of his success and is, for all intents and purposes, a woman called Liu Cui. Following the Moonlight Monk's elaborate conversion, in which she is finally convinced of her true identity, Liu Cui changes back into male clothing. Her body does not change. To accept this, and to accept the evisceration of the former self that it implies, means to acknowledge that identity exists somewhere either in one's state of mind or in one's outward show of clothing, but not within the physical body itself. Even when Liu Cui accepts her "proper" identity, she has no other choice but to take leave completely of the mortal world. This is, of course, how Yutong left the world for the first time, too. Complications of gender thus add another layer to the inherent comedy of limitless roles within all four plays, how the role one plays is transmitted to others, and how roles can be read and understood.

As with all of the *Four Cries of a Gibbon*, *Zen Master Yu* playfully explores the notion of playing false. *Mi Heng*, as argued in the previous chapter, presents a warning that falsehood (Cao Cao's) will eventually be found out. *Girl Graduate* and *Mulan* will both present secondary characters (the retried criminals and Leopard Skin, respectively) who have been accused of falsehood or who have taken on false roles in contexts that act as foils to Mulan and Chonggu's morally pure and selflessly motivated decisions to change their identities. Xu Wei effects a two-part play that contains opposite perspectives on the functions of play-acting. In the first half, deception is poisonous; in the second half, deception is redemptive. *Zen Master Yu* focuses our attention on how we construe deception, a theme that is present everywhere in *Four Cries of a Gibbon*, but never so concentrated and starkly presented as it is in this play.

Curiously, *Zen Master Yu* has received the least critical attention of the four plays. *Mi Heng* is singled out for its literary qualities, *Mulan* and *Girl Graduate* are noted for their feminist undertones,[3] and all three lend themselves to interpretations of the text as an allegory for the dissatisfied literatus, giving vent to his frustrations that his talents have gone unrecognized. *Zen Master Yu*, on the other hand, is noted primarily as a chronological marker for arranging the plays (see Wang Jide's comments in note 2, within). Elsewhere, some have employed it in attempts to date the play, though this dating cannot be proven; and subsequently, others have tried to do the reverse, drawing autobiographical connections by linking it to a time when Xu Wei was known to have stayed at a nearby monastery. It has even been suggested that the play was written after Xu Wei murdered his wife, as an expression of his regret and hope for her reincarnation into a better life. Wang Zhiyong's comparative study of the play with the Buddhist deliverance play *Delivering Liu Cui* (*Du Liu Cui* 度柳翠) and *Honglian zhai* primarily concerns plot differences and provenances rather than critical analysis.[4] This chapter will consider the ways that *Zen Master Yu* crystallizes the essential questions that reverberate throughout *Four Cries of a Gibbon*. It even suggests some of the answers, all in the raiment of an equal parts lurid, vulgar, ridiculous, and utterly enjoyable play.

Themes of Deliverance in Zen Master Yu

Zen Master Yu can be categorized as a deliverance play (*dutuoju* 度脱劇), a fairly large subgenre of Yuan and Ming *zaju*. Broadly speaking, deliverance play plots, whether Buddhist or Daoist, feature a minor immortal who resides in the mortal world but is not consciously aware of that fact. He or she is approached by another immortal, who has been sent to the dusty world on a mission to "deliver" or return the immortal to his or her proper place. Not surprisingly, the message is received with incredulity, and the deliverer is compelled to ever more dramatic ploys to secure the immortal's awareness of his or her true immortal identity, thus ensuring a passage to heaven. The best-known deliverance play is the Yuan *zaju* by Ma Zhiyuan 馬致遠 (1250–1321) entitled *Yellow Millet Dream* (*Huangliang meng* 黃梁夢), which relates the Daoist deliverance of the scholar Lü Dongbin 呂洞賓 (Tang dynasty) by one of the Eight Immortals, Zhongli Quan 鍾離權. In the play, Lü is an aspiring scholar who stops at a guesthouse on his way to the examinations. In the time it takes to cook some yellow millet, he experiences the vicissitudes of a lifetime: he achieves astronomical political success, only to then witness the complete dissolution of his personal life into betrayal and eventual murder. Awakening just as his dream self is about to be murdered, he finds that the yellow millet put to boil when he fell asleep is not yet cooked. Thus convinced of the utter futility of earthly desires, he devotes himself instead to following Zhongli Quan.[5]

Another Daoist deliverance play, the anonymous play *Lan Caihe* 籃采和 found in the *Supplementary Selections from the Yuan Dramas* (*Yuanqu xuan waibian* 元曲選外編), emphasizes the play's use of interventions and even deceptions to reveal greater truths.[6] The eponymous Lan, one of the lesser-known Eight Immortals, has to be delivered from the mortal body of Xu Jian 許堅. The Immortal Zhongli Quan descends to urge Xu to abandon his earthly career as an actor. When Xu refuses, Zhongli Quan sends Lü Dongbin to impersonate a magistrate, who has Xu seized and punished, setting the stage for Zhongli Quan to offer Xu his only escape by serving him. Xu chooses to go with Zhongli Quan, but his earthly family soon discovers his whereabouts and prevails upon him to return home. Xu refuses, but years later, when he is finally reunited with his family, now itinerant players, and just as he is preparing to join them for good, he is again whisked away by Zhongli Quan and Lü Dongbin to feast with the Queen Mother of the West. This play about actors is a fascinating exploration of how falsehood can expose truths. *Lan Caihe* is about how a mortal actor (who is actually an immortal but does not know it) must be awakened to his true identity by immortals who *do* know that they are immortals but who must resort to acting as mortals to achieve their goal. Of course, all of this effort in the way of play-acting paradoxically instructs the audience to completely and utterly reject the play-acting world of falseness.

Deliverance as a theme, whether or not with analogous religious premises, is a perennial favorite in popular entertainment from Yuan drama to contemporary Hollywood film, because it gives a character an opportunity to see or experience life as it might have been lived—without having to commit to that life. The experience of witnessing how one's life might have followed these alternate paths turns the character around to live life differently. A lost soul does not necessarily need religious arguments to try to forge a different path. In contrast to other traditions, however, the philosophical underpinnings of the Buddhist and Daoist deliverance plays are not satisfactorily resolved with the protagonist's choosing a different kind of life. Instead, he relinquishes the world and all earthly desires and ambitions; he gives up *all* roles, not just a specific one. On the topic of *Delivering Liu Cui*, one of the sources for *Zen Master Yu*, Wilt Idema writes: "The plot . . . closely parallels the [D]aoist deliverance plays, but, in contrast to those, it does not only include allegorical episodes, but is allegorical in its basic conception."[7] The Buddhist play, more so than the Daoist one, is based in a tradition of expedient means that uses allegory as a teaching tool and as a way to view the world. Thus, it makes use of internal allegory, as when the Moonlight Monk is identified with the moon and the delivered soul Liu (willow 柳) Cui with the willow, suggesting further associations in Buddhist iconography.[8]

Delivering Liu Cui, which is discussed in greater detail below, is the source for *Zen Master Yu*'s second act. The full name of the play, written in the Yuan dynasty by Li Shouqing 李壽卿, is *The Moonlight Monk Delivers Liu Cui* (*Yueming heshang du Liu Cui* 月明和尚度柳翠).[9] The play is simply about Liu Cui's deliverance, with no mention of Red Lotus at all, and *Zen Master Yu* barely resembles *Delivering Liu Cui*. The Yuan play involves dream sequences, religious debates, and a boat trip. Insomuch as it is an antecedent, it lends familiar names and a deliverance situation, but it is hardly copied, or even adapted, by Xu Wei. It does, however, give us some insight into the subgenre of the deliverance play, demonstrating the potential that anyone, even a common prostitute, can assume the proper path: What could be a more persuasive argument for the malleability of roles than that?

It has been speculated that the deliverance play originated in entertainments performed at funerals, as the kinds of rites that would assist spirits in finding their way to paradise. As the plays developed into Yuan *zaju* form, they became exclusively reserved for birthday celebrations, because they celebrated themes of longevity.[10] It is not difficult to see how this would be so; the deliverance plays, especially as the celebrant's age advances, offer an alternative to mortality. The delivered is reminded of the futility of earthly ambition and embraces instead a new identity as an immortal, or perhaps is invited to feast with the Queen Mother of the West. How inferior the splendors of this very birthday celebration must be, the plays suggest, when considered in light of the promised delights of the next world.

The deliverance play functions in part as a reminder to the audience of the potential for redemption within all of us, and it does so in the broadest strokes, so that even the basest of humans, not just a fêted official at his birthday party, might seem capable of being redeemed—an actor, perhaps, like Lan Caihe, or a prostitute, perhaps, like Liu Cui. We cannot ignore the significance of plays about actors or those other practitioners of "performance" art, prostitutes, which will in turn be performed by actors, who were historically interchangeable with prostitutes. One might even make the argument that the performance of such a play enacts a public cleansing, a purification not just of the characters on the stage, but of the viewers gathered to watch this ritual celebration.[11] Xu Wei's *Zen Master Yu* can hardly be taken seriously as a religious document warning about the dangers of worldliness. It does, however, adopt the existing vocabulary of the deliverance play, casting familiar character types into a familiar plot structure. The innovation here comes with the way the same characters cast in the same plot become opposite versions of themselves from the first act to the second, perceived differently according to their changing circumstances. The malignant and cunning vixen from the first act is contrasted with the prostitute forced into the profession by her family's dire straits in the second act (whose fate is determined by her father's sins, not her own). The daft monk of the first act, who follows all directions literally, is unwittingly reborn as a prostitute and contrasted with the Moonlight Monk, who comes to redeem his fellow monk with metaphors and sleights of hand. *Zen Master Yu*, although its conventional cast and concluding abjuration are typical of the deliverance play, is less about ritual purification and Buddhist doctrine than it is about entertainment. The entertainment is not effected through the realization of Liu Cui's renunciation; this is already a foregone conclusion. What matters here is *how* that resolution is reached, and that conclusion says more to us about language and how we speak and dress ourselves into existence than it does about religious epiphany, political hypocrisy, or public purification.

Reading Between the Lines

The first act of *Zen Master Yu* begins when a *sheng* playing the role of the Zen Buddhist monk Yutong 玉通 enters the stage. Yutong explains that he and Moonlight Monk are both ancient bodhisattvas from the Western Heaven, but whereas the elder monk has left the world, he himself has not yet reached enlightenment and still resides on earth in Yutong's body, practicing Zen Buddhism at the Water and Moon Monastery (*shuiyue si* 水月寺). Yutong goes on to declaim exhaustively about the arduous process of rising in the ranks of Buddhism, likening it to the government official system, and detailing the perils of one mistake that can wipe out years of striving toward higher levels of being. He finally interrupts his own musings to recall that he has to tell the audience his story.[12] As Yutong explains it, Yutong has refused to join a welcoming party for a newly arrived official who is both young and talented, Liu Xuanjiao 柳宣教, claiming that it would violate the cloistering he has long maintained. This detail is followed quickly by the entrance of Red Lotus (*Hong Lian* 紅蓮), played by a *tie*,[13] who tells the audience that she has been hired by the offended Liu to teach the monk a lesson. She comes in filial dress, pretending through her costume to be a virtuous widow who, having gone to sweep her husband's grave and make offerings, gets caught in the rain on her way back to the city and finds herself locked outside the city gates. Yutong offers her shelter but demands that she sleep far away from him. Undeterred, Red Lotus cries out in agony, claiming that an old stomach ailment is bothering her. She tells Yutong that the only cure for this excess of cold is for him to take off his pants and rub his warm belly against hers.[14] Unable to resist her pleas, Yutong rushes offstage with her. When the two return, the arias have already begun to sound, announcing his fall into her "carnal snare."

The songs that make up this act contain Yutong's laments at twenty years of dedication to an ascetic life wasted, and these songs are interspersed with Red Lotus's mocking retorts. Yutong then curses Red Lotus, telling her that she will surely come back as an animal in the next life for her misdeeds. He determines to seek his revenge by being reborn into Liu Xuanjiao's family as a daughter who will become, like Red Lotus, a prostitute. After writing a response anticipating Liu's missive, and a last will and testament for his acolyte, Yutong leaves his body behind. When his acolyte discovers the corpse, he at first mistakenly assumes that Red

Lotus was the bodhisattva Guanyin, come to initiate his master. He eventually discovers the letters that explain the true circumstances. Shortly afterward, a messenger comes from Liu's home; finding the recipient's corpse, he wonders how he will bring back an answer to his master. The act closes with a foreboding aria sung by the acolyte.

Structurally, the second act is almost identical to the first; this time, another monk, played by a *wai* (extra male), enters the stage carrying numerous props and making a long speech also filled with religious jargon. He identifies himself as Moonlight Monk, who has come from the Western Heaven in response to a fear expressed in Yutong's parting note that his new incarnation would not know that she was Yutong. Moonlight Monk tells the audience that Yutong's wish has been fulfilled; he is now a member of the Liu family, which suffered a decline so severe that the daughter Liu Cui (who is, as Yutong had feared, unaware that she is Yutong) has been forced into prostitution. Moonlight Monk, pitying her unenlightened state, has come to show Liu Cui who she really is. Knowing that she has an appointment with a customer at the Great Buddha temple, he has come to meet her there. Liu Cui arrives, but a servant tells her that her date has been delayed by his son's illness. She notices Moonlight Monk sitting in meditation and asks him where he has come from. Instead of replying, he pantomimes a response, pointing to the western sky, which she interprets correctly as "Western Heaven." Convinced that he is mad, she continues to question him, and he continues to refuse to speak, miming instead the different component parts of the characters for reincarnation, which she also correctly identifies. As Liu Cui begins to sing, she senses something uncanny about the monk's reference to reincarnation, but she does not know what he means. When she asks for clarification, he stubbornly refuses to speak, putting on hats and masks and acting out various poses and gestures that suggest hilarious potential for comedy when performed.[15] Gradually, Liu Cui comes closer and closer to understanding what he means, and she even realizes that her father played a part in the business. But when she concludes incorrectly that the reincarnation is yet to come and that she must be pregnant, the frustrated Moonlight Monk finally resorts to reading Yutong's letter aloud. At last, Liu Cui understands that she herself is really Yutong, immediately changes into a monk's cap and plain clothes, and departs together with Moonlight Monk toward the Western Heaven.

Zen Master Yu *and Its Previous Incarnations*

Zen Master Yu clearly demonstrates Xu Wei's inventiveness in the way that he weaves a series of disparate sources into a neatly paired set of interactions. The two acts of Xu Wei's play are actually derived from two separate and unrelated plots that are culled from short stories and a play. The discussion that follows details the extensive grafting and manipulation that was managed in creating this seemingly effortlessly balanced and lighthearted play, suggesting that the emphases on precise role reversals were deliberately calculated and manufactured by Xu Wei. The first of the two stories used for the first half of *Zen Master Yu* is a brief anecdote involving a Zen Buddhist monk named Apprehension (Zhicong 至聰) and a young woman named Red Lotus (Honglian 紅蓮). The anecdote occurs in Zhang Bangji's 張邦畿 (dates unknown, Song dynasty) *Shi'er xiaoming lu* 侍兒小名錄 and proceeds as follows:

> During the Five Dynasties Period, there was a Zen monk named Apprehension. He cultivated himself for ten years on Zhurong Peak, living a life of austerity, without fear of seduction. Then, one day he descended from the mountain and, reaching the roadside, he saw a beautiful woman named Red Lotus (Honglian 紅蓮). One look and he was taken, and he immediately trysted with her. The next day, the monk got up to take a bath, and he and the woman were transformed. There is a song that goes:
>
> There was in the mountain a monk, Apprehension,
> Who in ten years never left Zhurong Peak.
> All the Bodhi water he accumulated in his belly
> Spilled right into a Red Lotus leaf.[16]

The next time Red Lotus appears, it is in the vernacular short story (*huaben* 話本) "The Zen Buddhist Abbot Wujie Has Sexual Relations with Red Lotus" (*Wujie Chanshi si Honglian ji* 五戒禪師私紅蓮記), or "The Zen Buddhist Abbot Wujie." It differs significantly from the Song dynasty anecdote.[17]

The basic story of "The Zen Buddhist Abbot Wujie" follows an old abbot named Wujie (Five Precepts 五戒) and his junior companion, the monk Mingwu (Bright Enlightenment 明悟).[18] On a snowy day, Wujie's acolyte Qingyi 清一 finds an abandoned baby with a note stating her birth date and the name Red Lotus attached to her clothing. Qingyi brings her back to the monastery with the Abbot's permission, where she is raised until she is sixteen. When she turns sixteen, Wujie sees and desires her, and demands to be left alone to despoil her. When Mingwu finds out, he mocks his old friend with a suggestive poem on the subject of the lotus flower. When Wujie realizes the meaning of Mingwu's poem, he departs from the world, leaving behind a farewell poem (*ci shi song* 辭世頌) of his own to explain himself. Wujie is later reborn as the poet Su Shi 蘇軾 (1037–1101), and the story addresses the historical Su Shi's initial disdain for and later dedication to Buddhism. Mingwu, in pursuit of Mingjie, is reborn as Su Shi's friend and teacher, Xie Ruiqing 謝瑞卿, and later given the Buddhist name Foyin 佛印 (Buddha Seal).[19] Under Foyin's influence, Su Shi eventually follows Buddhist teachings and changes his name to Su Dongpo (Su of the Eastern Slope 蘇東坡). Aside from a handful of obvious similarities (a Zen Buddhist monk gives in to his desire for a young woman named Red Lotus, thus ruining many years of Buddhist cultivation. The monk is reborn as someone else who is unaware of his former life, and is then delivered from the former life by a friend who has been reborn to "chase" and save him), there are few correspondences between the story and Xu Wei's play. More significant to us is the use of letters and poems as evidence. The written word identifies the players: the note attached to the baby identifies her to the monks as Red Lotus. The written word also reveals what knowledge one may possess, as when Wuming lets Wujie know of his awareness of Wujie's indiscretions through a poem, and when Wujie lets Wuming know that he's leaving the world through his farewell poem.[20]

The source for the addition of Liu Cui in the second act of the play is Li Shouqing's (1616–17) *Yuanquxuan zaju* "Delivering Liu Cui." This play exists only in late Ming editions, and the earliest bibliographical sources list its name as *Moonlight Thrice Delivers the Crossroads Willow* (*Yueming heshang du linqi Liu* 月明和尚度臨岐柳).[21] The most significant of Feng Menglong and Xu Wei's borrowings from Li Shouqing's play may be its title. Although the Yuan play's full name echoes the GJXS 29 story title, "Moonlight Monk Delivers Liu Cui" (*Yueming heshang du Liu Cui* 月明和尚度柳翠), there are few other similarities. There is no indication in the Yuan play, as there is in Xu Wei's *Zen Master Yu* and Feng Menglong's GJXS 29 texts, that Liu Cui is related to the Liu family; in fact, in Li Shouqing's version, Liu Cui is not a Liu by birth but takes her madam's (surnamed Liu) family name.[22] What the Yuan play mainly lends to Xu Wei's *Zen Master Yu* is the situation of a courtesan in an unpleasant situation. Liu Cui is twice fallen. She is first a willow in Guanyin's vase, then a mortal in the Zhang family, and later, after falling on even worse times, a prostitute. In the figure of Monk Yutong, we see a reverse transformation: the mad monk, who is really the most clear-sighted, spends the greater part of the play convincing Liu Cui of her true identity.

Although Xu Wei does not reproduce the specific methods of awakening in *Zen Master Yu*, his play generally represents the methods used in the deliverance play. No reasonable person should be expected to accept the news that he or she is a reincarnation of a frond in a vase. The subject is, instead, edged toward this realization through methods of indirect persuasion. Signs need to be read and riddles puzzled out gradually, so that the convert might even begin to feel that she made the discovery naturally. This is certainly a scenario that Xu Wei adapts and takes to new heights, emphasizing how these games quite literally spell out who the characters are, and who the characters are meant to be; along the way, one might be led to speculate as well on who we are, and who we are meant to be. These themes in Li Shouqing's version shed light on our reading of *Zen Master Yu*, as they introduce the difficulty of expressing what is deliberately inexpressible.

Delivering Liu Cui opens with a wedge act (*xiezi* 楔子) that introduces Moonlight Monk and Liu Cui, explaining that Liu Cui was once a willow branch in Guanyin's vase. Found to be impure, the willow branch is sent down to Earth to be a mortal, and Liu Cui becomes a courtesan, patronized by Niu Lin 牛璘.[23] The wedge also introduces Liu Cui's madam, from whom Liu Cui (born to the Zhang family) gets her surname. Madam Liu orders rites to be held for her husband from the Xianxiao Monastery 顯孝寺 with money given to Liu Cui by Niu Lin. The abbot, needing ten monks to complete the task, has no choice but to call in Moonlight Monk, who is known to be mad. True to his reputation, Moonlight walks in carrying a moon and singing its praises. Moonlight Monk is played by the *zhengmo* and has a singing role in the play.

Act 1 follows the wedge act, with the monks arriving at Madam Liu's to perform the rites. Moonlight Monk continues to profess his exceptional status even while acting erratically, and, upon meeting Liu Cui, tries to encourage her to leave multiple times while refusing to answer any of her questions directly. He repeats his attempt to convert her three times, and is eventually thrown out of the house by Madam Liu. Act 2 involves a number of dreams that Liu Cui reports to the audience. She first recounts a dream about being a cat and tries to find out what the dream means while avoiding Moonlight. Naturally, Moonlight Monk knows exactly where to wait for her, and there he accosts her, revealing that he already knows about her dream. Her interest thus piqued, Red Lotus is engaged by Moonlight Monk's knowledge and later is induced into a dream state by Moonlight Monk. Finally, Moonlight Monk explains her dream to her, and she is converted as his disciple. The tripling of the dreams echoes the three attempts made in act 1. Wilt Idema also notes that the dream that occurs in the middle of the act "finds its counterpart in many other deliverance plays and is one of the most frequently employed devices to convince the convert of the inconstancy of life."[24] In act 3, Moonlight Monk accompanies Liu Cui when she returns home to Madam Liu and Niu Lin. In this act, Moonlight Monk destroys Liu Cui's clothes and then takes her on a ferry ride to cross (*du* 度) over to the next shore. In the fourth and final act, Moonlight delivers a speech on the Law, defending it against questions from the abbot, the novice, and Liu Cui. Liu Cui leaves her body in the seated position, demonstrating that she has purposefully left her earthly form to enter Nirvana; later, Moonlight Monk disappears as well. At the end of the play, Moonlight Monk presents Liu Cui to Guanyin, returning her to her original source.

Moonlight Monk's introduction in the wedge is comedic, playing on language as it develops its themes. When Moonlight Monk arrives onstage carrying his moon and extolling its poetic origins, a novice teases him and eventually smashes the moon into pieces:

> Novice: Truly a mad monk, carrying this . . . I don't know what! It looks like a big bright fried cake. You don't sell cakes, what are you doing with that? Let's break it! [Breaks the moon.]
>
> Moonlight: No! No! No! With one stroke he destroyed the Moon Palace!

The joke here, of course, is that Moonlight's prized piece of moon is a folly; only he sees it, as he sees himself, literally. To the novice, it is simply evidence of Moonlight's insanity:

> Novice: You are a monk who just wants to drink alcohol and eat meat. Truly you are a false monk.
> Moonlight: Who is the real monk? Who is the false monk?
> Novice: I am the real monk, and you are the false monk.
> Moonlight: Who is the real monk? Who is the false monk?
> Novice: You are the real monk, and I am the false monk. Bah! I've got it mixed up.
> Moonlight: Why are you bickering with me about identity? The grave mounds of Chu and Han, where are they all? Go try!
> (Sings) All alike, evanescent in the Moonlight.

Lighthearted though it is, the exchange introduces basic questions that are topical to drama in general, and crucial in plays of this kind. Moonlight has to make Liu Cui realize who she really is, and the difficulty of doing so is underscored by his own unreliability. We know from the wedge that Moonlight is Guanyin's messenger, but the novice and the abbot have their doubts about his sanity, let alone his provenance. Liu Cui's problem is not one of simple amnesia, or confusion. Her problem is even greater because she is someone else entirely; in fact, she is not just someone else but something else.

Following the wedge, when Liu Cui and Moonlight first meet in act 1, we again witness an exchange emphasizing the conflict between saying what something is, and what it really is:

> Red Lotus: May I ask, sir, where do you come from?
> Moonlight: I come from where I come from.
> Red Lotus: Now where are you going?
> Moonlight: I am going where I'm going.
> Red Lotus: This monk really knows where he's coming from and where he's going!
> Moonlight: Silence! Saying horse does not a horse make, naming it a cow does not necessarily make a cow. Let's both stop here and cease a while. On this is there anything left to say? Please, Liu Cui, quickly say so.[25]

This is an example of the kind of wordless doctrine basic to Zen Buddhism; the universal truths cannot be spoken, but have to be nearly happened upon by its converts. The riddling continues on throughout this act, with Moonlight Monk insisting that Red Lotus leave her home (*chu jia* 出家) and telling her of her origins as foliage, repeating her name (Liu/Willow 柳) and urging her until he is eventually pushed out by Liu's madam. It is not until the sequence of dreams that Liu Cui believes the Moonlight Monk and goes off with him. Certainly none of these scenes are included in Xu Wei's *Zen Master Yu*, but the spirit of the seemingly mad monk's enterprise, and the difficulties of convincing the skeptical courtesan, are present in the later play.

One other version of the Liu Cui and Red Lotus story, popular among Suzhou storytellers during Xu Wei's time, conflates the two stories and highlights how Liu Xuanjiao's machinations lead to his daughter's disgrace. The story, which is collected in the thirteenth *juan* of Tian Rucheng's 田汝成 (*jinshi* graduate 1526) "Guide to the West Lake" (*Xihu youlan zhi* 西湖遊覽志), claims to relate a Song dynasty tale about Lui Cui.[26] The plot contains the deception conceived by Liu Xuanjiao, the dispatch of Red Lotus to Yutong as a redress for slighting Liu, Yutong's resulting departure from earth, Yutong's rebirth as Liu Cui, and Liu Cui's deliverance by monks from Yutong's monastery.[27] This appears to be the version on which Xu Wei's play is based. The story, as told in "Guide to the West Lake," leaves out Red Lotus' ruse about stomach pains to seduce Yutong, which Jeannette Faurot traces to Huang Wei's 黃暐 (b. 1438, *jinshi* 1490) *Classified Records from an Overgrown Window* (*Pengchuang leiji* 蓬牕類紀).[28] The story also changes Moonlight Monk to monks named Ruhui 如晦 and Qingliao 清了. Like GJXS 29, it leaves out the elaborate pantomimes used to awaken Liu Cui.[29] I would also argue that the most important structural aspects of the story are here, specifically the systems of recycling characters and overlapping players from earlier situations and lifetimes. The particulars, such as what methods are used to seduce or redeem, are less crucial to the stories' development. One can, however, appreciate how adjustments to those details can heighten the play's dramatic and structural effect and create a more or less satisfactory experience for the reader or viewer. Although the various sources help clarify the context of Xu Wei's play, it is clear that *Zen Master Yu* delivers a new and economical hybrid of the Liu Cui and Red Lotus stories; Xu Wei has taken advantage of the structure of his play to invoke the repetitions, using that model, along with comic turns on language and identity, to create a consistent argument about where, exactly, one's identity might reside.

"You Haven't Changed a Bit!": Being True to Oneself

Virtually all critics of *Zen Master Yu* have discussed the parallels between its first and second acts, from similarity of events, character types, and so on down to the song sequences. I-Cheng Liang notes the perfect mirror images of a monk overcome by a courtesan in the first act and a courtesan converted by a monk in the second. He suggests that Xu Wei is using this repetition to make a comment that "evil could overcome right and that right could also destroy evil, whenever a person, who has true emotion and real virtue, will rise to heaven and find the truth," and he further theorizes that the play satirizes hypocrisy and affirms Buddhist salvation.[30] Luo Qiuzhao notes the way that the structure causes the audience to contemplate the complexity of character so brilliantly; by setting up a situation where one courtesan in the second act is directly affected by the actions of another courtesan in the first act, Xu Wei demonstrates how a single "type" of person can contain polar opposite subtypes.[31] It should be noted, however, that though the character type of the courtesan is the same, Xu Wei allows role type to trump character type by having the Red Lotus version of the courtesan sung by a secondary female role, *tie*, and the Liu Cui version sung by a lead female role, the *dan*. More significantly, both the deception of the first act and the salvation of the second act are produced using the same method: play-acting. It is hard to believe, then, that Xu Wei was using opposites in his play simply to enact a battle between evil and good, as Liang suggests. Roles here are too fungible to be taken so seriously; to understand this play simply as a depiction of the battle between good and evil, or between heaven and hell, is precisely the kind of mistake that the play warns against. After all, the prostitute Liu Cui turns out in the end to be the old bodhisattva Yutong! *Zen Master Yu* artfully uses the inverted structure to question just how much is at stake every time we present ourselves, and how changed we are every time, whether it is in minor adjustments or in complete transformations. By overlaying its supernatural elements with the mundane elements of miscommunication, it draws attention to the exigencies of everyday life.

Jeannette Faurot, in her discussion of the structural parallels of the play, sees manifestations of Buddhist doctrines of repetition and recurrence within the play. Noting the nearly identical song sets from the first to the second act, Faurot argues that this structural duplication is significant in terms of Buddhism.[32] She goes on to posit that it would be more dramatic if the same actor played both the role of the *sheng* in the first act and the *dan* in the second, and I agree. Unfortunately, we lack evidence of performance history and can only surmise of how the roles were played; it may have varied even during Xu Wei's time, depending on which troupe was performing it, if it was ever performed. In the case of Chinese drama, the appearance of different actors would not be as significant as different role types: where once the audience saw a *sheng*, they now see a *dan*. Still, the conventions of drama apply, and this duplication of song sets is nostalgic and certainly creates drama. It is even more dramatic for the very fact that the same song tunes are first performed by the *sheng* in the first act and then the *dan* in the second, echoing a reverse application of onstage gender change that we will see in *Mulan* and *Girl Graduate*, and serving as a constant reminder throughout the second act of what has occurred in the previous one.

The audience's complicity is crucial to the play; the first step of their acceptance is basic to drama: the character (in this case the *dan*) appears onstage and introduces herself as Liu Cui, and the audience accepts her announcement, and also accepts the *dan* as that character. However, having already watched the first act and Yutong's announcement, they also accept that, in fact, Liu Cui, who is played by a *dan* in this act, is somehow also the *sheng* from the first act who was Yutong, as they know that she is his reincarnation, and consequently also his previous incarnation as a bodhisattva. The overlap need not be physical, or visual, for it to remain in the mind of the audience member who saw or read the first act.[33] This fact is brought home with every song repetition in the second act, especially as they are used to express different emotions from one act to the next. Whereas in the first act Yutong used the songs predominantly to express his rage, Liu Cui uses the same song tunes to express her confusion about what Moonlight Monk is trying to tell her about herself.

As discussed above, the play's sources provide the characters' names and some basic situations, but they do not bear much similarity to Xu Wei's version. Although the curious repetitive structure of the stories of acts 1 and 2 in the play are not entirely unfamiliar from the subgenre of Buddhist deliverance plays, the way that they are exact mirror images in terms of song as well as situation is certainly Xu Wei's own innovation. The extended guessing game of act 2, in which Liu Cui is forced to puzzle out her past by piecing together clues as given to her by the Moonlight Monk's charades, is unique to Xu Wei's play. This riddling scene is crucial to our understanding Xu Wei's play and illuminating in its exploration of the transactions that encumber our ways of comprehension. It calls attention to the rhetorical structures that make drama distinct, and demonstrates how these patterns of sense-making are as real to our world and our experiences as they are to the stage world. *Zen Master Yu* deliberately draws the viewer's or reader's attention to concerns about drama, while stressing the larger questions of communication, imitation, and originality, and the complex ways of reaching understanding via language. The subject matter is similar to that of a deliverance play, as the second half of the play involves the Moonlight Monk "delivering" the Zen monk Yutong, who now resides in the body of Liu Cui. However, the play so delights in its display of trickery and misunderstanding—mixed with plenty of ribaldry—that it cannot be taken only as a doctrinal Buddhist text meant to instruct its reading or viewing audience on the Buddhist themes of retribution and reincarnation.

The central problem of the drama is precisely the structure that stresses the disparity between merely similar and completely identical, and it is enacted throughout the repetitions of the play. The self-identifications in *Zen Master Yu* move beyond the simple conventions of drama. Characters are called upon to announce and present themselves to each other, a self-presentation that is distinct from the conventional address to the audience. When Red Lotus first comes to the temple, Yutong's servant asks her who she is three times before allowing her entry; when Liu Ciu first comes to the temple in the second act, she has to ask Moonlight Monk who he is three times before she receives a response. The repetition of groups of three is a common trope in deliverance plays,[34] and the number three as a requirement in religious and folkloric plots is almost universal. The reason for the necessity of a third trial or object is found in simple mathematics; three is the minimum number necessary to determine the relationship between units, thus establishing a pattern. This repetition, echoed in many other patterns and words, emphasizes attempts to find out or to expose identity. Although the play as a contained performance offers the audience an opportunity to read significance into such repetitions, implying that they are placed there with a knowing hand from which we can read meaning, how different is it from how we read meaning into lived experience? Even if we choose to be less philosophical and to withhold from reading deeper meaning into the need for asking anything three times, we are still faced with the message of this repetition. The question is repeated because the answer is uncertain, and the uncertainty is in response to a basic question: "Who are you?"

Spelling Things Out

Spontaneity and expressions of the "natural" would not qualify as such without the deliberate orchestrations that allow them to occur: this play also resides in a paradox that challenges our ways of making sense. *Zen Master Yu* makes two simultaneous arguments: that language is obfuscating, used to deceive and confuse, and that language is illuminating, used to enlighten and redeem. I use the term "language" broadly, extending its meaning beyond words to include the language of signs, such as gesture and dress. Xu Wei's *Zen Master Yu* explores more than the limits of drama; it explores the limits of human understanding through communication. The subject of *Zen Master Yu* is particularly revealing, as the themes of conversion and reincarnation are in fact structurally similar to drama itself. Whereas conversion entails the enlightened self replacing the ignorant self in the same body, and reincarnation entails the same "self" leaving one body for another, drama offers itself up as the most flexible structure as it allows for both to coexist. One actor can play multiple roles, where different selves inhabit the same body; and multiple actors can play one role, where the same "self" enters different bodies. By the logic of Xu Wei's poem, which claims that one must be a gibbon to understand a gibbon, drama is *more real* than life, as it allows for the authentic experience of another, accepting the possibility that one person can fully become another. While this seems an entirely impossible feat, Xu Wei's play suggests that these transformations are actually quite simple. The characters literally identify themselves by using language: they transmit themselves to (and into) others through their words.

In the first act of *Zen Master Yu*, Yutong dismisses the Bodhidharma's teaching of Zen Buddhism through long hours of meditation and oral transmission rather than by studying written texts.[35] He makes his remarks in passing—and they are delivered with the same degree of lightness as the rest of his rambling speech—but they contain an essential tension found throughout the play about the transmission of knowledge through words. Words are particularly compromised in Xu Wei's play, which carries the burden of being a text in a tradition where readers were just as apt to read the play as they were to watch it in performance. Here, both aspects of words are taken into consideration, regardless of whether the play is read or watched. Just as there are moments where a reader would be forced to consider the sounds of the words, there are moments where an audience member would be forced to consider their shapes. Plays on words recur in all the interactions between characters, culminating in the riddling scene but certainly present in cases of mistaken identity. The structures of concealment and revelation extend beyond words and their physical shapes in the form of literal disguise, too, with the various props and costumes that "identify" a character as someone he or she may not in fact be. Language is figured as a costume, bearing outside traces that may be read incorrectly, or that may be "misread" correctly.

To explore the power of the written word as bearing witness to an event, one need look no further than Yutong's letters, which travel from the first act to the second. Yutong, determined to avenge himself in the next life, sets down a response written in anticipation of a note from Liu, and leaves a message for his servant telling him where to find the reply. The use of a letter as proof and evidence is a curious aspect of drama, as it is a concrete example of the written word at work on stage. Perhaps the most famous example in English literature is the traveling documentation that Hamlet's companions, Rosencrantz and Guildenstern, carry with them. When Hamlet discovers that the letters bear orders for his execution, he changes the death sentence, forging his companions' names instead of his. The orders are dispatched, and his friends are executed. The audience witnesses how the written word can be betrayed, whereas the enacted scene cannot (consider Hamlet's other ruse, the play "The Mousetrap," which he produces to accuse his uncle of murder). Here in *Zen Master Yu*, the letters are the only stage prop that Moonlight Monk successfully uses to effect Liu Cui's transformation.

Yutong writes a note because he expects that Liu Xuanjiao will expect word from him. The *words* that Yutong means to send will not be what Liu expects. Yutong describes his intent to be reborn as a scandalous woman who will destroy the reputation of Liu's household, and anticipates this turn of Liu's fate:

> It's just that this impudent Willow (Liu) seeks to use this to insult me. He will certainly send someone to inquire about me, and I must prepare a few sentences in response. I shall write a few words to Lazybones to instruct him to prepare this and that. Then I shall sit upright and send off my spirit, where it will speed off on a trip to the Liu house.
> (*Acts out writing a note, then acts out reading it*)
> Since I entered these Zen gates, I was without a care.
> For fifty-three years, my mind was centered.
> Because of this single deviating thought,
> I broke the Buddha's precept against lasciviousness.
> You sent Red Lotus to destroy my chastity,
> I now owe Red Lotus a payback for one night.
> My body's moral behavior bore your harm,
> Your household's reputation shall bear my destruction.
> (*Again acts out writing a letter for his monk, and then acts out reading it*)
> Left for my serving man, Lazybones: "If there should be a messenger come to the temple from the Willow's establishment, you can tell him that there is a letter of response at the foot of the incense burner."

(*Recites*)
Red Lotus made a monkey out of me,
So I shall hide for a springtime in the skin of a Green Willow.
Waves beat the duckweed, every one of them gets struck;
But my only fear is that when I return you will not recognize my self of old.
(*Acts out leaving his body*).[36]

This monologue expresses the problem that occurs in the transition from act 1 to act 2. We know from Yutong's introductory statements that he believes words interfere with truth. Yutong also knows that in order for his reincarnated self to find his own self in the future, he will need to send some physical evidence ahead of him. As we will see when his disciple finds his body, Yutong is right to take precautions; if not for the letter, there would be nothing to tie him to the events of the next act.

When, after writing his letter, Yutong chants aloud: "But my only fear is that when I return you will not recognize my self of old," he uses the word *shen* 身 for self; this is the same word that would be used to refer to his body, emphasizing the way that identity and body are intertwined, yet troubled. It is not his former body that he will encounter, but his former "self," whatever that might be. Yutong is clearly aware as he writes his will and testament that his jumping into another body, his seeking vengeance in the future as Mi Heng sought retribution in the underworld, might not offer the same satisfaction that it would in this world. His "self" will not quite be what it was, certainly not the same physical self, but it might not have a memory of the past, either. He thus leaves a record behind for Liu Xuanjiao, hoping that Liu will regretfully recall the letter when future misfortune arrives. As an added precaution, Yutong leaves another copy of the letter at his home temple.

Both of the letters prove crucial, as they are the only concrete objects that travel from the first act to the next, serving as a "witness" to the truth of what has happened. When the servant returns to the temple, Red Lotus is gone, and Yutong is already a corpse; if not for the letters, the servant would continue to believe that Guanyin has come to take his master's soul back with her. The repeated reading of letters onstage emphasizes the importance of the written document. First, Yutong's acolyte discovers the two letters under the incense burner and reads them. Then, when Prefect Liu's messenger arrives with his own letter inquiring about what has transpired, the monk reads Prefect Liu's letter aloud. Convinced of the truthfulness of Yutong's letter based on the contents of Prefect Liu's letter, the monk then hands Yutong's letter of reply over to the messenger. All of these exchanges remind the audience of the surrogates we accept for direct communication; if we cannot be there "in person," we must accept substitutions as presence.

The letter becomes the only evidence that matters in the second half of the play, as when the Moonlight Monk shouts out in frustration and brings out Yutong's letter after his complex of pantomimes has failed to awaken Liu Cui:

> All for naught! Waste of energy! Waste of energy!
> (*In a loud voice he reads out*:)
> Red Lotus made a monkey out of me,
> So I shall hide for a while in the spring in the skin of a green willow.
> Waves beat the duckweed, every one of them gets struck;
> But my only fear is that when I return you will not recognize my self of old![37]

It is the first time that he speaks aloud to Liu Cui, and it is only through the information contained in this letter, or perhaps hearing the words spoken aloud, that Liu Cui comprehends the content of Moonlight Monk's ultimately futile pantomime. In fact, so effective are these words that she becomes converted almost instantly and casts off her clothes in exchange for a monk's habit. So why does the Moonlight Monk hold back instead of simply reading the letter to Liu Cui? Certainly a primary factor is that it would deprive the audience of an extended scene of slapstick, in which the Moonlight Monk acts ridiculously and Liu Cui incorrectly guesses the answer to a riddle repeatedly to the entertainment of the audience that already knows the answer. The relationship between sound and meaning is an odd one. Moonlight Monk says in his introduction that explaining Liu Cui's origins to her is not something that can be done through language: "But as for this thing, it is not something that language can do."[38] This assertion is overturned when he gives up and simply reads Yutong's words to her, and this sequence of events highlights the mistrust of language, while emphasizing the fact that language cannot be avoided.

Sound and meaning are drawn into an even deeper tangle with the Moonlight Monk's pantomimes earlier in the second act. When Liu Cui asks him how he could have come from the Western Heaven, the following exchange occurs, and it is echoed every time the words for reincarnation are used:

> Liu Cui: One hand points west, one hand points to heaven, so you don't mean you are from the Western Heavens? What nonsense! All right, so tell me, what are you doing come down here to the world below from the Western Heavens?
> (*The* wai *uses his hand to strike his head once. Using his hands, he forms a three cornered* si 厶 *character, then acts out a four-sided square, to make the character* kou 口, *then acts out a circle, to make a full moon.*)
> Liu Cui: That three-cornered thing is a *si* character, the four-sided one is a *kou*, putting them all together, it makes a *tai* 台 character. The round thing is a moon (*yue* 月) character, but since he first hit his head (*tou* 頭) once, it must mean that this is a way of saying reincarnation.[39]

The scene is a comic one, playing upon the same basic conventions familiar to Chinese riddles in which puns on words (homophones) can be complemented by visual puns, as well, when the character's physical shape plays a part in the depiction of meaning.[40] It takes on especially comic value because the shapes of the characters are mediated by one more degree of visual meaning, in that they are depicted by Moonlight Monk's physical contortions rather than with a pen or brush. The construction of the term "reincarnation" (*toutai* 投胎) is quite complex, relying on Liu Cui's ability to navigate different aspects of language and demanding her literacy in order to decipher this puzzle. To solve riddles of this register, one must not only hear the words, but be able to visualize them.

The pun on *tou* 投 which Moonlight Monk demonstrates by striking his head (*tou* 頭) is a basic one, relying on the homophone. Another case of pure puns is seen when Moonlight Monk urges Liu Cui to guess again by pulling on her earring (*[er] huan* [耳]環) and miming a finger guessing game (*cai [quan]* 猜 [拳]) to act out the two characters for "guess again" (*huan cai* 還猜).[41] In contrast, the construction of the character "*tai*" (胎) involves much more navigation, and a knowledge of the shapes of the characters. First, Liu Cui has to recognize the component parts of the character by "reading" Moonlight Monk's gestures, because the first two marks—of the three-cornered "*si*" (厶) and the four-cornered "*kou*" (口)—are related to the word by shape, not by sound. The circle provides an even more complex challenge, as it signifies neither a character that is a circle nor a character that is homophonic with the sound for "round"; instead, the gesture is meant to signify a circle that *suggests* the shape of a full moon, which then is understood as the (non-circular) left "moon" (*yue* 月) radical of the character "*tai*." This elaborate explanation may seem quite tedious for such a short moment in the play, but it serves to demonstrate the sophisticated processes involved in interpreting language, and points to the connection between the shape of things and their meaning. This begs the question: What exactly is the relation between exterior appearance and meaning? The riddle and the scene of interpretation clearly suggest that there are occasions where the surface appearance of a thing is the absolute key to understanding it, while at other times only sounds will suffice.

If language, even when it is part of a performed dramatic text where the visual and aural dominate, has the qualities of a kind of costume that bears signs on its exterior, it can, like costume, provide a key to understanding what resides within, even when it lies. This is a troubling thought. It certainly troubles the plot of this play, in which disguises run rampant and are used both in wicked ploys to deceive, and in well-meant attempts to enlighten. Red Lotus arrives on the scene in act 1 dressed as a virtuous widow, and this disguise gains her entrance into the monastery for the night. Her calculated cries of agony from the mysterious stomach ailment, and the story about how it can be soothed, are lies told to seduce Yutong into ruin. Yet costume, disguise, and assumed identities cannot be discarded wholesale. Just as Red Lotus "acted" (*zhuang* 妝) pained to ensnare Yutong, Moonlight Monk "acted" (*zhuang* 妝) out the revelation of Liu Cui's old self to her (him!). The word for acting naturally carries with it the meaning of acting as something actors do on stage; but carries the meaning, too, of performing, of dressing up, and also of the deceit that can attach to these actions. One is acting when one does or says something that one does not mean. All of these vectors, while making acting something threatening, also present it as something ordinary; they go further still to slyly suggest that acting and clothing can even provide a window into enlightenment.

The play's climax follows a series of quick changes by Moonlight Monk, all executed in silence. With a few hats and a mask, he plays Yutong, Liu Xuanjiao, and Red Lotus, acting out every crucial moment that the audience had already witnessed firsthand. This, then, is a revisiting of the first act, understood by the audience as communicating the same already-seen essential information, yet in a completely different way. Now, one person plays all of the roles, and that player, Moonlight Monk, was not even party to the original events when they occurred. He is an actor, revealing the truth surrounding a chain of events that he did not see himself, following a script penned by the bilious Yutong seventeen years before. Moonlight Monk's onstage audience of one, Liu Cui, as well as the external reading or viewing audience, must accept the conventions of drama that make his various roles believable. The scene is initially confusing to Liu Cui, but she eventually comprehends the basic information. She recognizes similarities to her father when Moonlight Monk dons an official's hat, and when Moonlight Monk furrows his brows in anger, she comprehends that her father has engineered actions that have angered a monk. This time, the play-acting is only partially effective. To be sure, Red Lotus herself suggested that her acting was not the only cause of Yutong's fall: if he had not been already weak, her acting would have been in vain. In this act, Moonlight Monk's performance offers only a partially satisfying message, because it requires the existence of the written documents and his spoken words to clarify their meaning.

Liu Cui, confused by the miming, completely misinterprets the action. She has gleaned that both an official and a monk have been enraged, and that a woman is involved in this mess. She bemoans her own life as a courtesan, recalling that in past years she had indeed swindled a monk as well as a scholar. Making this connection with Moonlight Monk's continuous talk of reincarnation, she concludes that she is being punished for a few past misdeeds in her own lifetime. She eventually comes to the conclusion that she will bear a child who is the reincarnation of someone she has offended, and she muses aloud about how she had better make arrangements for an abortion. This is finally too much for Moonlight Monk, who shouts out what he had been trying to wordlessly relate to her.

Liu Cui's conclusion is perfectly plausible, especially given the circumstances of her vocation, her limited understanding, and Moonlight Monk's complicated explanations. At this point, Moonlight Monk has to admit defeat; his methods of teaching retribution without words are useless, and he concedes the necessity of speech. The moment he reads Yutong's letter, Liu Cui cries out that she understands. Shortly afterward, she sheds her women's clothes.[42] It is a scene of stripping in which she puts on a new costume, a new identity that represents the old one that she had nearly lost. In a neat reversal of the theme of Xu Wei's next two plays, which both feature women played by female role types who remain women while dressed as men, *Zen Master Yu* is a play in which a female played by a female role type actually *is* a man, despite all outward appearances. Before she even puts on the monk's clothes, she becomes a man not through changing bodies, nor even through changing clothes, but because she has changed her state of mind: she was, in fact, a man all along! Moonlight Monk has told her that she is Yutong, and she ultimately comes to accept that fact.

Written a few hundred years earlier, Ji Junxiang's 紀君祥 (ca. thirteenth century) Yuan dynasty *zaju* entitled *The Orphan of Zhao* (*Zhaoshi guer* 趙氏孤兒) tells the story of an orphan who has been raised and tutored by a man named Cheng Ying 程嬰. Through a series of schemes and tests of loyalty, Cheng Ying has kept the orphan's true identity hidden over the years. Eventually, Cheng Ying decides that it is time for the orphan to understand his past and to seek vengeance for the murders of his family members. He silently leaves a scroll depicting the various events that led up to those murders on a table in the orphan's study. The orphan, puzzled by these vivid drawings, describes what he sees. This is presumably for the benefit of the audience, though they are already familiar with the details. He asks Cheng Ying to explain what he sees in these pictures, and Cheng Ying does so, but without telling him that the story is about him. Gradually, the orphan grasps the truth, and only then can he begin his quest for justice. The similarity in strategy to *Zen Master Yu* is striking: both plays are about a return to self that is not a physically obtainable journey. The orphan and Liu Cui/Yutong have been the same all along; each was just not aware of this true self until confronted with a depiction of biography that is first transmitted wordlessly. Both plays beg the question of how selves are constructed, and explore the limits of our own self-knowledge, let alone our knowledge of others.

Lies and acts of obfuscation abound in this play, but perhaps the most interesting one is the one made unwittingly. When the *dan* enters the stage as Liu Cui, she makes the conventional self-introduction, which distinguishes this *dan* from, for example, the girl graduate played by the same *dan* in a different play. But by the time Liu Cui enters, the audience has already seen the first act, and witnessed Yutong's announcement that he will be reborn into the Liu family. The audience has also seen Moonlight Monk's prologue, in which he tells us that Yutong's wish has been fulfilled and that he has come here with the express purpose of meeting and converting this girl. When Liu Cui enters the stage, then, we know who she is even though she herself does not. In all fairness, she is, of course, also Liu Cui, daughter of Liu Xuanjiao, but we all know that it is not her *true* identity. She has been the same bodhisattva from the Western Heaven for much longer. Still, Liu Cui introduces herself thus: "I am Liu Cui" (*An shen Liu Cui de bian shi* 妾身柳翠的便是).[43] This moment of disjunction, where truth is inseparable from lie, and where seeing is not necessarily believing, points out the curious ways that truth is situational. Bearing witness may provide proof, but getting that truth across is not quite so easy. Communication labors to make the right distinctions; but perhaps in the final moment the truth of a statement, like the truth of identity, comes from guessing again.

3

The Namesake: Costumes of Words in Mulan

Of the four plays in *Four Cries of a Gibbon*, the plot of *The Female Mulan Goes to War in Place of Her Father* (*Ci Mulan ti fu congjun* 雌木蘭替父從軍), or *Mulan*, is the most familiar to the English-speaking world. Although the play is based on a poem that was thought to be a thousand years old by Xu Wei's time, there appears little evidence to suggest that it had been a popular literary topic before then. Indeed, Xu Wei's play may be responsible for the late imperial interest in Mulan as literary heroine, and certainly is the first of what would become a long tradition of dramatic works based on Mulan, proliferating in the Ming and Qing dynasties and generating adaptations and analysis well into the twenty-first century.[1] For all that followed after Xu Wei's play, *Mulan* itself, though it had little to prove in terms of staying true to its original source, does not stray far from the elements of the ballad. The story of a girl whose formation of an external identity relies on what she wears is also a natural fit for *Four Cries of a Gibbon.*

As *Mi Heng* does for *Zen Master Yu*, *Mulan* serves as a preamble to *Girl Graduate. Mulan* presents a quasi-historical example of a girl who takes over her father's legacy and achieves tremendous success, thus introducing the audience to a deeper, and gendered, exploration of the patterns of interaction between people discussed in the previous two plays. Thus far, *Mi Heng* and *Zen Master Yu* have taken up the tensions that result from discerning how a person is identified through different aspects of performance, aspects that compete or unite to ultimately form a coherent self-definition. Whereas *Mi Heng* engages with how one performs one's "self" to allow authenticity alone to shine through the boundaries of the body, *Zen Master Yu* takes the question a step further. What if, it asks, instead of defending ourselves after death in the Underworld, we can return to the mortal world in different bodies to avenge insults borne by our original selves? What if that body is a different gender? *Mi Heng* requires a recapitulation of events in the Underworld in order to set things straight; *Zen Master Yu* requires a complete change of bodies to redress incurred wrongs. In contrast, *Mulan* rejects the otherworldly aspects of the first two plays and is set in the mundane world. The play asks the same questions about where one's true and original self resides, but there is hardly a trace of the fantastical that we saw in the first and second plays. In fact, *Mulan*'s simplicity has radical implications, and even more radical conclusions: changing one's identity does not require anything as extreme as the changing of bodies. Identity is altered by something as quotidian as the changing of clothes.

Mulan does not exploit the radical possibility that identity is transportable, but deflates it. The play has been criticized for being the least interesting of the four,[2] although perhaps contemporarily its lackluster existence as reading material was mitigated by its display of a player's physical prowess, whether in the lurid removal of foot bindings, or in the displays of martial artistry onstage. The play is problematic because it offers a contradictory claim that is not resolved at the end. On one hand, it takes names and appearances as its premise: Mulan stands in for her father, taking his name. She goes on to "make a name" for herself, gaining honored titles and emoluments that build up her family's reputation. On the other hand, it emphasizes the importance of the body at key moments throughout the play. At the end, Mulan dissociates herself from the "Hua Hu" persona in which she is attired for the greater part of the play and immediately returns to her female form, with feet re-bound and virginity intact. Stranger still, when reflecting on her accomplishments in the field of battle, Mulan denies having had anything to do with it. The body had been imagined as a vessel in *Zen Master Yu*, when Yutong's spirit entered the Liu family in the form of their daughter, Liu Cui. Here in *Mulan*, it is more closely associated with the sartorial and superficial—to the point that thing like a soldier's uniform or a young girl's bound feet are viewed as existing within the body's boundaries—than viewers may be prepared to accept.[3] Indeed, Mulan and those who look at her rely so much on these artifices that the artifices take on active power. Rather than the body (including its covers) serving as a protective vessel for the self, the self is simply a way to animate these vessels. In *Mulan,* the vessel is empty. Can Mulan really mean that because she was in men's clothes during those battles, "she" wasn't actually there?

The switching of appearances from female to male and back again is the central element of the plot, and the source of the play's entertainment. In Mulan's final song of the play, she alludes to the anecdote of the two hares running together in the fields from "The Ballad of Mulan," noting that she passed under thousands of eyes without her true gender being known. Although the physical differences between a man and a woman may be hard to distinguish in the figure of a uniformed soldier running swiftly through the fields, there is never a question that these differences are, in fact, important. If Mulan's gender did not matter, there would be no plot. Yet rustling at the very surface of the play is the sense that even as crucial as it is to be able to differentiate, the difference has little effect on the outcome. Just as Mulan the character constructs a self out of clothing, postures, display, and self-description, *Mulan* the play uses the same elements to construct its entertainment.

In song-drama, the obvious site for open, lyrical, and personal expression is the aria, but the songs in *Mulan* predominantly dwell on clothing and accessories (in act 1) and on battle (in act 2). Interestingly, even the most emotional of the songs, in which Mulan contemplates the sacrifices of her parents and her solitude as a soldier, is expressed using the language of clothing. The tension between concealment and revelation, so much the source of the audience's pleasure in watching the play, is also the play's subject matter. How this tension is introduced and resolved reflects something about the relationship between drama and its audience, and between the play's audience and their world. As we watch drama, we believe that these actors, dressed up as other people, are what they claim to be. Mulan's statement, then, is an extraordinary one, because in a staged performance, this actor (actress?) starts the play dressed up as a girl, and later dresses up as a man, then dresses up again as a woman, and explicitly denies the "reality" of those proceedings, which took place in the "reality" of the play. She was acting all along, she implies, so she really didn't do these things. If this is not a definition of drama, what is?

Managing Life as a Woman Warrior

Mulan is divided into two acts. The first act, set during the Northern Wei among the Xianbei tribe, begins with the protagonist, played by a *dan*, introducing herself as Hua Mulan. Mulan notes that all men of age are being conscripted to subdue the rebellion of a bandit leader named Leopard Skin. Concerned that her father is too old and frail to serve, Mulan decides to take his place, citing two model women who were willing to sacrifice themselves for their fathers' sakes. This decision is followed by an offstage shopping excursion for trip supplies that launches a series of songs.

The middle of the act is taken up with a lot of stage work, described by the songs. In the third aria, Mulan removes her foot bindings. One can easily imagine the entertainment value of this action, and its potential for visual comedy. Mulan changes her feet back "into floating boats," but assures the audience that she will be able to return them to their golden lotus glory with the help of a secret family recipe. She proceeds to change out of her women's clothes and into the soldier's uniform. Having taken on a soldier's appearance, she demonstrates her fighting skills by performing a series of martial arts moves with sword, staff, and bow and arrow. She receives her parents' blessing and leaves with two fellow soldiers, heading toward Leopard Skin's lair.

Although Mulan exclusively sings the arias in the first act, various characters sing arias in the second act, beginning with Mulan's commanding general Xin Ping. Act 2 begins in the heat of battle, with Xin Ping employing Mulan to lead the raid on Leopard Skin. He alternates songs with a chorus of soldiers, during which they successfully invade the bandit hideout and capture Leopard Skin. "Hua Hu" is praised for his part in the capture and is given cap and girdle as a symbol of his promotion to a position in the Imperial Secretariat. Mulan is thus sent home, still as a man, in the company of two fellow soldiers, to await her new appointment.

Mulan sings an aria about how the one who captured the bandit king was a fraud, and therefore she cannot take credit for the victory. As she travels with the soldiers, they comment on how strange it is that they have never seen Hua Hu use the toilet. Mulan mysteriously tells them about a statue in her village whose face changed to that of a goddess. When she returns home, she first puts on the face makeup of a woman, and then greets her family. She shares her successes with her parents, showing them the cap and girdle she has been granted, and then confirms that she returns to them as a "dogwood bud," or virgin. After her amazed fellow soldiers leave, a *sheng* also wearing cap and girdle enters; he is the neighbor, Master Wang, who recently passed the exams with flying colors. The two have been conveniently matched by their parents and are immediately married on stage. The wedding is another one of Xu Wei's innovations in the Mulan story; Luo Qiuzhao suggests that this reflects the influence of Ming dynasty *chuanqi* plays, which conventionally end with a reunion scene or wedding.[4] If Mulan can't keep the official's cap and girdle herself, at least she can marry someone who possesses them. The play ends with Mulan singing this song:

> I was a woman till I was seventeen,
> Was a man another twelve years.
> I passed under thousands of glances,
> Who among them could tell cock from hen?
> Only now do I believe that to tell cock from hen, you can't rely on eyes.
> Who was it that really occupied Black Mountain top?
> The girl Mulan went to war for her Pa.
> The affairs of the world are all such a mess,
> Muddling boy and girl is what this play did best.[5]

A Brief Historical Background

The final song about the ways that outward appearances can be deceiving refers to the more curious ending of Xu Wei's source, "The Ballad of Mulan" (*Mulan shi* 木蘭詩). The ballad is found in the *Collected Poems of the Music Bureau* (*Yuefu shiji* 樂府詩集), the Song dynasty anthology compiled by Guo Maoqian 郭茂倩 (fl. 1264–69). Guo Maoqian claims that "The Ballad of Mulan" is taken from the *Musical Records, Old and New* (*Gujin yuelu* 古今樂錄), a no-longer extant text that dates from approximately the sixth century CE.[6] The ballad is traditionally thought to have been written in the Northern Wei between the fifth and sixth centuries. Xu Wei fills in details about his protagonist based on the dating of the poem, making her a member of the Xianbei tribe that ruled the Northern Wei.[7]

"The Ballad of Mulan" begins with the image of Mulan performing the typically female task of weaving while lamenting her situation:

> A sigh, a sigh, and then again a sigh—
> Mulan was sitting at the door and weaving.
> One did not hear the sound of loom and shuttle,
> One only heard her heave these heavy sighs.
> When she was asked the object of her love,
> When she was asked who occupied her thoughts,
> She did not have a man she was in love with,
> There was no boy who occupied her thoughts.
>
> "Last night I saw the summons from the army,
> The Khan is mobilizing all his troops.
> The list of summoned men comes in twelve copies:
> Every copy lists my father's name!"

Reasoning that her brother is too young to go into battle, Mulan resolves aloud that she will take her father's place. Her first decision is simply to get a saddle and a horse; there is no discussion at all about her disguising herself as a man:

> The eastern market: there she bought a horse;
> The western market: there she bought a saddle.
> The southern market: there she bought a bridle;
> The northern market: there she bought a whip.

Rather, her transformation into a man predominantly involves taking up arms and putting on the right costume, suggesting that it will be her deeds that distinguish her.

> At dawn she said good-bye to her dear parents,
> At night she rested by the Yellow River.
> She did not hear her parents' voices, calling for their daughter,
> She only heard the Yellow River's flowing water, always splashing, splashing.
>
> At dawn she left the Yellow River's bank;
> At night she rested on Black Mountain's top
> She did not hear her parents' voices, calling for their daughter.
> She only heard the whinnying of Crimson Mountain's Hunnish horsemen
>
> Myriads of miles: she joined the thick of battle.
> Crossing the mountain passes as if flying.
> Winds from the north transmitted metal rattles,
> A freezing light shone on her iron armor.
> A hundred battles and the brass were dead;
> After ten years the bravest men returned.

The ballad's emphases are subtle, but significant: the middle section, quoted above, details Mulan's departure from home and her life as a soldier. The descriptions are expressed primarily through sound, whether it is the clacking of the shuttle, the girl's sighs, the wind whistling, or the horses whinnying. With the exception of the cold light on her armor, the listener's emotions are captured through sound, not image. This will not be the case in Xu Wei's play, which, though it relies on the roles of speaking and hearing in the production of knowledge, conveys its message mostly through the visual. The irony of the emphasis on visual enjoyment should not be lost on those who will remember the equal emphasis on rejecting visual evidence at play's end.

When Mulan returns home, she changes back into her female clothing. Here the poem describes the removal of her soldier's garments and the steps she takes to return to her old self, moving from east to west in her chambers. We see Mulan taking off her soldier's buffcoat and putting on her skirt and makeup:

> Hearing their daughter had arrived, her parents
> Went out the city, welcoming her back home.
> Hearing her elder sister had arrived, her sister
> Put on her bright red outfit at the door.
> Hearing his elder sister had arrived, her brother
> Sharpened his knife that brightly flashed in front of pigs and sheep.
>
> "Open the gate to my pavilion on the east,
> Let me sit down in my old western room.
> I will take off the dress I wore in battle;
> I will put on the skirt I used to wear."
> Close to the window she did up her hair;
> Facing the mirror she applied makeup.
> She went outside and saw her army buddies—
> Her army buddies were all flabbergasted:

The ballad ends with the strange hare analogy appended as a sort of moral to the story, describing the surprised reaction of her fellow soldiers:

> "We marched together for these twelve long years
> And absolutely had no clue that Mulan was a girl!"
>
> "The male hare wildly kicks its feet;
> The female hare has shifty eyes,
> But when a pair of hares runs side by side,
> Who can distinguish whether I am in fact male or female?"[8]

The analogy is an intriguing one: there are concrete ways to tell apart the male from the female. The hares have specific gender characteristics, but they are obscured by the activity natural to animals with a nervous spring and wandering eyes: they are always in motion, and when they are in motion, those characteristics are hard to see. The analogy does not propose that Mulan's gender was unidentifiable because she was always in motion, of course. Men and women, unlike hares, do not have gender-determined eyes or legs. They do have natural physical differences, and culturally-imposed physical differences like bound feet, but these too can be obscured. The human analogy for the evasive effect of hares running side by side is clothing. When hares run, their physical differences are obscured; when people dress, their corporal differences are obscured.

When Mulan dressed as a man, her brave actions and her assertions were accepted without question as a man's. Interestingly, it is female characteristics that are regarded as qualities that can be put on or taken off; little mention is made of dressing up as a man, with the exception of battle wear. As noted earlier, the most important transition for Mulan in becoming a male soldier in the ballad is to obtain the appropriate equipment, and it is no more difficult for a woman than it is for a male civilian to do this. The category of soldier is associated with a certain type of clothing, but it is not specifically marked as a gender category. Sufen Lai writes about the contrast between the scenes of changing into a male and changing back into a female: "Such contrasting treatments in describing Mulan's transforming herself and assuming different roles suggest that women's cross-dressing was still a taboo subject even under the Confucian premise of filial piety. Therefore, her transformation into a warrior is suggested with the purchasing of a gallant horse and its necessary gear, while her return to womanhood is detailed with feminine motions, objects and sentiments."[9] Lai makes a convincing argument that the ballad's audience would not have been as accepting of a woman's cross-dressing, but the reasons behind the contrast go beyond audience prudery and suggest the possibility of a different way to read maleness and femaleness. Mulan had been introduced at the beginning of the ballad accompanied by the tools associated with femaleness: the weaving loom and shuttle melodically click their reminder of what constitutes the women's work that fills her days. But when the soldier's buffcoat is taken off, and her hair restyled and makeup reapplied, it is not in response to a service or social role: she is putting on femaleness. Or, to put it the opposite way: here in the ballad, femaleness is a kind of social role, an addition to the essential humanity of the male role. As the visual vocabulary and the hare metaphor seem to imply, gender, like one's social role, is something that can be put on or taken off as circumstances require.

Discussions of Xu Wei's play have aligned with the readings of the ballad and have not made much of their differences; those scholars who do discuss the theme of cross-dressing in Xu Wei's *Mulan* mainly discuss it in terms of its place in the literary tradition on Mulan;[10] as evidence, rather dubiously, of incipient feminism in Xu Wei's work;[11] or as testament to thc triumph of patriarchy, with Mulan's acquiescence to womanhood at the end.[12] Written a few decades before the spectacular end of the Ming dynasty, Xu Wei's *Mulan* does not use the female figure as a critique of the ineffectual male who could not act appropriately in service of his country.[13] The discussion in this chapter accepts the conclusion that the transgressions in *Mulan* as such are not really that transgressive after all: Mulan takes expedient means to carry out a task and, having succeeded, seems to return to exactly who she was before she began. This chapter will examine the case of "who she was" in the beginning, "who she was" at the end, and "who she was" in between. Something strange occurs in Xu Wei's play. It is not the obvious fact of the switching from female to male and then back again, but rather the complete disavowal that this is at all strange or unusual, that is most affecting. The play, for all its apparent superficiality and inadequacies, proposes some crucial questions about the performance of the self.

Here again, the question of how identity is constructed through the lens of gender crops up. Xu Wei's play engages such questions in a much more complicated manner than the ballad does. The play presents a case of performance, a performance whose success is critical both personally and nationally for Mulan. Then, when she succeeds in this performance, the heroine dismisses her actions as if she had nothing to do with them. Recall the aspects of performance I discussed in the chapters on *Mi Heng* and *Zen Master Yu*. Mulan uses the same strategies of costume and speech to create a self, only to mock the notion that sight can be trusted, leaving the audience with a puzzle concerning what they have just witnessed. If the actions performed in the battle scenes were as if performed by someone else, to whom do we direct our appreciation? Similarly, when we watch a play, what constitutes our experience of what happens onstage? Does the presence of actors and actresses nullify the sincerity of all actions performed, because they were conducted in disguise?

Gender, Performance, and the Cross-Dressing Heroine

The remainder of this chapter will first consider how the vocabulary of hiding and revelation play a crucial part in the performance of identity in *Mulan.* The crises of category are principally enacted in the male/female modulations, but they are only the most obvious example of the many fluctuating categories throughout the play. This chapter will conclude with a discussion of the difficulties that arise when one "body" harbors distinct selves: the result is not surplus but rather deficit. Most scholarship on cross-dressing and gender in the last two decades bears the influence of Judith Butler's path-breaking work in the field. In works such as *Gender Trouble* and *Bodies That Matter,* Butler builds an argument that emphasizes the implications of gender as performance, exploring what forces are at play in the construction of heterosexually codified binaries of gender, and even sex.[14] Although this chapter does not pursue analysis of the political engagement of those readings, Butler's vocabulary of performance as taken from the perspective of social culture rather than theater arts informs the following reading. Butler criticizes theater, and phenomenology, for assuming an essential gendered self prior to performances; she argues in the article "Performative Acts and Gender Constitution: An Essay in Phenomenology and Feminist Theory" that there is no essential self, and that a "natural" idea of gender is constructed by authoritative forces in our culture.[15] Taking aim at the binaries of gender and sex as products created by repeated speech and behavior, she demands the inclusion of queer identities as a destabilizing force against the vocabulary of absolutes when talking about gender and sex: homosexuality is as "unnatural" or synthetic as the distinctions between genders and sex.[16] Extending the work of speech act theorists beyond the confines of ritualized moments of speech ("I now pronounce you man and wife"), Butler argues that all speech codifies and categorizes, such that "the naming is at once the setting of a boundary, and also the repeated inculcation of a norm."[17] Although she uses the word "performative" and illustrates this in earlier works with readings of drag performance, she disavows the immediate impulse to find correlatives of the stage in real life, saying: "The publication of *Gender Trouble* coincided with a number of publications that did assert that 'clothes make the woman,' but I never did think that gender was like clothes, or that clothes make the woman."[18] Butler is keener to emphasize that the formative moment occurs first; impersonation exists before there is a "one" who puts anything on.[19]

One of the publications that Butler refers to obliquely in her mention of clothes making the woman is Marjorie Garber's *Vested Interests*, published two years after *Gender Trouble* in 1992, in a decade that saw many academic conferences, scholarly publications, and even popular movies take up the theme of cross-dressing.[20] Also interested in interrogating the binaries of male and female designations, Garber examines the phenomenon of cross-dressing in film, music, and theater, as well as in transvestite groups. Garber looks, literally, at the cross-dresser. Her focus is less on the implications of a man playing a woman, or a man playing a woman playing a man, than on the foundation of gender disparities. Noting the proliferation of work on cross-dressing, she writes: "The appeal of cross-dressing is clearly related to its status as a sign of the constructedness of gender categories. But the tendency on the part of many critics has been to look *through* rather than *at* the cross-dresser, to turn away from a close encounter with the transvestite, and to want instead to subsume that figure within one of the two traditional genders. To elide and erase—or to *appropriate* the transvestite for particular political and critical aims."[21] The cross-dresser creates a "category crisis" that should not be glossed over in preference to a gender-specific reading; instead, Garber calls for finding the categorical crisis elsewhere, beyond the comparatively simpler category of male/female.[22] Garber argues that the category crisis exists for its own sake, and for the sake of those very categories, by representing something essentially primal in the origins of divisions and the meanings we make of them.

Butler shows how life performs gender by repeatedly stating it into being, imposing it on objects where no pre-existing categories exist; *Mulan* the play performs precisely that argument. Just as Butler's theory runs through Xu Wei's play, so too is Garber's crisis of categories clearly present in Xu Wei's *Mulan*, more so than in the two preceding plays; the gender questions that provided so much of the comedy in *Zen Master Yu* are performed quite as a matter of fact. As in *Mi Heng*, the audience is exposed to some onstage stripping; but in *Mulan*, the audience could interpret the stripping as necessary for a deception with good intentions at best, and as cheap titillation at worst, rather than as an announcement of a character's true intent. *Zen Master Yu* played with gender, but the cross-dressing was confined to the staged world, kept in the audience's memory of who the character had been in the first act. This is not the case with Mulan, who purposely dresses up as a man while remaining "herself" beneath her soldier's clothes and behavior. As with *Mi Heng* and *Zen Master Yu*, clothing and its role in making meaning are central to the plot, but *Mulan* presents it in the most plausible scenario yet, in the sense that it all takes place in the "real world" (albeit on stage). Are *Mulan* and, later, *Girl Graduate*, different from the first two plays because they present a more believable situation? Or should an audience conclude the alternative: that the premise of a woman succeeding in a male world (and, in fact, bettering her male counterparts) is just as fantastical as a man redeeming himself in the underworld or through reincarnation?

My analysis concludes that both readings are possible, and although such ambivalence may seem defeatist, it is a necessary frame for a play about how roles are occupied. Although some critics might feel disappointed that Mulan unquestioningly returns to her former life, what brings a greater disappointment is the sense of absolute hollowness that comes from the playing out of all roles in general. This play, more than the others, is about stage work and role-playing in "life." It is hard to feel sadness about Mulan relinquishing one thing for another, because Mulan as a distinct person does not exist. Instead, we have a series of roles and performances always setting up binaries, some that can be easily reversed and some that cannot. The situations that are not easily reversed bear hardly a trace of emotion, with age being the only slight exception. Virginity and biologically designated sex are both caught in the pervasive web of concealment and revelation that infects the whole play. The object must be concealed and preserved at all costs, but, paradoxically, it only attains its full value when it is exposed.

It is only fitting that this play, with its emphasis on the visual—in service of both proof and deception—would bear an intriguing stage direction present in the earliest printed version, but excised from the modern punctuated edition in use today, that reads: "When Mulan tries out a weapon and changes clothes and shoes, she absolutely must do wonderful kicks and jumps. When each part of the stage work is done, then she can sing, or else it will be a mess."[23] The instructions draw attention to the play's most memorable scenes. *Mulan* is distinguished neither by its language nor its narrative; it can only be understood as relevant in terms of its potential as physical entertainment. Verbal lyricism is exchanged here for slapstick humor and displays of technical skill. In fact, the arias do not describe the character's inner turmoil so much as they describe her physical action.[24] The action goes from Mulan's undressing and dressing, to military strategies, and then back to another scene of dressing before it concludes with a wedding. Over the course of these scenes, patterns of pairing insistently proliferate. The audience is exposed to double meanings from different perspectives: a pair of feet can mean different things depending on how they are presented, and a needle and thread can mean different things depending on how they are used. Moreover, things that cannot be reversed are presented in two stages: before and after. Different as they all are, they share the state of being revealed, for a while, for the pleasure of the viewing audience, who, with repeated exposure, comes to be immunized to any search for deeper meaning within these gestures.

The most basic substitution used throughout the play concerns names. The audience in a theater never suspects that a character is not who he claims to be, even as it knows that this character is played by an actor who is, by necessity, someone else. In the world of theater, this is not a troubling substitution, for the dramatic contract guarantees that both parties understand this aspect as part and parcel of a play. Outside the world of theater, however, the behavior of taking on another name and identity is a deception of the highest order. Although most viewers can be trusted to understand the difference between acting when on stage and simply lying when offstage, the threat of overlap is ever-present. In *Mulan*, the question of false names is both the complication and the solution.

The question of names, it turns out, has given rise to the need for war and, subsequently, conscription in *Mulan*. The Tuoba Khan is drafting men into his army in direct response to a conflict involving names: someone is claiming the title of ruler in an already-claimed territory. Mulan enters the stage and shares a conventional self-introduction that identifies her name and background, including her family's generational history and her own place in the family.[25] She then continues: "Yesterday I heard that Black Mountain's bandit chief, Leopard Skin, led hundreds of thousands of men on horseback in rebellion, and is now calling himself king (*cheng wang* 稱王). Our great Wei's Tuoba Khan sent down to our district, calling up troops. The army rolls have been arriving, twelve in a row, scroll after scroll bearing my father's name."[26] The situation presents a conundrum. The need for men arises from the rebel's assumption of a title that does not rightfully belong to him. The only way that Mulan can protect her father and serve the Khan is to take a name that is not rightfully hers. In doing so, she ultimately receives a title that should belong to her, but she does not accept it, because, she claims, the heroic act was not technically performed by *her*. This is not the only parallel between Mulan and Leopard Skin; in addition to taking on names other than their given name, the two have a parallel existence of hiding and exposure. Later in the play, Mulan will take the credit for driving Leopard Skin out of his hiding place, thus enabling his capture, even as she herself commits all her acts of bravery in disguise. Her perfidy is arguably more drastic than simply hiding in the mountains.

Mulan's concealment extends to the corporeal, involving the body's trappings and its bearing. These acts of concealment make up the bulk of the first act. Male dress lends credibility to Mulan's performance as a man; moreover, she claims that her success in impersonating a man makes her superior to her cross-dressing predecessors. Instead of likening herself to a historical combatant, Mulan compares herself favorably to Qin Xiu and Tiying. The two women were distinguished not for their willingness to cross-dress, nor for their abilities as war heroes, but for their filial piety. Although both of these women were considered model daughters devoted to their fathers, Mulan suggests that she does them one better by expressing her filial love for her father while in male dress. After praising them for their loyalty, she remarks: "But, weren't those two still putting their buns in hairnets instead of wearing male caps? Didn't they go on wearing their girls' skirts and jackets?"[27] In other words, although they performed their acts of piety commendably, what Mulan is about to do is superior because she will manage it not in female but in male clothing.

After this speech comes the change of clothing that Xu Wei presumably wanted performed slowly and deliberately, for the viewing pleasure of his audience. Although Mulan presumably has to remove some of her clothing and hair ornaments to turn into a man, the scene of transformation as it is written more heavily emphasizes putting things on, not taking them off, with one exception.[28] In order to ready herself for battle, Mulan says: "If I want to practice martial arts, I've got to first let out these feet, and change to this pair of boots."[29] Anachronistic though they might be for the Northern Wei period, bound feet were *de rigueur* in Xu Wei's milieu, and their display would provide an irresistible stage scene.

Interestingly, although women did not actually bind their feet during the Northern Wei, the image of bound feet was, especially during later centuries, intertwined with a romanticized vision of the Northwest. Specifically, this was Northern Wei territory from 298–494 CE, with its capital in Pingcheng 平城 (Datong 大同 now, as it was in Xu Wei's time). Male writers from the seventeenth and eighteenth centuries projected their desires on to an imagined Northwest, a "geographical location . . . [that] was a cultural imaginary in which indecent male desires could find concrete and socially acceptable expressions." Datong in particular had a "centuries-old reputation as the mecca of footbinding" and was mythologized as a site for foot festivals, or competitions, dating back to 1000 CE.[30] In spite of the problems with chronology, the geographical associations of Mulan and the Northern Wei would do away with any reservations a reluctant observer might have in enjoying this scene.

Joseph Allen, writing about Mulan imagery in the later tradition, notes that the emphasis on legs and feet might have more to do with an acknowledgment of male riding style, as it is an "index to a particularly important aspect of the sartorial code of her disguise. The spreading of her legs is not simply an acknowledgement of the male riding style, for Chinese women also rode astride, but rather it displays her trousers and boots that were part of the male military costume."[31] Mulan does make much of this shedding of her most female characteristic; though she later speaks of face powder and beauty marks, her bound feet are physical proof of her femininity to her companions. She acts out pain in removing the bindings, and sings an aria on this version of stripping:

> Just-removed, the half-folded "tiny ripple socks" bindings,
> How it hurts!
> It took me several years to bind together these phoenix-head points.
> Now I quickly turn them into floating boats.
> How will I now fill up these boots?[32]

Mulan's sacrifice is not as devastating as it may seem, however; her letting out of her feet, the product of years of binding, hardly a typically reversible procedure, has a loophole, thanks to a family recipe:

> When I return, I'll still want to get married. So what can I do? Well, no need to mope about that! My family has a method for shrinking golden lotuses: just take a bit of saltpeter, boil it, and use it to wash the feet. In this way, we make them even smaller!
> (*sings*)

> Take the raw saltpeter,
> Boil it so it is white like snowflakes,
> And in a thrice, you've shrunk them back into golden lotus petals.[33]

Xu Wei takes the usually fixed boundary of the bound foot and makes it a category that can easily be broached, at least for the Hua family. The visible trappings of female difference become simply a procedure that requires a bit of time: "wait, wait, until my feet have unfolded,/And with big steps I can stride again."[34]

When Mulan puts on clothes and equipment and changes the way she moves, she is merely performing procedures. Before announcing her decision to take her father's place, Mulan is determined to first practice her male self: "And I'd better go over my martial arts once or twice. Only then can I tell my family about my aim to take dad's place."[35] She waits to present herself as a finished product to her parents, to which they respond: "Why are you dressed up (*daban* 打扮) like this today?" Their response emphasizes play-acting through their use of a term that is reserved for dressing up in the context of playing a part.[36] Most of the songs in the first act describe Mulan's putting on armor or trying out equipment; just as Mi Heng beat the drum while calling out each of Cao Cao's crimes with each aria, Mulan sings each song to accompany her stage of dress. After the above-mentioned unbinding song to "*Youhu lu*," she sings to the tune "*Tianxia le*" as she dons the newly purchased armor.[37] Following the dressing-up songs, Mulan runs through a series of songs describing her fighting styles with sword, staff, and military bow. Kathleen Ryor's recent article on Xu Wei's career as a military aide and strategist may go some distance in explaining the very technical and specific terms used for the equipment in Mulan's songs.[38] However, such a careful inventory of these masculine details emphasizes the importance of clothing and postures in the performance of being a man, specifically a military man. The distinction is crucial: Mulan is putting on an entire male identity, not just a gender, and in doing so she completely wipes out her former self. As she puts it: "I shall sweep away the traces of old rouge from my flower cheeks with my sable cap."[39]

The transformations are detailed through the putting on of clothes and the display of certain behaviors, demonstrating to the audience that the bulk of one's gender is something that one puts on, like a costume, and that any deeper differences are mainly incidental. Mulan is, after all, not the only character on the stage defined by her dress. The audience cannot forget that all the *actors* on stage are defined by their dress, which signifies their role type; but in *Mulan*, characters are known by their appearance. When Mulan and her companions draw near to the battleground, she observes:

> Several banner flags are raised.
> In tattered caps, and worn shirts,
> They are not very intimidating,
> This must be an officer of the guard!
> Is he not like us, one of the same kind?[40]

She unselfconsciously identifies with the officer of the guard, as their clothing marks their shared association. Later, when Mulan distinguishes herself in battle, she is rewarded with the cap and girdle of officialdom. When she returns to her parents, she uses the cap as a synecdoche for all of her accomplishments: "This black gauze cap (*wusha* 烏紗) came from the khan himself."[41] She enters the second act wearing the official's cap and girdle. At the end of the act, she is back to wearing women's dress before being married to Master Wang, who happens to have just won the cap and girdle, thus keeping it happily in the family.

Mulan asserts that men and women are not so very different, and that women's capabilities are equal to men's. Speaking again of Tiying and Qin Xiu, she says, "They were both my female companions, in skirts and hairpins./Standing on the ground, holding up heaven,/What's all this about male heroes?"[42] The question of category is not even necessarily one of using different objects, but of things having different purposes. Throughout her transformation from daughter to soldier, Mulan and her parents describe the circumstances with the metaphor of needlework: "why aren't my hands sore with pain, used as they are to threading the loom's shuttle?"[43] This talk continues with the image of needle and thread, which Mulan has used for domestic work and which are now presented to her as a going-away gift, alluding to a tradition of mothers sending off their sons.[44] As Mulan readies herself for departure, her mother gives her a needle and some thread for her new life on the road. Remarking on how she has been turned into a soldier, Mulan notes "Dropping the needle's point, I've slung on my strung bow."[45]

Just as simply as she drops her needle and thread, Mulan assumes a new identity with a change of clothes: "Dressed up, I daresay I'm a senior campaigning officer."[46] At the end of the play, as in the ballad, when Mulan returns home, she goes to a mirror and transforms herself back into a woman before greeting her parents. Yet in spite of the language of dress-up, there is an implication that the old Mulan may no longer be familiar to her family members. As she became the senior campaigning officer by changing her costume, it is conceivable that, when she returns a decade later as Hua Hu, she will not be recognized as their daughter, Mulan. The costume is too opaque to be seen through.

Mulan's need to hide her true self, and her equally strong need to reveal it at the end of the play, are amplified in her searching out the other imposter in the play: Leopard Skin. Leopard Skin's attempts to hide, however, are mocked for their futility and myopia: "Black Mountain's little bandit is truly shortsighted!/ He continues to hide himself—what can he accomplish?"[47] Leopard Skin provides an alternative model to Mulan's narrative; while she successfully transforms herself and maintains her cover, even while surrounded by men, he cannot conceal himself, even when isolated in the mountains. This deliberate contrast begs the question of why Leopard Skin should fail, as it appears from Mulan's example that disguise is not inherently futile. Whether it is a question of intent or skill that sets them apart, Leopard Skin's pursuit and eventual capture underscores the danger in these transgressions.

Not all categories may be crossed with such ease, and, indeed, anxiety over the boundaries of those categories drives the play. Mulan determines that she must join the army on behalf of her father because of his age. In this play, at least, there is no room for redemption in the Underworld, and her father has clearly made the transition from one stage of life (and even gender association) to another. The parallels are presented in Mulan's description of her father:

> To think, how
> In earlier times,
> He fit an arrow to hunt the hawk, piercing it with its white-feathered shaft.
> Now, ah,
> He leans on a staff to watch the wild geese, counting them against the blue sky.
> He calls in the chickens, and feeds the dog,
> He stays in the village, and minds the fields.
> For training falcons, his wrist is too weak,
> For chasing hares, his back is too bent.
> He leads us sisters by the hand,
> He combs the hair of us little girls.
> Seeing us in front of mirrors touching up rouge, he laughs out loud,
> Hearing about swords raised in battle, his brow furrows in frowns.[48]

Her father's transformation is described with symmetrical accuracy: whereas he used to hunt birds of prey, he now only directs his gaze upward to look at the geese. The sight of daughters putting on makeup delights him in a way that the sound of swords once did. Now, Mulan has to take part in both activities in order to spare him.

The category that she absolutely cannot cross, however, concerns her virginity, which is tied in to the ultimate marker of her being female: the concealment of the fact that she lacks a penis. Her parents are not as concerned about her going off to war for fear of violence from battle; the scenario that her mother especially fears is that she will lose her virginity. This anxiety is captured in the following exchange between Mulan and her mother:

> Mother: And another thing, if you go, you are still, after all, a girl. Through a thousand provinces and a million miles, you'll be marching with men and keeping their constant company—breakfasting together in the morning, lodging together at night—how can you keep your you-know-what from showing? Don't you think that this will create problems?
> Mulan: Mom! Don't worry. I will return to you as a virgin.[49]

Mulan's only concern throughout the play is the preservation of her virginity, which, unlike her tiny bound feet, cannot be reclaimed; neither can the men around her be trusted to resist her feminine charms. To that end, a few scatological jokes are accommodated by the curious fact that Mulan refuses to go to the toilet in front of her fellow soldiers, who assume that it is a sign of her cultivated ways. As her mother says, she must prevent her fellow soldiers from catching a glimpse of her unclothed body, and Mulan succeeds in doing so, even as she is engaged in the pursuit of "exposing" Leopard Skin from his hiding place. She returns to her parents with her virginity still intact, a triumph that was accomplished through, in her words, a ruse (*jiguan* 機關).

The success of the ruse, and the conclusion of the play itself, raises some intriguing questions about the themes already presented in the earlier plays. Whereas *Mi Heng* explores how one's true self could be revealed by stripping bare, and *Zen Master Yu* looks at how one's true self could be revealed by the use of costumes and stage props, Mulan presents a strange assertion of the absence of self, or of a self subsumed by costume. Even more troubling is the question: To what self can Mulan possibly return when her only concern was the preservation of her virginity? Toward the end of the play, Mulan reflects on the situation as she sings a compelling song:

Everything is—when I think of it—an illusion, after all;
Why should I boast that I succeeded in this scheme?
The "I" who killed bandits, and captured their king,
Was a female officer who switched to a man.
After all, these successes did not cost me a drop of sweat.[50]

This is the most personal of the arias in the sense that it is the most self-reflective. It is also the most impersonal, as Mulan categorically denies having had anything to do with the person who carried out the acts of valor. This is a chilling and startling claim: Mulan dissociates herself from the "I" who went to war, retreating into vague Buddhist talk about everything being illusory. Instead of clothes being the extension, or helper, of the body, they begin to dominate the body. The male dress that went off to war performed the action, and there was nothing beneath it. The irony is that, for all her protests and all her efforts to keep the male "self" separated from the other men, and her female self separated from her male self, there was something essentially appealing about Mulan/Hua Hu regardless of her gender. When she departed with two fellow soldiers, they commented to each other on "his" attractiveness: "That Hua Hu doesn't look bad at all. He doesn't look like a senior officer, but he'd be a nice morsel."[51] Yet, though Xu Wei nudges the audience with these sly insinuations, he does not pursue this possibility's potential for either comedy or danger, and the audience hears nothing further of it.[52]

Mulan, with its subject of cross-dressing and then its serious and strange assertion that perhaps it is not just dress that has changed, raises questions about the nature of performance and gender roles. What happens when we watch onstage cross-dressing and, potentially, the cross-dressing of a male actor, playing a female character, who is dressing up as a man (if Mulan was, for example, played by a male *dan*)? Although much critical space has been occupied by questions of whether a man is better equipped to perform a woman, we ought to also consider whether it is any less significant when a woman performs a woman. *Mulan* demonstrates that the putting on of different dress is just as much an altered state of being as reincarnation or revivification in the Underworld, and these separations reveal how much of our real lives are taken up with performance. We are asked to contemplate whether acting is always an empty and unworthy act, and whether people are constantly changing and different. Such a perspective also brings a certain degree of potential, however: if outward show is all that matters, what we become is limited only by our imaginations. Perhaps this is why the Mulan legend has endured so many adaptations and interpretations, entertaining us year after year, century after century. The comic dimensions of mistaken identities, the uplifting dimensions of potentially limitless options, the seeming assurances that no boundaries can defeat a full heart, all conspire to distract us from the fact that underneath it all there might be nothing there.

4

The Woman Who Took Herself for Himself: Truth, Evidence, and Identity in The Girl Graduate Rejects the Female Phoenix and Gains the Male Phoenix

"Je pense: on devrais dire: on me pense. . .Je est un autre"
Rimbaud, "Letter to Georges Izambard"

In October of 2006, *The China Daily* published a story about a woman named Li Xu who purchased false papers to pass herself off as a male officer in the People's Liberation Army in China. Unlike Mulan, she was not using these papers to demonstrate her filial piety. Instead, posing as a man named Li Zhanyu, she met a woman on the Internet and defrauded her with a story that "he" would like to marry the woman's daughter if only "he" could afford to break off "his" existing engagement to another girl. The story was noteworthy not because the imposter was pretending to be an army officer, nor because he was feigning interest in a girl he had no intention of marrying, but because he was in fact a woman. A photograph of the suspect shows a burly, unsmiling figure in a crewcut and officer's uniform. Internet scams are certainly unremarkable, and misrepresentation on dating websites is so ubiquitous as to be expected, but this story gained an international readership because of the nature of the deception. Cross-dressing women, and their reasons for wearing men's clothes, remain a topic of fascination and entertainment. In this real-life story of cross-dressing, the happy marriage conclusion is thwarted, if not because of the taint of fraud, then certainly for the wickedness of its motives, not to mention the legal impossibility. Not so with Xu Wei's heroines, Mulan and Huang Chonggu, who only resort to costume for noble reasons and are thus rewarded with marriage.

The final play in *Four Cries of a Gibbon* presents a case study of the many ways that people represent themselves, and the many ways that those representations are tested by others. Huang Chonggu is the heroine in this, the longest play in the quartet: *The Girl Top Graduate Rejects the Female Phoenix and Gains the Male Phoenix* (*Nü zhuangyuan cihuang defeng* 女狀元辭凰得鳳), or *Girl Graduate* (*Nü zhuangyuan* 女狀元). This play, which continues and expands the female cross-dressing theme, is the most structurally distinct from the other three plays; it comprises five acts and nineteen characters and features an exclusively southern roster of songs. Therefore, the majority of critical attention given to the play has thus far been devoted to its structural innovations.[1] Although the play's structural innovations are important, I will argue in this chapter that the play has much more to offer than simply serving as a milestone in the development of a genre.

Girl Graduate, with its plot involving a girl who dresses in her father's clothing to enter and succeed unimaginably in an exclusively male world, is a natural pair for *Mulan*, and the juxtaposition of the two plays makes for effective contrast. I suggested earlier that *Mulan* functions as a preface to *Girl Graduate*, in much the same way that a parallel, shorter story or anecdote prefaces a longer and more complex story in a short story collection. Huang Chonggu, like Mulan, navigates changes of identity without any supernatural intervention in a mundane setting. This time, the story takes place during the Five Dynasties and Ten Kingdoms period (907–960/979) following the fall of the Tang dynasty setting, in the Shu state. In many ways, the three preceding plays could be seen as somehow lending nuance and entry into this longer play. *Girl Graduate* represents the culmination of many threads begun in *Mi Heng* and *Zen Master Yu*, as well as *Mulan*. The theme of dressing and undressing is revisited in this play, with both the heroine and her trusted wet nurse dressed as men and working in the exclusively male profession of investigating and settling legal cases. The trial scenario that is the basis of *Mi Heng* is also the primary plot apparatus in *Girl Graduate*; this time, instead of serving as the defendant, the protagonist is the adjudicator of criminal trials.

Courtroom Trials and the Trials of Everyday Life

The courtroom trial is a natural setting for a play, sharing as it does many of the qualities of drama and allowing features of the plot to be revealed in a "natural" expository manner.[2] The third act, placed at the midpoint of the play, is a series of actual trials with characters dutifully presenting themselves and telling "their story" to the audience, just as Mi Heng did to the Underworld audience and the play's real audience. Similarly, the judge can act as the audience's surrogate, asking the accused for more details and testing the veracity of their accounts by querying complicated details. The courtroom setting brings the structure and formality that imply that truth will, and should, be told here: the law demands sincerity. Court cases allow for a reconsideration of "facts" that cannot be repeated but, within the framework of compulsory truth, will be corroborated by witnesses to create a simulacrum of the actual moment. This is no doubt why people follow real court cases with such interest, and why court cases have so frequently been the subject of dramatic works. The proliferation of Judge Bao plays in the Yuan and Ming dynasties testifies to the public's strong interest in courtroom cases, especially ones in which justice was meted out against all odds.[3]

Act 3, in which Huang Chonggu demonstrates her skill at adjudicating true and false, is framed by two acts in which Huang Chonggu's own person is tested and assessed. In act 1, she is called upon to bear witness to herself through language. In fact, the examination scenes, in which a student displays his scholarly prowess, were so common a feature in Southern Song drama that they were, like displays of martial arts or stage foolery, usually left to the actors' discretion. Idema writes: "The basic pattern of such a scene is so conventional that its text is often omitted in printed editions of *chuanqi* plays; it is even so conventional that exceptionally it has even dictated the pictorial representation of examinations in woodblock illustrations in printed editions of *chuanqi*."[4] In *Girl Graduate*, however, the dialogue is completely scripted. Of course there are many potential interpretations of the significance of this inclusion, but here, especially, the scene reinforces the repetition of a trial of sorts. While the criminal trials of *Girl Graduate* are the most obvious example of trials on stage, most of the other interactions that Chonggu has throughout the play take the form of *de facto* trials as well. Just as the trials in the second and third acts are enacted in threes, the trials that make up the storyline of the play (civil exams, criminal appeals trials, and "informal" social-literary trials) appear in triplicate. This proliferation of trials surely speaks to an undercurrent of anxiety in *Girl Graduate*. How people's claims of authenticity are tested and verified, and whether these claims can actually be tested or verified, are at stake in this play.

All interactions may be construed as trials of a sort, but the very visual presence of the cross-dressed character heightens the audience's awareness of the ease of deception. Readers familiar with *The Merchant of Venice* might notice thematic parallels with Shakespeare's cross-dressed heroine and the "trials" that are central to that play. At the beginning of the play, Portia puts each suitor to the test, judging his character by his choice from among three boxes she presents. In another repetition of threes, the play shows the suitors being tested: the Prince of Morocco fails first, followed by the Prince of Arragon. Finally, the successful candidate, Bassanio, makes the right choice and wins Portia's heart. This trial is followed by a real courtroom trial, also presided over by a now cross-dressed Portia, who is assisted by her lady-in-waiting, Nerissa, also cross-dressed and masquerading as her clerk. During the trial, Portia impresses all with "his" wisdom by finding a loophole in Shylock's contract. Like *Girl Graduate*, Shakespeare's play ends with a trial that tests the worthiness of a marriage; in the final act, Portia and Nerissa demand to see their husbands' wedding rings as a test of their oaths of fidelity. Of course, the husbands cannot produce these concrete objects, but all is resolved when the wives laughingly reveal that they were in fact the lawyer and clerk who had previously taken the rings as payment. In Shakespeare's play, as in *Girl Graduate*, the device of cross-dressing is the most immediate reminder of the unreliability of judging someone by their looks. Like *Girl Graduate*, the resolution (a happy wedding) of *The Merchant of Venice* is secured through the parsing of language.

One need not cross both land and sea to find evidence of a general audience interest in female cross-dressing. *Mulan* is just one story within the tradition of cross-dressing women warriors, covering the exclusively male domain of warfare. Huang Chonggu breaches the civil counterpart, participating in the exclusively male domain of officialdom. Another famous female cross-dresser in the Chinese tradition is Zhu Yingtai 祝英台, a woman who disguises herself as a male student, sharing a room and falling in love with her classmate, Liang Shanbo 梁山伯.[5] The lovers are thwarted, Liang dies of heartbreak, and Zhu jumps into his grave to join him in death. The two are turned into butterflies. It has been suggested elsewhere that Zhu Yingtai and Liang Shanbo's ultimate tragic ending results from Liang's failure to recognize Zhu Yingtai's true gender.[6] This problem of recognition is clearly a problem that appeals to a theater audience, and masking of gender is one of the most efficient and immediate ways of representing this problem; at least this seems to be the case with the story of Huang Chonggu, which was taken as a subject or as a source of inspiration by many women playwrights in the eighteenth century.[7] With *Girl Graduate*, cross-dressing plays a part in the narrative tension of the play and its resolution, but it is not the fundamental topic of the play. The problem, a basic one of recognition that transcends questions of gender, is this: it is difficult to understand another person, and it is difficult to make oneself understood. The ubiquity of costume and disguise are given immediate concreteness when represented on a cross-dressed heroine, making gender an expedient dramatic device.

Girl Graduate is Xu Wei's most thorough consideration of the nature of truth-telling; yet, the exposure of one's true self, and one's truth, comes mediated by language, often highly ornamented language. If *Mi Heng* emphasizes exposing one's true self, and *Zen Master Yu* and *Mulan* explore the fluidity of one's identity and the means people take—even to the extremes of deception—to express that identity, then *Girl Graduate* combines these themes into a play about forgery. The primary forgery is the hero/ine's: Chonggu's first words of introduction align her with the female dress of a red head scarf, but soon enough she is transforming herself into a (male) scholar who takes part in an exam where the participants are asked to write, conveniently for a song-drama, songs (*yuefu*). When Chonggu wins the top prize and takes her post presiding over legal appeals, the nature of her work is precisely to sift through evidence to get to the heart of the matter. Significantly, when she addresses the first case of forgery, she blames the viewers for not seeing through an obvious fake. Later, Zhou Xiang calls her to his home to be unwittingly tested as potential son-in-law material, and her assignment is to write some verse on his behalf. The echoes of acceptable and unacceptable forgeries abound throughout the play, as Xu Wei presents, on the one hand, cases where forgery is too ludicrous to be taken seriously, and, on the other hand, examples of "forgeries" that are just part of an accepted writing convention between a mentor and his protégé. The culminating moment of sincere self-revelation is Huang Chonggu's confession at the end by way of a poem, a literary creation that delivers its message indirectly. It is fitting that Chonggu demonstrates that the lyrical and formally constricted forms of a poem are better suited to her sincere confession than to plain speech, subtly underscoring that the person masquerading under a different identity can still be sincere in intent. The cross-dressing, which, as noted before, would have been even further emphasized if the *dan* were male, reminds the audience that any deep consideration of authenticity is qualified by the fact that it is presented by actors in costume.

Studies of *Girl Graduate* have treated it in much the same way as *Mulan*, often grouping the plays together. Both plays about women who dress up as men and succeed beyond expectation are naturally considered in terms of their successes and failures as feminist texts, whether furthering the feminist cause or eventually subverting it by conforming to the existing patriarchy.[8] Following a synopsis of the play and a brief survey of its literary antecedents, this chapter will instead give special attention to the way the performative aspects, such as costume change, contribute to a larger sense of stage-audience interaction. The ways that counterfeits and impersonations are engendered, exposed, and then incorporated in *Girl Graduate* provide us with a model for reading *Four Cries of a Gibbon*. These structural elements in the play also model the way that actors present themselves to the audience, reminding us once again that in our own interactions with others, we are spectacularly close to the world of performance.

The Girl Graduate

The first act of the play immediately introduces the heroine, who begins singing as she enters. She does not tell us her name, but only identifies herself as female by referencing her clothing. She reveals that both of her parents are dead, and that the money she has managed to cull from selling family jewelry is running out. Following the song, she identifies herself as Huang Chuntao, the daughter of a prefect whose honesty prevented him from building up much of an estate. As a result, after her parents' death, she and her former wet nurse, Auntie Huang, were forced to eke out a living with their spinning. Well aware of her talents, Huang Chuntao decides to sit for the imperial examinations, because success in the examinations would guarantee her a viable living. The decision is phrased purely in terms of economic necessity; they need to be able to buy food, and this is the only way they can manage. She changes into her father's old clothes, removes her makeup and ornaments, and leaves with Auntie Huang. Chuntao's description of her transformation into a scholar like a soldier going into battle underscores the parallels with *Mulan*. "If I, Chuntao, could change my costume for just one battle (*gai zhuang yi zhan* 改妝一戰), I could easily take first place in the examinations."[9]

Act 2 takes place in the examination hall, where the exams are presided over by the Prime Minister, Zhou Xiang. Huang Chuntao, who is now in disguise as a man named Huang Chonggu, is tested along with two other candidates, Jia Lu and Balderdash (his name Hu Yan 胡顏, a pun on "*huyan*" 胡言, means "nonsense," or "balderdash"). Zhou Xiang announces that he wishes to hear a song from each of the candidates composed on a theme he selects. He will provide the song tune and the rhyming words at the ends of certain lines, which must be maintained in all of the songs. Huang Chonggu is chosen to present first, and s/he is asked to compose on Sima Xiangru's 司馬相如 (179–127 BCE) removing his kingfisher robe in order to support Zhuo Wenjun 卓文君 (second century BCE). The situation of a talented writer's removing his clothes in order to pay for food is naturally familiar to Chonggu, who composes a poem that Zhou Xiang finds to be "especially subtly rhymed."[10] When Jia Lu is asked to compose on Du Fu 杜甫 (712–70), he too does a satisfactory job, but not so the comic figure of Balderdash, who is played by a *chou*. Balderdash is given another famous Du Fu scene—that of a neighbor woman knocking down dates from his tree. True to his nature, he immediately protests and constantly misinterprets words, spouting out hilariously disastrous, yet unintentionally fitting puns. Nonetheless, Zhou Xiang is impressed at Balderdash's guilelessness: "What I like about him is that he doesn't conceal from me his true nature" (*ke quchu zhi shi bu cheyan zhe ta de zhen xingqing* 可取處只是不遮掩著他的真性情).[11] Zhou Xiang passes Balderdash, too, even giving him the appropriate rhyming lines for a winning essay.

In the middle act, Huang Chonggu is titled Regional Administrator, managing records and documents as an associate judge. She has held the same position for three years and is frustrated that she has not been promoted. Prime Minister Zhou, who has in the meantime been promoted to Municipal Prefect, sends her suspicious closed cases of three convicted criminals petitioning for reconsideration. Expected to review the cases to see if they demonstrate a miscarriage of justice, Huang Chonggu does not know that these difficult cases have been chosen specifically by Prime Minister Zhou to test her skills and measure her worth. Here, as in the second act, there are three cases to be heard, and the first is that of Huang Tianzhi ("Heaven knows"), who has been accused of forging seals. The second case involves a woman, Madam Wu, convicted of poisoning her husband based on the accusations of a thwarted admirer. The third case involves an itinerant drum-singer, Zhen Kexiao ("Truly Laughable"), who is accused of robbery. Huang Chonggu ably dispatches each case, finding the weaknesses in the accusations and exactly interpreting the true facts of each situation. In the case of Madam Wu, she ferrets out a witness who corroborates Madam Wu's story with further damning details. Huang Chonggu determines Zhen Kexiao's innocence based on analyzing his responses to her questions. Huang Tianzhi's case, which involves a personal seal made in imitation of an official seal, is also dismissed. The scene concludes with a grateful chorus by the defendants in praise of Huang Chonggu's wisdom.

In the next act, Huang Chonggu is invited to Zhou Xiang's home on the pretense that Zhou wants Huang to report on the three cases investigated in act 3, when in fact Zhou Xiang is investigating Chonggu's suitability as a son-in-law for his talented daughter, Fengchu. After congratulating Chonggu, Zhou Xiang asks him to compose verses for various monuments on his property, including a temple to Mulan. Chonggu churns out verse after verse, each time pleasing Zhou Xiang to no end. Chonggu then paints a picture, performs a song on the *qin*, and beats Zhou in a game of *Go*, which impress Zhou Xiang all the more. At the end of the act, Zhou sends an envoy to propose his daughter in marriage to Chonggu, to which the bemused Chonggu replies in verse form, finally revealing her sex:

> Ever since I stopped collecting kingfisher feathers at Brocade River's edge,
> Poor and keeping a humble thatched hut, I composed *fu* and poems.
> Since I donned the blue gown of a graduate to take on official duties,
> I had long cast away the *luan* bird mirror used to paint eyebrows.
> Establishing myself with the bearing of the green pines,
> I willfully maintained the carriage of tinkling white jade.
> Now, minister, if you seek me to be your son-in-law with bared belly,
> I beg Heaven to quickly change me into a man.[12]

The final act of the play begins with Chonggu trying to decide how to behave now that her identity has been revealed. On the one hand, she is embarrassed that she had to reveal her true female self to the man who so trusted her. On the other hand, she is socially beholden to him and would insult him if she does not go to congratulate Zhou's son Fengyu on his examination success. This decision to ready the horse to go in congratulation marks Chonggu's difference from Mulan who, after becoming a woman again, denies any relationship to the acts she performed as a man. Here, Chuntao goes to do what is socially expected of the male Huang Chonggu, even though she is now publicly identified as a woman. Happily, Zhou Xiang is only delighted with her and has already resolved to pair her with his son. This "happy ending" might strike a dissonant chord with modern feminist readers, who might chafe at the way Huang Chonggu is quickly stripped of her titles (and accompanying cap and girdle) and thrust back into female clothes. We also cannot forget the lot of the put-upon Fengchu, who not only loses a prospective husband but is immediately dispatched to help "him" get dressed up as her sister-in-law. Fengyu returns and eventually marries Chonggu, and the pair even receives the Emperor's express approval.

Chonggu's Literary Antecedents

Wang Jide, in the above note on the genesis of *Girl Graduate* (also called *Huang Chonggu*), writes that he suggested the story by Yang Shen 楊慎, called "Huang Chonggu: The Tale of Chuntao," which is no longer extant.[13] An extant early source is the classical tale in the *Taiping guangji* 太平廣記 entitled "Huang Chonggu" 黃崇嘏.[14] The tale gives the period and setting of the story that Xu Wei uses for his play. Instead of meeting Chonggu through the regular examination system, however, Zhou Xiang meets Chonggu because she is on the wrong side of the law. Having been convicted of arson, she has protested the accusation in the form of a poem. Impressed by the poem, Zhou has Chonggu summoned to court, where Chonggu claims to be a thirty-year-old *jinshi* scholar. Zhou Xiang is impressed with Chonggu's responses and frees "him." Zhou Xiang "not only appreciates his extraordinary intelligence, but also admires his elegance [beauty] and sophistication" (*Zhou ji zhong qi yingcong, you mei qi fengcai* 周既重其英聰。又美其風彩).[15] Impressed even further by Chonggu, Zhou Xiang decides to make him his son-in-law, whereupon Chonggu refuses the offer through the poem that we know from act 4 of the play. When Zhou realizes the truth after reading the poem, he questions Huang and discovers the details of her past. Zhou, along with everyone else who has witnessed these events, is impressed by her chastity and purity. Huang Chonggu returns to her former life as a recluse in Linqiong, and thenceforth nobody knows what becomes of her.

Xu Wei preserves most of the details from the *Taiping guangji* tale, using the poem of refusal. The changes and additions are naturally suited to the themes of his play, as forgery and impersonation run throughout *Girl Graduate.* A choice is always constructed between two entities: the true and the false, the real person and the impostor. Xu Wei's introduction of the character Fengyu allows for the traditional happy ending (*tuanyuan* 團圓) native to *chuanqi*, but it is also necessary to maintain symmetry. Fengyu is the obvious foil for his sister, Fengchu, who immediately drops in status from potential wife to handmaid once Chonggu is found to be a woman. He is also, however, necessary as a foil for Chonggu. Now that she is a woman again, she cannot be a real top graduate, and he conveniently steps in to fulfill those duties, wearing a cap and girdle like the ones that Chonggu has to give up. This chapter will argue that these changes and additions are not accidental, but rather reinforce the theme of double identities, and the need to distinguish between them. In this reading, then, the third "lawsuit" act is not just "of minor importance to the development of the story."[16] Although it certainly provides the same kind of entertainment as a standard courtroom drama, and establishes Chonggu's skills as a judge, it also provides a frame to view Chonggu's own situation as a perpetrator of deceit and impersonation, even as our evaluation of her is tied to her skill in judging right from wrong, and true from false.

Identity on Trial

The prevailing reading of courtroom drama of the Yuan and early Ming dynasties is that the trials function as allegories about Mongol oppression.[17] George Hayden, in his book *Crime and Punishment in Medieval Chinese Drama*, dismisses this reading, arguing instead that the judges' ability to solve dilemmas "reflect an equation of intelligence (an equation strongly Neo-Confucian in tone) with man's innate ability to distinguish right from wrong. In its most extreme form, this insight allows the detective to determine from a mere glance at a subject's physiognomy and bearing his innocence or guilt."[18] Recalling the trial scenes in act 3, the reader might agree that the farther along Chonggu goes in reviewing the three cases, the more astute her judgments, and the less hard evidence she requires to make her decisions. She goes from retrieving documentary evidence in clearing Huang Tianzhi, to relying on verbal (and conceivably coerced) testimony in clearing Madam Wu, to a sensible prognosis based on an oral interview in clearing Zhen Kexiao. The more dazzling her displays of intuition and wisdom, the farther away the connection between case-solving and "evidence" as we know it. Chonggu relies on intuition in all cases, but her decisions are supported less and less frequently with concrete evidence as she progresses.

The conventions of a wise and all-seeing judge seem to apply, whether referring to the Yuan and early Ming plays Hayden discusses or to Xu Wei's late Ming creation. The more we marvel at Chonggu's perspicacity, the more the other characters lose credibility. When our respect for Huang Chonggu heightens with each demonstration of her ability to distinguish true from false, our esteem for Zhou Xiang decreases, as he obtusely fails to recognize Chonggu's deception. One could also argue that Zhou Xiang is actually an astute judge of character, one who does see Huang Chonggu for all that is worthwhile and talented about her, judging a horse not by its color, but by its abilities. The fact that she is a woman would then be irrelevant, her deception committed out of necessity. This is a generous reading, but not incompatible with the play. After all, *Girl Graduate* makes an argument for the implausible, whether it is with the convenient switch of groom for bride at the end of the play, or the equally extraordinary transformation and triumph of an impoverished girl in the civil examinations. Unlike *Mulan*, which deals in absolutes, *Girl Graduate* works through the same dichotomies but ultimately suggests a greater degree of flexibility.

Throughout the play, the emphasis on evidence contrasts with Chonggu's hints at her female identity; it shows through like the flashes of red azalea in the springtime. Some circumstances escape notice even when in plain view. It is incumbent on the viewer to notice things as they are, or, when it is more convenient, not to notice them at all. The first statement made in the five-act play is a visual reference. Although it is the convention for the characters to introduce themselves to the audience upon entering, Huang Chuntao/Chonggu's introduction sets the tone for the audience to see how identity is formulated. The character, played by a *dan*, does not say, "I am a girl in a headscarf," but rather uses the synecdoche "A [girl's] pointed headscarf" (*yi jian guo* 一尖幗) as the subject of her sentence. I emphasize her identification with the sartorial because clothes are a crucial plot element, as they were in *Mulan*. The *dan* continues, referring to outer visual cues rather than any personal pronouns: "Wasting away, this jade-like body,/Colorful sleeves in winter's cold."[19] The question of how a self is defined continues to be a prominent theme in this play, as it has been in the other plays within *Four Cries of a Gibbon*. Mi Heng knew which self he wanted to show and demonstrated it by flouting the expected uniform; Liu Cui needed a mental shift to realize that she was actually Yu Tong; and Mulan sends only her body in men's clothes, separate from her "self," into battle. Everyone experiences the familiar feeling of a divided self, and each of these characters literally embodies the strangeness of one body containing multiple selves. Yet none take on these multiple identities as comfortably as the protagonist of *Girl Graduate*. Visual reference is at the center of this state of multiple selves, as the play maintains the conflicting threads of anxiety about being exposed and the valorization of exposing what is hidden. Both are tied together by the element of the hint, or clues. The device of the hint epitomizes how this play works: clues are scattered about, neither invisible nor obvious, amplifying the need for a canny viewer. In the discussion below, I will first look at the references to costume and body that recur throughout the play, and the issues of exposure and duality that arise from these, before turning to how these images are echoed and reinforced on smaller and larger scales.

Dressing the Part

Huang Chuntao, as she is called at the beginning of the play, knows that if she can "change [her] costume for just one battle, [she] could easily take first place in the examinations," asserting that only clothing stands in the way of her talent.[20] Chuntao's wet nurse, Auntie Huang, reacts in the same way Mulan's parents do when they hear their daughter's plan, and needs a bit more convincing. The playful, improvised dialogue that ensues sheds light on how much one's face is tied to what one wears, as Chuntao responds to Auntie Huang's concerns about her girlish face with the solution that she will change her clothes to solve the problem:

Auntie Huang: Great! Great! If you go and take the exams, you will certainly make it, but what are you going to do about changing your girlish face?
Chuntao: What difficulty is there with that? I will take my father's old clothes, shoes, head-wrap and hat and put them on, in exchange for my own skirt, jacket, and coiled-up chignon. Anyone seeing me would never be able to tell that I am a girl, and not a man!
Auntie Huang: This really makes sense.
(*Auntie Huang acts out clowning around*)
Chuntao: Let's not talk nonsense anymore. Quickly go and prepare father's old clothes and bring them out. I will change costume. And you also need to be ready to impersonate an older servant. We will call you Huang Ke, and I will take the name Huang Chonggu, and that's how we will go together. Command your son, Number Two, to take care of the house, and that should do it.[21]

Gender is determined only by clothes, hat, and hairstyle.[22] Here, as with Mulan, the characteristics that constitute the female identity are ones that are put on, like so many ornaments and additions, so that the process of Chuntao's becoming a man involves her stripping down and taking off these encumbrances, echoing Mi Heng's exposure. Chuntao's, now Chonggu's, exposure also involves a covering up, as she is disguising herself as a man. The first order of business is to remove the traces of her femininity:

Facing the mirror, I wipe off the red rouge,
Take off the lotus ornament, and from now on wear green robes.
A sail full of wind helps one a little,
Brushing the rosy clouds, a solitary duck.
My source of words will overturn in Qutang's waters,
My literary style is wholly free of the vulgar habits of rouge and powder.
My cloth-wrapped bundle is tied up tightly, my chignon fastened into a snood,
I will come back wearing gold flowers of success stuck into my cap.[23]

Of course this is simply replacing one type of ornamentation (rouge and powder) for another (the ornaments of a top exam candidate), but clearly the former is unacceptable, while the latter is desirable. The ornament of makeup is mixed up with ornament in writing, and Chonggu abjures these "vulgar" (*su* 俗) elements from her face as she will, later, from her writing. Red will still come creeping back at various moments in the play, just as the ornament of lyric—an unavoidable feature of song-drama—continues to inhabit its scenes.

Chonggu willingly acknowledges that, having changed her costume to impersonate a role, she must continue acting. Indeed, anyone who attains a higher position has to "act" appropriately to that role. At the beginning of act 3, she comes in to introduce herself, now dressed in official's cap and girdle. She expresses her anxieties about fulfilling her role in office in terms of clothing and color, using the term used to refer to those serving a high official: "Black curtains and blue gowns are easy to put on,/Clear waters and red lotus are difficult to emulate."[24] The language of acting and clothing comes naturally to her musings on her new public role. Musing on how she should act toward an official, she remarks:

> Even though the Postmaster General is haughty,
> If I have to seek an audience with him, what harm is there in doing so?
> I only consider it a play on a stage (*zhi zuo xichang kan* 只作戲場看),
> And bend my waist as if it were soft cotton.[25]

As easy as it is to put on the costume, she still has a role to fill. Chonggu's reference to her greeting the official as a "play on a stage" refers not so much to her playing the part of a man but to her playing the social role of a low-level official facing a superior, underscoring the fact that her cross-dressing is not the source of anxiety as much as a fear of failing to succeed in that role.

Inevitably, however, Chonggu's hand is forced by Zhou Xiang's proposal of marriage to Fengchu. She has to reveal the fact that she is not a man in order to refuse his offer. Act 5 begins with the news of Zhou Xiang's son, Fengyu, having succeeded in the imperial examinations. Chonggu is faced with an interesting dilemma: how will she present herself to Zhou Xiang when she offers the obligatory congratulations (*ke ba shenme zuilian qu jian zhe laoshi* 可把什麼嘴臉去見這老師)?[26] The sentence can be taken figuratively, of course, since Chonggu is well aware of the implications and punishments that could befall someone who has so seriously deceived the prime minister. At a minimum, she has embarrassed Zhou Xiang first by deceiving him, and then continuing to deceive him, exposing his lack of perspicacity. In the most basic sense, she is also asking, "How can I face him?" but the words could be parsed, "How dare I show my face to him?" There are practical considerations, as well, and the sentence could be taken quite literally: "What am I going to wear to meet him?"

The answers to all the questions are, in a way, unanswerable. She readies her horse immediately and leaves as Chonggu, in male clothes. Happily for her, Zhou Xiang takes everything quite in stride, and has already come up with a resolution to the problem of incorporating her into his family. The way he phrases this plan demonstrates the difficulty of the situation. Although the Chinese language generally accommodates the avoidance of gendered pronouns, Xu Wei takes pains to emphasize the comical situation caused by the gender switching when Zhou Xiang says, "Master Huang must be the daughter-in-law" (*Huanglang zhege xifu, bu pa bushi ta de* 黃郎這個媳婦，不怕不是他的). He then goes further to equate his son to the prospective daughter-in-law: "My son and that Chonggu, ah,/are like two identical pearls, wept by a mermaid."[27]

Needless to say, this kind of confusion will not do, and so the hapless Fengchu is put to the task of helping her ex-betrothed to change into a ceremonial dress and hair extensions fitting for a bride.[28] Surely Chonggu's return to female clothes helps lessen the blow when Fengyu returns home expecting congratulations and meets instead with this exchange:

> Fengyu: Who is this?
> Zhou: All this time you were in the examination quarters, I didn't want to embarrass anyone by sending word to tell you of these matters. This person is your brother from your generation of students, Regional Administrator Huang, whom, it turns out, is a girl. Just yesterday I wished to make your sister Chonggu's wife. Once exposed, she came out with everything.
> Fengyu (startled): How on earth could this happen! And why has she changed dress now!
> Zhou: As she cannot be my son-in-law, I have changed my topic, and sought to make her my daughter-in-law, to be married to you. She could not refuse, so I called on your sister to help her change clothes, and we have been waiting for you to come to get married.[29]

The two are then hurried into a marriage ceremony to neatly cover over the discomfiting complications. To further ameliorate the tensions she has created, Chonggu justifies her choice to disguise herself as a man as one made solely from desperation:

> It's not that I made a show of falseness,
> But only that my poor existence was too forlorn.
> I guessed that if in a palace gown I could steal the brocade,
> I would not have to live behind a twig and bracken door.
> I am humbled that the Prime Minister saw me as an immortal talent fit to ride the phoenix,
> And invited Xiao Shi to be the fine man mounting the dragon with his bride.[30]

She further strokes her mentor's ego by suggesting that he recognized her talent rather than something as superficial as her sex.

The unfortunate erstwhile bride, Fengchu, sings a concession that is truly tragicomic:

> This fine son-in-law pleases father,
> Who would have thought you, Regional Administrator, would be of my kind.
> To sum up, the teacher set out a banquet,
> But alas the guest turned out to wear curled shoes!
> Changed anew from man to my sister-in-law, entering the kitchen,
> Sending me off to taste the soup vegetables for her mother-in-law.[31]

She, who had nothing to do with the deception, has had to go through a role change as well, from bride to sister-in-law cum lady-in-waiting, from bridal altar to kitchen stove. To add to the levity that would befit a comedy, the audience is treated to the vulgar corollary to Chuntao's dignified and literary exposure of her true self. Auntie Huang, the erstwhile Huang Ke, in a fit of fury that Chuntao's chastity has been impugned, foregoes a poem of explanation for a more efficient response. She contests the distinction of looks versus reality, asking: "Take a look at this old man. Do you still say that I am really a man?" (*Ni kan wo zhe laohan, ni jiu shuo zhen shi yige hanzi me?* 你看我這老漢，你就說眞是一個漢子麼?). With these words, she makes sure that all doubts are cast aside.

> I have pulled open my collar, and dragged out nipples to rival yours,
> That young lady—
> I nursed her myself until she was three years old,
> Needless to say
> I was her constant companion at home,
> And on the road, would never have allowed a man to be her companion![32]

Auntie Huang does what Chonggu, the *dan*, could never do. She is Chonggu's proxy, asserting her ward's chastity by being simultaneously the eyewitness and the visual evidence. Presumably the eyeful that the audience receives does little to detract from the entertainment value of this play. As we know from the various trials that occur throughout *Girl Graduate*, concrete evidence does away with speculation.

Hiding in Plain Sight: Exposure and Evidence

Auntie Huang's bold display of physical proof acts as a counterpart to the subtle clues scattered throughout the play that Chonggu is, in fact, not who she says she is. The hints, ranging from pointed comments about other cross-dressed women to admissions of play-acting, are signaled by the scatterings of red throughout the play. Very early in the first act, when she is still dressed as a girl, Chuntao refers to herself as a red flower. Using metaphors of flora to describe her orphanhood, she chants: "Since those two elms were ravaged by the fifth watch's winds/ Now who will care for the bereft cherry apple tree? The red azalea (*dujuan hong* 杜鵑紅)!"[33] Chuntao is not the only character to use the metaphor of a red flower to describe herself; Auntie Huang also identifies Chuntao as the "red leaf" (*hongye* 紅葉) that she carries on her back.[34] Again in act 3, Chonggu (as she is called, by this time) calls herself a "red lotus" (*honglian* 紅蓮).[35] And at the very end of the play, a chorus of the characters sing in thanks to Auntie Huang that, "The peony would be burnt by the sun if not for the green leaf's cover,/Such was Auntie Huang's doting care."[36] The astute viewer will remember the connection between Chuntao and red flowers in act 4, when she drops hints during her interview with Zhou Xiang. The imagery will also become uniquely weighted with meaning in act 5 when Zhou's son Fengyu returns, having won the top prize and referring to that accomplishment using the conventional phrase of breaking off the red branch.[37]

In act 4, when Chonggu has been summoned to Zhou Xiang's house to report on the cases from the day before, she is unaware that though she has already passed the official imperials exams, and passed muster as an appeals judge by making sound legal decisions, she is about to be tested once again. This time, Zhou Xiang intends to test her literary abilities in a social setting, in order to evaluate her further. Chonggu is asked to write a poem on Zhuo Wenjun's "Zither Terrace." Zhuo Wenjun and Sima Xiangru were already the subject of one of Zhou Xiang's exam questions in the second act, and the object of particular interest was Sima Xiangru's sale of his kingfisher robe. Chonggu writes a poem about the mountains awash with red azaleas, for which Sichuan's landscape is famous, and Zhou Xiang specifically praises her use of the azalea imagery.[38]

Immediately following this piece, Zhou Xiang reads Chonggu's piece of parallel prose on Mulan. The topic of Mulan is directly relevant to Chonggu's own situation, and her response is riddled with hints about the similarities between them. She quotes the line from Mulan about hares running side by side whose sex is indistinguishable when in motion, and adds an allusion to the horse expert, Bole 伯樂, who explains to Duke Mu that it is the inner quality, not the outer appearance, of a horse that is the measure of its worth. This work so impresses Zhou that he pronounces of Mulan: "To take on the disguise that she did was all good luck for her old man,"[39] which no doubt gives Chonggu some confidence. In response to all of Zhou's praise, she blurts out, amid claims of drunkenness: "When will Mulan's debt be repaid?" When Zhou Xiang questions this, she claims drunkenness again and makes up an excuse for her indiscretion and remarks: "I almost gave myself away!"[40] Here the fear of exposure is quite directly addressed. Chonggu is well aware of the tenuous hold she has on her disguise and how easily her true face can slip out when she is not careful.

All's Well That Ends Well

Like its three companion plays, *Girl Graduate* is about how multiple people can coexist in one body. With respect to the relationship between stage and earthly world, any theater audience is already well aware of how an actor's body contains both the actor and the character he plays. But in Xu Wei's play, this problem is situated singularly in the stage world, which presents a different challenge. Do the inhabitants of the staged world manage to accept the multiple identities embodied in Huang Chonggu/Chuntao in the same way that a theater audience accepts the duality of an actor, or the suppression of the actor's self in favor of the character he plays during the duration of the performance? In *Girl Graduate*, at least, this is the scenario that is tested, achieved, and, once achieved, set aside. The combination of two qualities, in this case male and female, residing in one body is repeatedly raised as a nearly impossible, yet admirable, achievement. As Auntie Huang says at the beginning of the play: "The talented poet, the beautiful woman—surely they exist,/ But when have they ever been combined in one body?" (*caizi jiaren xin you zhi, yi shen jian de gulai shei?* 才子佳人信有之，一身兼得古來誰？).[41] The joining of the conventional pair of talented poet and beautiful woman into one person finally ceases at the end of the play, when Fengyu and the restored Chuntao are married. It is the eventual separation of the talented poet from the beautiful woman (from one person) and the metaphorical joining of two people (Fengyu and Chuntao in marriage) that allow the characters to jubilate at the end: "On whom do the good deeds of the world depend?/If not a man, then a girl (*shijian hao shi shu he ren?/buzai naner er zai nüzi* 事間好事屬何人／不在男兒而在

女子)!"[42] This phrase seems to have less to do with feminist causes than with an affirmation of the inevitable separation of male from female: mixing and overlapping is all well and good for the duration of the entertainment, but the happy ending requires this resolution.

Chonggu's many accomplishments are only fully appreciated when the efforts she underwent to mask her true self are revealed and the disguise is removed. This play sympathizes with those who take extreme measures to reveal, and preserve, their true nature. These sympathies abide even when the heroine is someone who can only preserve her true nature by putting on a disguise. Zhou Xiang passes a clearly incompetent exam candidate, Balderdash, because he feels that "what I like about him is that he doesn't conceal from me his true nature (*zhen xingqing* 真性情), which is quite unlike those who, though they are arrogant and stingy in their hearts, act magnanimous through their mouths."[43] Zhou Xiang values Balderdash's spontaneous, original expression over his acquiescence to the rules. This evaluation coexists with Zhou Xiang's ranking Chonggu above all the other candidates. Which of the two has best represented his true self in the contest? Perhaps a certain degree of play-acting is necessary in order to reveal the truth; this is certainly the case in the third act.

To conclude, I would like to return to a moment in the third act where Chonggu, dressed now as a male official, is called on to determine whether a committed forgery was a criminal act. The first case is that of Huang Tianzhi (黄天知), whose name (Heaven Knows) implies his predicament: he is innocent, but lacks the means to prove it. Huang Tianzhi has been convicted of trying to pass off a personal seal as an official seal; he willingly confesses to having had a copy of the official seal made, thus committing a technical act of forgery. However, further questioning from Chonggu reveals that the seal is substantially smaller in size and, what's more, is clearly marked with Tianzhi's own full name carved on its face. When the chits that he marked with the seal are eventually produced, Chonggu pronounces:

> The case against him makes less and less sense. This is clearly a case of a small child making a muddy cap and sash from clay, and pretending that he is a Prime Minister or general, or something. Everyone knows it's just make-believe. But to take it as the real thing would be inconceivable even to babies not old enough for solid food! Piteous![44]

This statement is made even more fascinating by the fact that it is spoken by Chonggu, who is pretending to be someone she isn't: she is dressed in cap and girdle (*guandai* 冠帶), like the child's toys made of mud that she speaks of. It is up to the audience to decide whether her pretense is so clearly visible that it is the viewers' obtuseness alone that prevents them from noticing, or that her pretense is extremely well executed, unlike those made of mud, in which case the deception is more severe. Either way, it is clear from this scene that the greater part of understanding who or what another is depends on the viewer's abilities. Chonggu sums up Huang Tianzhi's case using the language of performance: "His true name was not concealed/Like one playing a large toad while hiding that he was a little tadpole!" Having already made the point of someone playing (*ban* 扮) a part, Chonggu goes on: "If it's not a case of forcibly appointing Tang Shuyu,/Then it's a play (*xi yi chang* 戲一場) about cutting a pawlonia branch to serve as a jade tablet."[45] Invoking an anecdote about Tang Shuyu, who received his title when his brother, the king, playfully gave him an appointment, and was forced to honor the command, Chonggu underscores the function of authority in constructions of understanding and meaning. With Tang Shuyu, something is forcibly said into being. When the words are spoken by a pretender or play actor, it is just a performance.

Of course the problem in this play is that one cannot simply distinguish between the person in authority and a play actor. If we take Chonggu to be an actor, like Mulan separating herself from the warrior, then are all her acts of wisdom and poetic compositions nullified? If we take her as the person whom she was playing, but know that she was playing a part, then how can we reach a meaningful definition of truth? We may find some hints of an answer in the comic exchange between Balderdash and Zhou Xiang during the examination scene. Balderdash has been told that his poem did not rhyme properly with the assigned words, and he responds: "What is so absolute about rhymes? Poetry rhymes are just like fates. If the examiner says that it rhymes well, then even if the rhyme doesn't rhyme, it will rhyme! If the examiner says that the rhyme is no good, even if the rhyme rhymes it won't rhyme. My fate resides with the examiner, not with me. That is why it is said: "Essays of the past cannot be relied on; one only relies on the nod of the red-robed examiner."[46] This comic tone, emphasizing the beholder's role in making meaning of what he sees, is echoed again when Chonggu refuses Zhou

Xiang's praises by likening herself to an ordinary rock who gets worshipped by the Song dynasty rock lover, Nanguan.[47] Mulan offers one solution, by transitioning from one role to another. She chooses to think of herself as having never been a combination of "Hua Hu" and Mulan the girl, treating those selves as two separate people. Chonggu offers an alternative. *Girl Graduate* instead suggests that all of these multiple meanings, conflicts, and clashes coexist freely in the world. The objects themselves are not the problem: they just need an astute viewer to make sense of it all.

Conclusion

The plays that make up *Four Cries of a Gibbon* present four variations on the same theme: a protagonist is aware of how he or she will be seen by others, and has to assert his or her identity by a series of actions that always involve donning or removing clothes. As I wrote in these chapters, this dramatic situation is especially suited to representation in theater, which intrinsically involves the putting on and taking off of costumes and makeup. Although each of these plays takes up the conflict between the real self and the performed self, *Four Cries of a Gibbon* does not explicitly depict acting and the theater world. In *Mulan* and *Girl Graduate*, the lead characters, Mulan and Huang Chuntao/Chonggu, respectively, pretend to be different people by donning men's clothes and assimilating into a male-dominated world. In *Zen Master Yu*, The Moonlight Monk uses masks and costumes to perform Liu Cui's history as the monk Yutong. The plays do not directly address acting as a profession. In this Conclusion, I will consider, by way of comparison, a play that does feature actors as characters. It bears the legacy of the themes already incipient in Xu Wei's *Four Cries of a Gibbon*, but it expands the themes in the languorous form of the *chuanqi* from the Qing dynasty rather than in the relatively abbreviated form of Xu Wei's *zaju*. Kong Shangren's 孔尚任 (1648–1718) *Peach Blossom Fan* (*Taohua shan* 桃花扇), which makes a brief reference to *Mi Heng*, uses historical actors, performers, and storytellers to merge issues of performance with identity against the backdrop of a historical moment.

Peach Blossom Fan is a play set in the dramatic period of the late seventeenth century, when China was in the painful process of transitioning from the Ming to the Qing dynasty. As the Manchus took over the Ming capital of Beijing, Ming officials attempted to maintain a Han capital in Nanjing, with a surviving Ming prince installed as the emperor of the Southern Ming. The heroine of the play is a young courtesan, Li Xiangjun, whose devotion to her true love, Hou Fangyu, is repeatedly thwarted by the machinations of other men who desire her. The play is unique for its achievement of transforming real events and people into an aesthetic form; scholars have commented that it is "the only play in the Chinese tradition to turn both history and the interpretation of history into part of the dramatic interpretation."[1] *Peach Blossom Fan* draws attention to the staged quality of the historical period; the Hongguang 弘光 (1644–45) emperor of the Southern Ming was a puppet emperor whose personal love of acting and drama only corroborated the likening of his brief "pretender" reign to a piece of theater. Additionally, the scenes are scattered throughout with real characters from history, including a few who were involved in the theater world: the playwright Ruan Dacheng 阮大鋮 (1587–1646), the professional storyteller Liu Jingting 柳敬亭 (ca. sixteenth–seventeenth century), and the demimonde music teacher Su Kunsheng 蘇崑生 (1600?–1679?). Lynn Struve has written of this phenomenon that "every play asks its audience to temporarily suspend disbelief in the players' actions and enter into an illusion of reality; but it also breaks this illusion by creating an aesthetic distance which the audience feels it can surmount both ways, into the illusion-as-real and back again. In historical drama, temporal distance of the audience from the events reenacted is an important element in maintaining and dispelling the illusion."[2]

Another element in *Peach Blossom Fan* that reminds us of the relationship between stage and the world is the presence of the heroine Li Xiangjun, who is a gifted performer. We first meet her as she is studying songs from Tang Xianzu's 湯顯祖 (1550–1616) *The Peony Pavilion* (*Mudan ting* 牡丹亭) with a music teacher who emphasizes technical fluency in performance at the expense of meaning. Li Xiangjun, however, sees herself in a different light, as a heroine who means what she says, even when those are lines of lyrical drama written by a playwright. When forced to perform for the detestable Southern Ming ministers, Xiangjun decides that she will use the floor to express her rage: "This will give me a chance of seeing the villains together and venting my pent-up rage" (*Zheng hao tu an xiong zhong zhi qi* 正好吐俺胸中之氣). She goes on to sing:

> The shameless flatterer will sit with the cruel tyrant,
> His face a powdered mask (*mo fen lian* 抹粉臉) of obsequious guile,
> Fawning on the despot's whim in a thousand odious ways.
> Soon the play called *Singing Phoenix* will be acted in real life (*yan chu zhen mingfeng* 演出眞鳴鳳),[3]
> And I shall resemble Mi Heng when he cursed and beat the drum (*An zuo ge nü Mi Heng, zhua Yuyang, shengsheng ma; kan ta dong bu dong* 俺做個女禰衡，撾漁陽，聲聲罵；看他懂不懂).
> It remains to be seen whether they will understand.[4]

Like Mi Heng, Xiangjun is subjected to her onstage audience's abuse for the impertinence of singing about her pent-up rage. Ruan Dacheng proceeds to physically abuse and then eject her when she uses the opportunity of performance to insult the gathered party. The play concludes with the actress, having seen the futility of trying to negotiate the "real world," renouncing it to become a nun. Li Xiangjun, more so than the characters in *Four Cries of a Gibbon*, struggles to assert her identity even as standards for self-definition are crumbling around her. Kong Shangren's play demonstrates how the lightness of play-acting can have all too serious implications: the character one plays affects who one is.

To turn from a literary example that references the real world to a real world example that references literature, consider the case of another moment of upheaval and transition with the crumbling of a dynasty. In *Peach Blossom Fan*, Li Xiangjun uses Xu Wei's *Mi Heng* to vent her feelings about the injustices she perceives that accompany the Ming collapse. At the turn of the twentieth century, Qiu Jin 秋瑾 (1875–1907), the youngest daughter of a well-to-do family from Xu Wei's hometown of Shanyin, left her husband and young children in 1904 to go to Japan, where she studied fencing and archery and experimented with various styles of dress, using Mulan as her role model. Upon returning from Japan, she edited a newspaper on women's issues and taught at a school in her native Zhejiang. Qiu Jin is celebrated to this day as one of the first martyrs of the revolution against the Qing imperial government. In 1907, she attempted an uprising against the Qing, was captured, and was summarily executed.[5] The photographic record she left behind reflects Qiu Jin's interest in the effects of the sartorial on creating personal identity. In these photographs, she alternatively appears in Japanese female dress (specifically, as a Japanese woman warrior), Manchu male dress, and Western male dress.[6] Qiu Jin sought role models from the universal canon of women warriors, from Joan of Arc to Hua Mulan.[7] Her patriotic *shi* and *ci* are insistently nostalgic for a Han era before the entrance of the "barbarians," in this case the Manchu ruling family.[8] Qiu Jin was also an outspoken opponent of footbinding, that corporeal marker of gender that Xu Wei's Mulan dismisses and regains with ease. The resonances between the real-life revolutionary who poses in various (and often male) costumes and the literary heroine whose abilities are released by a change of clothes are nearly too perfect. Both cases demonstrate how easily identities could be tried on and discarded at will; a persona can be put on just as simply as a costume. And both cases demonstrate the consequences of that ease: what remains underneath when all that matters seems to be surface appearances? Is there an essential body? Or is there only a carapace marked with a name? When Qiu Jin was surrounded and captured by Manchu troops in 1907, she reportedly refused to speak. She was given a brush with which to write out her confession. She wrote instead: "Autumn rain and autumn wind: the sorrow kills one" (*Qiuyu qiufeng chou sha ren* 秋雨秋風愁殺人).[9] Qiu Jin plays on her surname, Qiu (秋), which also means autumn, in these final, unspoken, words. Instead of speaking her words, she has written them down. Instead of inscribing her confession, she has inscribed her biography. Instead of writing her life story, she has taken her life and made it into lyric.

At the beginning of this book, I considered Xu Wei's criticism, and his admirers' interpretations of his criticism, of the Archaist schools that limited literature by focusing on imitating master texts. Xu Wei stood instead for freedom from imitation, arguing that one cannot learn anything about another by merely copying the forms. He suggested that the ability to represent another, which is a way of understanding another, can only be gained by becoming that other. The process of becoming another is distinct from simple impersonation. This distinction is muddled when it is expressed in drama, which is necessarily based on impersonation. One might question the feasibility of Mulan's becoming a soldier by unbinding her feet, removing her makeup, and changing into men's clothes. Is she not just impersonating, instead of inhabiting? She certainly suggests that she thinks she was not there; the men who fought with her, and the men who were vanquished, might not share that view. The distinction is also muddled, it turns out, in real life. What of Qiu Jin, who started on her path toward finding her role in the world by first trying on various personas? The woman she "becomes" is the result of those early imitations; she had to try them on until they fit. Even then, her success as a revolutionary was negligible if judged in terms of actually producing tangible results. Instead, her success lay in her transformation into a symbol of a patriotic martyr who would inspire later generations of revolutionaries. She did this by first applying the costume, and then by becoming that role; she set that process of becoming into motion by claiming it for herself. Finnane quotes Qiu Jin: " 'My aim is to dress like a man!' she proclaimed. 'If I first take on the appearance of a man, then I believe my mind too will eventually become like that of a man!' "[10]

Xu Wei's *Four Cries of a Gibbon* offers readers a consideration of how selves are created through the telling of a personal narrative. No matter how ridiculous the situation, the plays optimistically enact variations on the theme of speaking the self, with conclusions that tend to reassure the audience that beneath the costume and makeup, an unchanged and individual self exists. The stretches in the formations of identity are playfully executed, and they affirm the balance required from the static subject hidden beneath layers of outer personae and the discerning viewer who can see through to that static self. This layering motif serves as a powerful reminder that what we think of as a stable self may really just be the accumulation of projections, whether made in clothes or words. Each of Xu Wei's plays proposes and resolves strange cases of questioned identity, and the issues that are given political weight in the later dramatic tradition are already central in Xu Wei's quartet. The wonder of these concatenated themes is that they share a basic problem: How can you be sure that you are seen and heard as you want to be? In making the question of proving one's self the subject of each play, *Four Cries of a Gibbon* reminds us of how much drama serves not as a shadow of our world, but as its reflection.

Appendixes

A Note on the Appendixes

Yuan Hongdao discovered Xu Wei's works in the years following his death, and in 1598 Yuan oversaw the publication of *Xu Wenchang sanji* 徐文長三集, for which he and Tao Wangling 陶望龄 (1562–1609) wrote prefaces. The *Sanji* was compiled by Xu Wei's disciples and was a composite of *Xu Wenchang chuji* 徐文長初集, *Quebian* 闕編, and *Yingtao guan shi* 櫻桃館詩, none of which is still extant individually. This promotion of Xu Wei's works sparked an interest that led to the production of more extensive literary collections, such as the 1614 *Xu Wenchang quanji* 徐文長全集, which comprised the *Sanji* and *Four Cries of a Gibbon* with annotations by Yuan Hongdao. Works that had not been previously published in the *Sanji* were collected in *Xu Wenchang yigao* in 1623 by Zhang Dai. In 1925, Chinese scholars unearthed archived texts and published them as the *Xu Wenchang yicao* 徐文長佚草.[1]

The most complete collection of Xu Wei's works, first published by Zhonghua shuju 中華書局 in 1983 and reissued in 1999, is *Xu Wei ji* 徐謂集, a modern punctuated text without annotations. This edition comprises the *Sanji*, the *Yigao*, and the *Yicao*, eliminating repetitions from the *Yigao* and appending miscellaneous writings, famous prefaces by other writers, and the plays *Four Cries of a Gibbon* and *Singing Instead of Screaming* (*Ge dai xiao* 歌代嘯).[2]

Although many editions of *Four Cries of a Gibbon* have been printed, the variations among them are largely insignificant, with the exception of

1. Xu Wei, *Xu Wei ji* (*XWJ*), 3.
2. *XWJ*, 4.

the stage direction mentioned in my discussion of *Mulan*. There are two modern Chinese annotated versions of *Four Cries of a Gibbon* in Chinese: Liang I-Cheng's *Xu Wei di wenxue yu yishu* 徐渭的文學與藝術 and Zhou Zhongming's *Sishengyuan Gedaixiao fu* 四聲猿歌代嘯附.[3] I have made use of the above-referenced texts for comparison in the translations, but the translations below follow Zhou Zhongming's edition and detailed annotations, as well as a reproduction of the woodblock print of *Four Cries of a Gibbon* from the *Xu Wenchang sanji*. I cite significant differences, if any, in the notes, but page references are to the Zhou Zhongming edition, which is the most easily accessible annotated edition of the plays. I have not translated all of Zhou's extensive annotations to the text but have tried to incorporate as much information from them as I could into my footnotes. It would not be an exaggeration to say that this translation would not have been possible were it not for all of Zhou's excellent notes of clarification and explication. Any infelicities and errors in the translation, however, are completely my own.

3. Xu Wei 徐渭, *Sishengyuan Gedaixiao fu* 四聲猿歌代嘯附 (*SSY*), ed. Zhou Zhongming 周中明 (Shanghai: Shanghai guji chubanshe, 1984).

Role Types

chou	clown
dan	female lead
er	second
jing	"painted face" male role
lao	"old" as a prefix (for example, a *laodan* is an old female, *laomo* an old male)
mo	older male lead
sheng	"young" (used also to designated young male lead)
tie	"additional"
wai	"extra" (therefore, a *waidan* would be an extra female, and a *waimo* an extra male)
zheng	"main" (therefore, a *zhengdan* would be a female lead, and *zhengmo* a male lead)
zhong	"middle" (*zhongjing* would be "secondary villain")

N.B. In Chinese drama, arias are sung to set tunes from a musical repertory and are marked in the translation by indentation in the formatting and a heading in brackets that gives the song title.

I

The Mad Drummer Plays the Yuyang Triple Rolls[1]

(*A* wai *playing a Judge enters, leading in a ghost*)

Judge:

Our judgments here are very clear indeed,
Bad and good deeds, ultimately, cannot be denied.
As for those debtors, though they may hide, it's not for long,
Never does a debt go unpaid.

I'm surnamed Investigator, my given name is Obscure; I'm styled Moderator, my other name is The Sage of the Fiery Pearl. All my life I have been adept in settling cases and impartial in my judgments, and in the Fifth Palace of Prince Yama, I have been a good, clear-sighted judge. That day when Mister Mi Zhengping[2] brought suit against Old Cao Man,[3] I was the one in charge of the books. My Lord has always thought of Mister Mi Heng as a man of spirit and talent, a cut above the rest, so he drew upon his literary skills and had him draft all his documents,

---

1. The "Yuyang Triple Rolls" (Yuyang sannong 漁陽三弄) is a kind of drum song in which the verses are accompanied and punctuated by triple drum rolls. Yuyang is the ancient place name for modern Jixian in Hebei province.

2. Mi Heng 彌衡 (173–98) is styled, or courtesy named (*zi* 字), Zhengping (正平).

3. Cao Cao's childhood name ("little name" *xiaoming* 小名 or "milk name" *ruming* 乳名) was A Man (阿瞞). The "little name" is an informal and diminutive nickname given to a baby by his parents. To call him Old Cao Man (Cao Cao laoman 曹操老瞞) is not to use an alternative socially acceptable adult-given name, such as a style name (*zi*, see above note) but rather to show disrespect.

treating him as an honored guest. During yesterday's evening audience, My Lord said to me: "The Lord on High always employed Men of Letters on his staff,[4] but they've all been transferred to different offices. Now they plan to find men fit to replace those who have been taken, and Mister Mi is among them. Why don't you ready some things for sending him off, so that if he is indeed summoned, he won't miss his appointment?" This made me think back to the time when Cao Man was the one summoning guests, and how he had commanded Mister Mi to play the drums to entertain him, only to have him wild-eyed and naked, beating out a rhythm, banging the paddle, reinventing that ancient tune "Yuyang Triple Rolls." Feigning madness to vent his spleen, acting deaf and playing dumb, he exposed Cao's every fault so that he had nowhere to hide. Now wasn't that something to shake up Heaven and Earth? Wasn't it a wonderful sight like some grand wooden puppet show? Now he is about to ascend to Heaven, and I intend to summon him here, and at the same time release Cao Man, and have them reenact the age-old scenario of "Cursing the Host."[5] Having the two of them give such a performance will make for a good amount of conversation for those of us in the Underworld Offices. I will also let them see that bad and good deeds, ultimately, are just like debts that must be repaid: how can they not be! Attendants, invite Mister Mi for me, then also release Cao Cao, but allow him to bring one or two of his old attendants. Tell them to await my instructions in the Left Hall.

Ghosts: As you wish.

(*Ghosts exit*)

(*Ghosts reenter, leading in a* sheng *playing Mi, a* jing *playing Cao, and two servants*)

(*Cao and the servants wait on the left side*)

Ghost: Sir, Mister Mi has arrived.

(*The two greet each other. Mi ascends to the seat of honor, while the Judge descends to sit below him*)

Judge: Sir, that day when you took up the drums and beat them to curse Cao Cao, it amazed the world. Although I, in the time that I conducted

---

4. A "man of letters" is a literary secretary.

5. The host is Cao Cao, who has received Mi Heng into his court as his guest.

my official investigation, got to hear one or two pieces of evidence regarding this incident, I regret that I never had the chance to experience it firsthand. (*Rises and says*) And another thing: I must congratulate you on your special recognition from Lord on High. There is news that you will soon be summoned to become one of the Men of Letters, and as your turn to leave will come before too long, I would be disappointed not to have fulfilled my long-held wish. Mine is only a trifling matter. In our Offices here, among the officials and ghosts, this story should be spread about, rousing all to moral endeavor. I humbly beseech you: may I be so bold as to trouble you to return to the events of that long-past day? We'll also have Cao Cao perform in the position he was in that day, and you could act out that scene where you cursed your host, thus fulfilling this long-cherished wish of mine. Sir, what do you say?

Mi: How can I not? There's just one thing: when I cursed the host, that Cao Man's evil deeds were not yet as many as now, and those curses would be tepid and bland, boring and dreary. They would not be worth listening to. If I were to curse him today, ah, I would have to include the matter of the Copperbird Terrace and that business about dividing up the incense and selling shoes![6] Now that would gladden everyone's hearts!

Judge: Even better! Even better! Servants! Bring Cao Cao and his servants in. Cao Cao, today we want you to take on your former role of

---

6. Copperbird Terrace was constructed by Cao Cao and memorialized by his son Cao Zhi 曹植 (191–232) in a *fu* on the topic. Zhuge Liang 諸葛亮 (181–234) has to try to convince Sun Quan 孫權 (182–252) and Zhou Yu 周瑜 (175–210) to side with Liu Bei 劉備 (161–223) against Cao Cao, but the men are inclined to submit to Cao Cao to avoid further fighting. Knowing that Zhou Yu is married to the younger Qiao sister, and that the elder Qiao is the widow of Sun Ce 孫策 (175–200), under whom Zhou Yu had also served, Zhuge Liang tells him about Cao Cao's construction of the Copperbird Terrace and Cao Cao's intention to keep the Qiao sisters inside as the finishing decorative touch. The line linking Cao Zhi's poem to the Qiao sisters, "He'll hold [in the towers] the two Qiaos of the southeast, delighting with them morning and night" (*lan er qiao yu dongnan xi, le chaoxi zhi yu gong* 攬二喬於東南兮，樂朝夕之與共), is in Luo Guanzhong's *SGZYY* version of the *fu* (see *SGZYY* ch. 44). As for dividing incense and selling shoes (*fenxiang mailu* 分香賣履), this is an allusion to the lines in Cao Cao's "Final Orders": "Take the incense and divide it among the wives, not for offerings. As for the wives [after my death], there's nothing for them to do but to learn how to make shoes to sell [for a living]." This is taken to show how, even on his deathbed, he thought about the well-being of his wives, though this was still with himself in mind (see *SGZYY* ch. 78).

Prime Minister and, with Mister Mi, perform the affair of "Beating the Drum and Cursing the Host" from back then. If you pretend to be too afraid, or try to keep any of your wickedness to yourself, my attendant will give you a hundred strokes of the iron rod, and you will have to start over from the beginning.
(*Cao and his group prepare*)
Mi: Your Honor, you are always so generous and modest; if you don't agree to be part of the audience, it really wouldn't be much of a show.[7] That day when I cursed the host, honored guests were seated here.[8] Today I beg you to act as Cao Man's guest and sit as part of his audience; that will make a proper arrangement.
Judge: Your wish is my command. (*Bows and says*) Begging your pardon, sir, I take the liberty of sitting!
(*Judge on the left and Cao Cao on the right lift glasses of wine and sit; Mi comes in wearing his usual long gown and carrying a drum*)
Cao (*shouts*): Rube! As an official drummer, you have your own designated uniform; why aren't you wearing it? Go, change!
Cao's servant (*shouts*): What, you still haven't changed? (*Mi Heng takes off his old clothes and stands naked before Cao Cao*)
Cao's servant (*shouts*): Savage! With the Prime Minister before you, you dare stand there, all naked? Now I know why they say "the donkey's dick points east, the horse's dick points west!"
Mi: As for your dickhead Prime Minister, his dick points south while mine points north![9]
Cao's servant (*shouts*): He still hasn't put on any clothes! What nerve!
(*Mi mimes changing into a brocade scarf and an embroidered robe with braided sash*)

---

7. Mi Heng recognizes that the judge would think it rude to act like an audience member, casting Mi Heng as a mere entertainer. This is in contrast to the circumstances that have brought Mi Heng there, and to his condemnation of Cao Cao for the way that Cao Cao flouted courtesy by treating Mi Heng as a common performer.

8. Meaning that the guests would have been seated on the raised platform for dining, encircling the space where Mi Heng was commanded to perform. The platform, of course, is reminiscent of a stage.

9. Mi Heng's dirty joke also plays on the convention that the ruler faces south, and the subject faces north.

[To the tune *Dian jiang chun*]

Fleeing from trouble, I left my family,
Traveled down to Xu,[10]
And there climbed the tower.[11]
Turning my head to the horizon,
I never thought I'd have to crouch down and crawl between their legs.[12]

[To the tune *Hunjiang long*]

He held a banquet and reclined on the couch,
Told me to grasp my mallets, clack the clapperboards, and beat the drum,
And, in time with the drumbeat, I attacked him.[13]

---

10. Xu refers to Xuchang 許昌, in modern-day Henan province. With Luoyang ravaged by war, Cao Cao installed his court and the Han puppet emperor in Xu (named for the ancient state of the Warring States period) in 196, making it the de facto capital. It became the eventual capital of the Wei dynasty. When Cao Pi ascended in 220, he renamed the city Xuchang, which means "Xu Rising."

11. This alludes to Wang Can's 王粲 *fu* entitled "Climbing the Tower" 登樓賦. Wang Can was one of the "Seven Scholars of Jian'an" and an adviser to Cao Cao. Following the devastation of the western Han capital of Luoyang, Wang Can wandered southward, landing in Jingzhou where he sought to serve in Liu Biao's 劉表 (142–208) court. After being turned away, he wrote his "Climbing the Tower," a meditation on exile and nostalgia for home. A translation by Burton Watson is included in *Classical Chinese Literature*, ed. John Minford and Joseph S. M. Lau (New York: Columbia University Press, 2000), 311–14. A manipulated form of the story is told in the Yuan dynasty *zaju* "Wang Can Climbs the Tower" (王粲登樓 *Wang Can denglou*) by Zheng Guangzu 鄭光祖 (fl. 1300).

12. This is an allusion to Han Xin 韓信, who was a military officer under Emperor Gaozu of the Han, or Liu Bang 劉邦, and was considered one of the great generals and military strategists in Chinese history. It was said that once in his early years, when he lived in conditions of extreme poverty, he was confronted by a bully (in later renditions, several bullies) and made to crawl between his legs as a form of humiliation. At the time, Han Xin knew that if he were to fight back, he would be at a great disadvantage. So he did as he was told, realizing that the humiliation he endured at that moment would allow him to go on to greater glory. Indeed, he became one of the greatest strategists of his time. His biography may be found in chapter 92 of the *Shiji*. In the *SGZYY*, Cao Cao is said to be a reincarnation of Han Xin born to fulfill the circle of revenge, and Liu Bang is reincarnated as a weak Han Emperor.

13. This is an allusion to the *Analects* of Confucius when Confucius says: "The head of the Ji family was richer than the duke of Zhou had been, and yet Qiu collected his imposts for him, and increased his wealth. The Master said, 'He is no disciple of mine. My little children, beat the drum and assail him'" (Xian Jin 17, translated by James Legge).

My insults, sentence by sentence, were sharp points like flying daggers and spears,
My drumming, beat by beat, were crashing thunder churning up wind and sand.
Cao Cao! This drum skin is your body's husk.
This mallet is your own rib from elbow's height,
This nail hole is like your empty heart,
These clappers are those monstrous fangs in your mouth.
With these two sticks I'll beat your roguishness through your skin,
And in that space of time, I still won't be able to give your wicked heart its due honors.
Thus I'll start to count them from the beginning,
Wash out your ears, and listen.

(*Strikes the drum*)
Cao: Madman! I told you to play the drums, why do you gesture to the east and talk to the west, comparing people to beasts? This here bronze bludgeon[14] and iron blade of mine are fierce! You better be careful of that tongue and those teeth of yours.
Judge: This fellow really is uncouth!
Mi: [To the tune *Youhulu*]

First of all, you exiled Xiandi from the capital,[15]
Then ordered the murder of Empress Fu,
Sending Chi Lü to arrest her.[16]
Ai! What a pity that even nine concentric layers of imperial palace gates
Could not save the Emperor's wife.
He said to her, "Though you be first to go,
Most likely I shall follow closely behind you."
Also there were those two sons,
What a shame that they did not flower from a different tree,

14. The character for "bludgeon" (槌) is the same character that is used for drumsticks, or a drum mallet.

15. Xiandi 獻帝 was the reigning Han emperor Liu Xie 劉協 (181–234). In 196 he was captured by Cao Cao, who kept him in Xuchang as emperor in title only. When Cao Pi established the Wei dynasty in 220, he made Liu Xie the Duke of Shanyang 山陽公.

16. Empress Fu 伏后 was Xiandi's wife, Fu Shou 伏壽 (d. 214).

Both were the Liu family's own flesh and bone,[17]
Reared in the palace.
How could you make a dragon pup or phoenix seed into a jar of fish paste?

(*Strikes drum*)
Cao: He's talking about that affair of mine.
Mi: [To the tune *Tianxia le*]

There was a Consort Dong,[18]
Who was the Emperor's second-favored beauty.
What did she do to deserve this?
Weren't you in the wrong?
In her belly, she carried a three-month-old baby,
Yet you killed her father,[19]
And bound the two, womb and its fruit,
Taking mother and child both, and hacked them into bloody toads.[20]

(*Roll of drum is sounded*)
Cao: Madman! Often it's been said: "When the wind comes, the trees shake." "If a man hurts the tiger, the tiger will want to hurt the man." Empress Fu and Consort Dong and their lot were secretly plotting to harm me, which was why I did those things. It's not that I first harbored thoughts of harming them!

---

17. That is to say, from the royal Han family, surnamed Liu (劉).

18. Consort Dong is Xiandi's concubine mentioned above, the daughter of Dong Cheng, the Eastern Han official who had conspired with Liu Bei to assassinate Cao Cao. The plot was found out, and Dong Cheng was executed, but Cao Cao, unappeased, sought Consort Dong's death as well. He seized her as she was talking with Empress Fu about the secret decree entrusted to Dong Cheng (which, incidentally, had been written in the Emperor's blood and sewn into Dong Cheng's girdle, drawing attention again to how body and clothing are intertwined) and speculating about why there had been no action. The Consort, although pregnant, was taken into the courtyard and strangled (*SGZYY* ch. 24).

19. In other editions, father (*die* 爹) is 娘. Here, *die* refers to Dong Cheng, her father (n.b., in ch. 24 of *SGZYY*, she is said to be Dong Cheng's sister).

20. This verse was presumably made to rhyme with the last three words of the last song verse regarding Empress Fu, as "Xie-ha-ma" resonates with "Zha-yu-xia." Regardless, in the *SGZYY* the Consort is strangled.

Judge: The Prime Minister is right.
Mi: You think about it: why do you suppose they would have wanted to hurt you? You forced the Emperor of the Han to move to Xuchang, and you had him under such guard that he was like one of the ghosts here. He had nothing to wear, nothing to eat, no one to serve him. Even if he had wanted to send a strip of paper even three fingers wide, not even a ghost would have heeded him. You first killed Consort Dong, and they panicked. How long could you expect it would be before they plotted against you? You tell me: if the Emperor wants to kill a subject for no reason, can that subject then just drag the Emperor's woman right before him and, with one blow, chop her in two? Has the world ever witnessed such things?
Judge: This too, that the madman says, makes sense. Let's have another cup and hear some more of these silly excuses.
Mi: [To the tune *Nezhaling*]

> When he begged something to eat,
> You gave him a few pieces of stinking marrow from the cow's horn,
> When he begged something to wear,
> You sent him rough hemp.[21]
> When he occasioned to issue a decree,
> You sent a ghost to come and take it.
> Even a man of stone would be moved,
> Even a fool would be afraid,
> Even a sheep would bite at a man.

(*Roll of drum*)
Judge: Prime Minister, you really can't outtalk him on this.
Cao: If I could, I wouldn't be in this state now.
Mi: [To the tune *Queta zhi*]

> As for Lord Yuan's two families,[22]
> You annihilated them to the last scale of armor.

---

21. Mourning clothes are made with hemp, making this a suggestive gift in response to the Emperor's request.

22. The brothers (or cousins) Yuan Shao 袁紹 (154–202) and Yuan Shu 袁術 (155–90) were Eastern Han warlords. Both were defeated by Cao Cao, and both eventually died of illness as a result of those defeats.

As to Liu Cong and his party,[23]
You forced him to submit.
That Sun Quan, ah, he had a couple of close calls,[24]
And Xuande, ah, you twice kidnapped his lady.[25]
Everywhere, war horses roamed empty city walls,
Over years, cawing crows flocked on corpses.

(*A roll of the drum*)
Cao: Your honor, it was a time of disorder. It was not just I, Cao Cao, who was like this.
Judge: Yes, all the yamens of our underworld bureau here have such cases on the books.
Mi: [To the tune *Jishengcao*]

Your vaunted authority was just self-invention,
Promotion in rank did not depend on the Emperor.
Putting a daughter into the Empress' carriage,[26]
You, a cavalry officer, became the usurping ruler.
Your Copperbird Terrace was scaffolded into cloudy mists,
Your usurped carriage and flags made the court cower before you.
Once you nearly wrested away the Jade Emperor's goblet,[27]
And even now you have Prince Yama afraid.

---

23. Liu Cong 劉琮 (also pronounced Zong) was the son of the Jingzhou warlord Liu Biao (Liu Bei's key ally). Liu Biao's adviser, Cai Mao 蔡瑁, suggested the younger son, Liu Cong, as the successor, although Liu Biao eventually selected Liu Qi 劉琦 (d. 209). As such, Liu Cong followed Cai Mao in surrendering to Cao Cao. When Cao Cao lures Liu Cong to Jingzhou with the promise of appointing him the successor, Liu Cong happily gives up his military commission and seal and greets Cao Cao. Cao Cao then tells Liu Cong that he is being dispatched as the "protector" of Qingzhou, and sends him off, despite his protests, along with his mother. Cao Cao then sends his men to kill them both (*SGZYY* ch. 41).

24. Sun Quan 孫權 (182–252) was the founder of Eastern Wu during the Three Kingdoms.

25. Xuan De 玄德 is Liu Bei's style name (*zi* 字). Xu Shu 徐庶 (also known as Shan Fu 單福) was Liu Bei's adviser. In the *Sanguo yanyi* Cao Cao captures Liu Bei's wives and children and most of his troops. They are returned to Liu Bei eventually, but he is again forced to abandon Ladies Gan and Mi when Cao Cao attacks him at Jingzhou.

26. After the above-mentioned incident in which Cao Cao has Empress Fu executed for plotting against him, Cao Cao tells the distraught Xiandi—who has forsworn eating—that there is no reason to be sad, and that he is giving him his own daughter in marriage to be the new empress.

27. Meaning Xiandi's power.

(*Strikes the drum*)
(*Judge, in a low voice, gives directions to the ghosts, telling them to play singing girl musicians*)
Judge: There is nothing untoward about a prime minister's daughter becoming an empress by marriage, or about building a bigger house. Let's let the drummer stop a while. I've heard that the Prime Minister has some fine girl musicians, shall they come out and perform?
Cao: That was back then; how can we do that now?
Judge: Don't worry about it, just call for them and you'll have them. You may use them as you please.
Cao: As you command. Order a servant to call the singing girls to come out.
(*Two girls carrying the instruments for the "Crow's Sorrow" song enter*)
Cao: Today, you two must make up a verse, then play and sing to accompany us for three cups.
(*Mi squats, facing Cao*)
First Girl (*sings*):

> Over there a fat pelican,[28]
> (Ya-yi-ge-di-du, ya-yi-ge-di-du),
> Turned into a piebald pig (Di-da-du, da-di-du),
> Singing "The Partridge Song."
> (Ya-yi-ge-di-du, ya-yi-ge-di-du).
> When he sang it well, he could still carry on,
> (Ya-yi-ge-di-du, ya-yi-ge-di-du)
> When he didn't (Di-da-du, da-di-du),

---

28. This is an allusion to the *Book of Songs* (*Shijing* 詩經), from the "Odes of Cao" 曹風, "Officers of Escort" 候人. The poem notes the distinction between one's outward appearance and one's capacity or actual situation: "Those officers of escort, / Have their carriers of lances and halberds. / But these creatures, / With their three hundred red covers for the knees ! — / The pelican is on the dam, /And will not wet his wings ! / These creatures, / Are not equal to their dress! / The pelican is on the dam, / And will not wet his beak! / These creatures, / Do not respond to the favour they enjoy. / Extensive and luxuriant is the vegetation, / And up the south hill in the morning rise the vapours. / Tender is she and lovely, / But the young lady is suffering from hunger" (*Shi Jing* I.14., in James Legge, trans., *The Chinese Classics*, 151). The difference in appearance in the case of the pelican is that in spite of its plumage, it will not lower itself. The comparison is to someone whose inner worth is not equal to his position.

They called Butcher Wang.
(Ya-yi-ge-di-du, ya-yi-ge-di-du).

Cao: What are you talking about, "calling Butcher Wang"?
Girl: Butcher Wang kills pigs. (*Offers a cup of wine to the Judge*)
Second Girl (*sings*):

The Prime Minister does things too sneakily,
(Ya-yi-ge-qiao-xi, ya-yi-ge-qiao-xi)
Provoking all around him (qiao-da-xi, da-qiao-xi),
To gossip.
(Ya-yi-ge-qiao-xi, ya-yi-ge-qiao-xi).
Obscured by the snow, the egret is seen only when it flies,
(Ya-yi-ge-qiao-xi-, ya-yi-ge-qiao-xi)
Hidden among the willows, the parrot (qiao-da-xi, da-qiao-xi)
Is known only when it speaks.[29]
(Ya-yi-ge-qiao-xi, ya-yi-ge-qiao-xi).

Cao: Those last two lines are clichés.
Second Girl: Though clichés, they stick.
Cao: This girl leans to the outside.[30]
Second Girl: Facts are facts. I'm confessing now to avoid punishment later.(*Gives Cao a cup*)
First Girl (*sings*):

Rub in the powder, paint on the rouge,
You'll stay flushed for a while,
(Ya-yi-ge-dong-hong, ya-yi-ge-dong-hong)

Second Girl (*sings*):

Repaying kindness, bearing grudges
(hong-da-dong, da-dong-hong)
Is the breeze that fells blossoms.
(Ya-yi-ge-dong-hong, ya-yi-ge-dong-hong)

---

29. A popular couplet in calligraphy, it also closes Scene 15 of Zhang Fengyi's 張鳳翼 (1527–1613) "The Red Whisk" (*Hongfu ji* 红拂記).

30. Literally, her "elbow bends outward." She is supposed to be his employee, but she is disloyal and insults him instead.

(*Both girls sing together*)

All things in the world are beyond man's control,
(Ya-yi-ge-dong-hong, ya-yi-ge-dong-hong)
Add them up, and it's all (hong-da-dong, da-dong-hong)
A big nothing.
(Ya-yi-ge-dong-hong, ya-yi-ge-dong-hong).

(*Both girls bring cups*)
Judge: A fine song, in accord with our Heaven's Way.
Cao: Girls, you can go. I'm tired now.
(*Judge laughs. Mi rises and speaks*)
Mi: You may be tired, but my drumming and cursing are not yet finished.
[To the tune *Liuyaoxu*]

Duping other people with honey-coated words,
Harming worthy men is just a game to you.
You had one Yang Dezu[31]
Summarily executed beneath the army camp gates,
His blood rained down.[32]

31. Dezu 德祖 is the style name of Yang Xiu 楊修, (175–219) who was one of Cao Cao's officers; he was the son of the Han officer Yang Biao 楊彪 (142–225) and the nephew of Yuan Shao. He and Kong Rong 孔融 (153–208) are named by Mi Heng as the only two talents among Cao Cao's retinue. He was executed by Cao Cao in 218. Yang Xiu was a close friend of Cao Zhi's and is said to have written essays in a literary competition against Cao Pi.

32. The specific incident is described in *SGZYY* ch. 72. Cao Cao has retired to camp following a fight and is paralyzed into inaction by the fear of being defeated if he advances, and of being humiliated if he retreats. One night, while brooding over his soup, he distractedly says "Chicken tendons" when asked for the watchword for the night. When Yang Xiu receives this order, he tells his men to pack up all of their belongings. When asked why, Yang explains: "Chicken tendons are flavorless, but it is a pity to waste them." He goes on to explain that since Cao Cao knows that to advance would mean defeat and to retreat would mean embarrassment, there are no gains to be had from either course. Retreat would not mean profit, but at least it would not mean loss, so he anticipates that Cao Cao, realizing this, will opt for retreat. He chooses, then, to prepare himself for retreat. Upon finding this out, Cao Cao is so enraged by Yang Xiu's presumptuousness that he orders him to be taken out and beheaded, and for his head to be hung beyond the gates. It is a cautionary tale for all overzealous literary critics.

Master Kong[33] was a cinnabar and mercury immortal,[34]
A golden toad in the moon,
A rare *qiong* flower in the halls of the immortals.[35]
Like the *Book of Changes*, wondrous yet normative.
Like the *Book of Songs*, correct yet beautiful.[36]
The transgressions of these two men
Against you were but as big as the tip of a needle,
Moreover, theirs was but idle chatter.
Why quibble?
One was so clever,
He understood when you said "Chicken tendon."
As for the other, just one word was not in harmony with yours,
And yet both ended up buried in the yellow sands.

(*Strikes the drum*)
Judge: Prime Minister, this you can't deny.
Cao: I'm drunk. I want to take a nap (*mimes sleeping*).
Judge: Men, take him out and give him a hundred strokes of the iron rod, then make him start over from the beginning.
Cao: (*Hurriedly*) I'm awake! I'm awake!
Judge: You finally get it.[37]
Mi: [To *Yao*]

---

33. Master Kong is Kong Rong, the other talent in Cao Cao's court mentioned above. A descendant of Confucius, Kong Rong was one of the "Jian'an Seven" known for his literary talent. His contrary opinions to Cao Cao during his time in Xuchang led to his eventual execution. Kong Rong was also responsible for recommending Mi Heng to Cao Cao's court.

34. Cinnabar and mercury were common ingredients in alchemical formulas for immortality.

35. The flower referred to here as the flower that the spirits gaze on (仙觀瓊花) is the *qiong*, a rare flower that only grows in Yangzhou. Believed to have originated in the Han dynasty, it blooms for only two weeks out of the year. While emphasizing Kong Rong's rare qualities, the reference here may also suggest Kong Rong's recognition of quality in Cao Cao's rivals, specifically Chunyu Qiong 淳于瓊 (146–200), Yuan Shao's general and one of his most trusted commanders.

36. This phrase is from Han Yu 韓愈 (768–824) and his essay "On Studying" (進學解). It suggests that even the classics, which he considers the standard for correct behavior, can include the wondrous or the unexpected.

37. The Chinese plays on the homonyms for being awake and for understanding.

Ai! My background is without deviations,
It's all because of my literary skill that I was singled out for distinction.
Heroic aura ever growing,
I carried my calling cards to every door,
Yet my service was never employed.
Inlaid axe and golden staff,
Eastern Chambers, Western Flowering Palace,[38]
Not once did I pay them the least bit of attention.
Ai! That Kong Beihai really made a fuss over nothing.[39]
Saying there was a destined affinity between us,
He brought me to his home,
This was just an example of a toad in a well.[40]
With just one word out of harmony,
My anger could only grow.
Is it because I should have been agreeable and tight-lipped
That you, under cover, with hidden blade,
Sent me to Jiangxia's Huang?[41]
Then, too, to have that parrot nipping at me,[42]
My colorful brush filled the pages, enhancing my reputation.

---

38. The emperor's retainers who serve as his advisers live in the Eastern Chambers. Western Flowering Gate is the West gate of the imperial city. The fancy accessories and locales are meant to connote Mi Heng's worth.

39. Kong Beihai is Kong Rong, so named because he was once the governor of Beihai Commandery.

40. This refers to Cao Cao and means that his world is limited to the immediate enclosures around him, so much so that he lacks perspective.

41. After offending Cao Cao with his naked drumming, Mi Heng is seized and sent off to Liu Biao, where Cao Cao hopes to be rid of him. Liu Biao strategically refuses to execute him in spite of bearing his insults, and sends him off to Huang Zu 黄祖, the Prefect of Jiangxia (*SGZYY* ch. 23). Huang Zu is at first happy to have Mi Heng as a guest, but a fight soon ensues, and he orders Mi Heng beheaded.

42. This line refers to Mi Heng's famous "Parrot" rhapsody (鸚鵡賦), written while he was a guest at Huangzu's house and collected in *Wenxuan* 文選 (501–31). Mi had been befriended by Huang's son, Yi 射, who had a parrot and requested a poem on the subject from Mi. The poem speaks of the miseries of living in captivity and the impossibility of escape. See Graham, "Mi Heng's 'Rhapsody on a Parrot.'" Following his beheading, Mi Heng was buried on Parrot Island.

With waist bent, grasping a goblet, and as they urged Huang to drink,
I threw down the brush in less time than it took him to drink a cup of tea.

(*Roll of the drum*)
Judge: So that's how this disaster began. Be careful! "The Parrot" can bring disaster on you.
Mi: [To the tune *Qing Ge'er*]

Sun and shadow move across the window blinds,
Window blinds flicker a moment.
Drafts of rhapsodies cast down, the sound of metal,
The sound of metal.[43]
Huang Zu was wicked and cruel inside,
He flexed his scaly armor,[44]
And bared his claws.
Incense fears the blowing wind,
Powder blames the smearing hand of the whore.
Gentlemen envy talented men,
Women envy great beauties.
Yesterday a bodhisattva,
Soon to be a raksha.
Ai! Pity this head of mine, Mi Heng, ah,
Like a vessel gourd at autumn's end,

---

43. When Sun Chuo 孫綽 (314–71) of the Eastern Jin 晉 (317–420) wrote his "Rhapsody on Tiantai" (天台山賦), his friends all praised it, and he is reported to have said: "When I tried to cast it to the ground, it made a sound like metal and stone." In other words, the poem is "solid."

44. The following conversation is recorded in Chen Zhen's 陳震 biography in the Shu 蜀 chapter of *Records of the Three Kingdoms* (*Sanguo zhi* 三國志): "Zhuge Liang wrote to Chief Clerk Jiang Wan and Privy Councilor Dong Yun: 'Right before Xiaoqi [Chen Zhen's style name] went to Wu, he told me that Zheng Fang [Li Yan's style name] had scales [or armor] covering his chest, and that friends and neighbors found this to be intimidating. I had thought of those with scales that one should best stay clear, but not that he would be capable of deeds such as Su or Zhang, whose actions were insincere. Tell Xiaoqi this.'" Su Qin and Zhang Yi were Warring States strategists on the Qin side and on the side of its six rivals, respectively. In other words, Li Yan, and Huang Zu in turn, are insincere and dishonest.

Where the vine is cut, it cannot grow again
While frost hangs on the eaves.

(*Strikes the drum*)
Judge: This rogue really betrayed this man, after all.
Cao: Sir, don't listen to him. The other day my confession was forced out of me.
Judge: If that's the case, did he cut his own head off, too?
Cao: Lord Mi, forgive me!
Judge: No need to be falsely caring. Men! Where is the iron rod?
Cao: (*Acting panicked and angry*) Madman! I have good qualities, too! I sought out worthies, and returned three counties, yet are these good deeds all buried and forgotten?[45]
Mi: [To the tune *Jishengcao*]

You were eager to seek worthies only for your own sake,
Returning three counties—what's the big deal?
A few sesame seeds taken from a giant urn,
The false tears and wails of a greedy cat,
The hungry eagle hanging up half the intestines,
The fierce butcher setting aside his knives for a rest from the sheep
and pigs.
Who are you still seeking to dupe?
Even as a ghost you can't stop being slippery as oil!

(*Beats the drum*)
Judge: Well done! Well done! Let's have a large cup. Sir, please finish what you were saying.
Mi: [To the tune *Hulu cao hun*]

As for cases of your hurting the common people, ah,
Though there be a million, seven or eight more can still be added,
As for the killing of lords and ministers, ah,
How can they all be tabulated!

---

45. Cao Cao relinquished "three counties of twenty thousand households as his personal demesne, reserving only Wuping with ten thousand households, a measure Cao took to reduce criticism." See Luo Guanzhong, *Three Kingdoms: A Historical Novel, Complete and Unabridged*, Part 2., trans. Moss Roberts (Berkeley: University of California Press, 1991) 1053n2.

It's like taking a large grain measure to measure out sesame seeds,
Evil hearts and livers hung, still alive, on swords and spears,
Savage sights that could not be depicted, even in a painting's brightest colors.
With all your craftiness, how can I exhaust my curses in the haste of this moment?
Cao Cao, how come you aren't sending the dogs out the East gate,[46]
Or leisurely listening to weeping cranes at Flowering Pavilion Slope?[47]
Instead you obstinately raise a bother, wearing chains and carrying the cangue.

(*Strikes the drum*)
Judge: Old chap, let me tell you, even if I were to let you handle this case yourself, you wouldn't be able to pardon yourself. (*Turns to Mi*) Sir, finish what you were saying.
Mi: [To the tune *Zhuansha*]

You built Copperbird Terrace meaning to lock up the Qiao sisters,
Who would have imagined that your shameful goddess dreams[48]
Would feed that fiery conflagration at Red Cliff?
When you were near death, and taking leave of those chicks,

---

46. In the *Records of the Grand Historian* (*Shiji* 史記), in the "Biography of Li Si" (李斯傳), the following exchange is said to have taken place before his execution: "Li Si bade farewell to his son, then, turning, said: 'I have something to ask of you. Go back and release the yellow dogs at Cai's Eastern Gate; send out a wily rabbit; can they catch it?" See Sima Qian, *Records of the Grand Historian*, trans. Burton Watson (Hong Kong: Chinese University of Hong Kong, 1993), 179–207.

47. This is from "Lü Ji's Biography" 陸機傳 in *Jinshu* 晉書. When Lü Ji realizes that he is going to die, he says, "The cries of the cranes at Huating (Flowering Pavilion), / I shall never hear them again." This and the above reference are meant to illustrate how Cao Cao can no longer enjoy his past exploits, as he is now imprisoned in the Underworld.

48. This is an allusion to King Xiang of Chu 楚襄王 of the Warring States (ca. 475–221 BCE) period. Traveling in Gaotang Mountain, he had a dream in which he has a sexual dalliance with a mountain goddess. This is the topic of Song Yu's 宋玉 (fl. third century BCE) famous "Rhapsody on Gaotang" (*Gaotang fu* 高唐賦), written in response to King Xiang's command to commemorate the incident. It is the source of the term "clouds and rain" as an aphorism for lovemaking.

Still that nonsense about selling shoes and dividing the incense!
I commend your ability to feel no shame, telling them twice monthly, on the new moon and when it is full,
To face the Western tomb,
And to mourn, month after month,[49]
Never thinking once that those chicks, ah,
Wearing mourning robes, could embrace someone else.
Cao Cao, you tell us yourself!
Just stop talking of your worthiness.
On this topic alone, ah,
We'd need dozens of brushes to write it all down.
Ai! I'll let you off! I'm tired of playing the "Yuyang Triple Rolls" with this drum and mallet!

(Mo *playing an Attendant of Prince Yama enters*)
Judge: Attendant, quickly take Cao Cao and his crew back to their cell.
Ghost: Your Honor, the Jade Emperor sent me to summon Mister Mi. His Highness Prince Yama says we are pressed for time. He instructs Your Honor to give him a large amount as a parting gift, putting all expenses on his ledger.[50] My lord is currently busy with work and can't send him off himself, and he instructs your honor to apologize for him. Another day when he is attending in Heaven, he will pay his respects personally.
Judge: Understood. You may report the discharge of your mission.
(*Ghost assents and exits*)
Judge: Call the Ledger Keeper. Quickly prepare the finest-quality gold brocade and coins, fruit and wine for a send-off.
(*Shouts of assent from backstage*)
(*A* xiaosheng *playing a small boy, and a* dan *playing a girl, enter carrying a book and tally*)

---

49. Cao Cao had instructed that following his death, his women be installed in the Copperbird Terrace where they could gaze toward his tomb on the western slopes of Zheng, sacrifice daily for him, and carry out ritual offerings to his spirit on the first and fifteenth day of each month (new and full moons).

50. My thanks to Wai-yee Li for pointing out that this is a satirical reference to contemporary practice.

Boy and Girl:

The grass at Hanyang River sways under the spring sun,
Heaven's Emperor himself heard of the Parrot brush.[51]
Know that the Jade Tower was finished last night,
We don't need Longxi's Li Changji.[52]
We two present the Jade Emperor's seal and orders, and we have come here to summon Mi Heng. We must enter and announce the decree. Which one of you is the Fifth Hall Judge?

(*Judge kneels*) The Jade Emperor has ordered a summons for Mister Mi. Invite him to come over here to attend our good tidings.
(*Mi kneels with Judge, two officers mime presenting the document*)
Mister Mi, the Lord on High has summoned you; you can examine this tally yourself. When you go, you must bring it with you to present it back. We have to go soon, we mustn't be late.
Boy: [To the Southern tune *Shuahaier*]

Letters from the beginning have been priceless,
His words move the heavenly court, and the Jade Emperor welcomes him personally,
On flying ducks, a descending crane, treading on rosy clouds,
We invite you immediately to ascend to Heaven.
Repaired are ancient golden chambers, with dragon heads and ornaments,
Readied are new white jade prongs, of fish, unicorn, and lamb.
Pour the garnet spirit and thrice play "Great Heaven."[53]
The Lord Editor attends the fragrant tablets at the Jade Capital,
The Weaving Maid attends the fairy raft to cross the Milky Way.

---

51. This couplet refers to how quickly Mi Heng was able to compose the rhapsody. Wai-yee Li notes that the couplet also alludes to "Yellow Crane Tower" (黃鶴樓) by Cui Hao 崔顥 (Tang dynasty): "The clear river sparkles by Hanyang trees, Fragrant grasses crowd on Parrot Island" (晴川歷歷漢陽樹，芳草萋萋鸚鵡州).

52. Li Shangyin's "Biography of Li He" reports that when Li He 李賀 (790–816) was about to die, he had a vision that he was being summoned by the Jade Emperor, who told him that the White Jade Palace was completed and that he needed to come and serve as a literary officer there. Li He's ancestral home was in Longxi (Gansu province), and Changji 長吉 was his style name. The anachronistic implication is that Mi Heng beats Li He for the job a few centuries in advance.

53. Ritual court music for Heaven.

(*Delicate music from backstage*)
Girl: [To the tune *Sansha*]

Mister Mi,
You enjoyed a great reputation and were loath to toady,
Your rhapsody on the parrot written so fast, you didn't punctuate it,
Your brilliance in letters reached us here in Heaven.
Though wondrous birds and beasts are thought auspicious omens,
Leaning on the horse to carve dragons brought calamity![54]
Mister Mi, who else has had a fortune like yours, with such bad beginnings and such a good ending?
Who could make a copy of such a perfect result?[55]
Take dates to sweeten your mouth,
Once made sour by olives.

Mi: [To the tune *Ersha*]

I approach the Gate of Heaven; it is not far off,
The pain in parting from Lord Yama grows ever strong.
When shall I ever enjoy his conversation!
I sigh over the wind- and waveswept prison that you rule,
In the future, ah, the rich furs and fine horses in Heaven's Courts will be my home.

I have got something to say.
Judge: Speak.
Mi: Show your beneficence and pardon Cao Cao!
Judge: That is not for me to decide.
Mi: The destiny that lies before me is like the spring flowers after rain.

---

54. The Jin general Huan Xuanwu 桓宣武 (Huan Wen 桓溫) (312–73) was in such a hurry to write a memorial that he used the side of a horse in place of a table to write it out. The figurative terms such as "leaning on a horse" or "carving dragons"—beautifully crafted essays—typically used to describe great literary talent like Mi Heng's have only been a liability to him.

55. Here "copy" means to replicate an inscription by transferring it to paper by rubbing or daubing.

Judge: [To the tune *Yisha*]

I believe, sir, though you were as Mount Tai,
I was blinded as if by lightning.
From now on, ah, I shall sweep clean my study,
I shall hang up a scroll of your honorable likeness.
There you, in spirit-flight, shall travel at leisure through spring gardens,
Here I shall deal with the crowds of devils riling up my evening court sessions,
When will I have the chance to meet a literary genius again?
Another thing, if my three spirits happened to slander me,[56]
I hope it will be smudged out by your brush.

We have now come to the place where *yin* and *yang* meet. I do not dare accompany you any further beyond this border.
Mi: Please, return.
Judge: My Lord has a trifling gift that he wanted me to present to you. I hope you accept it. I myself have some wine and would like to invite you for three cups, to show my humble feelings of admiration.
Mi: I am undeservedly called to serve in Heaven, so what use do I have of such gifts? Please, bring them back with you with many thanks to your Lord. I ought to accept a toast, but I daren't keep the messengers from Heaven waiting.
Judge: Well, then, goodbye.
(*Both kowtow and sing together*)
Mi and Judge: [To *wei*]

Ere it's been said:
Better than reading ten years' worth of books,
Is spending one evening conversing with you.

---

56. According to Daoist belief, there are three spirits (*sanshi* 三尸) residing within each person that control the body, heart, and mind. The spirit residing in the body (feet) regulates its mechanics, the spirit residing in the heart (abdomen) regulates its emotions, and the spirit residing in the mind (head) regulates its reason or will.

To awaken people, one must point out the donkey to talk about the horse,
Certainly you can say that Manqian's riddles were not in jest.[57]

(*Mi exits*)
Judge: Having seen this Mi Zhengping's "The Yuyang Triple Rolls,"[58]
I laughed until my all-seeing eyes could barely see. Were it not for the thousand statutes of criminal law in Fierce Yama's Hell, all would say "Prime Minister Cao is a divine immortal in the Eight Grottoes."[59]
(*Exeunt*)

---

57. Manqian 曼倩 is Dongfang Shuo's 東方朔 style name. Dongfang Shuo was Han Wudi's 汉武帝 (156–87 BCE) jester and was famous for his riddles and jokes (see *Hanshu* ch. 65 and *Shiji* ch. 126 for biographies). His riddles often made use of metaphors or analogies to make a point, e.g., using a donkey to describe a horse. Something similar to, but not exactly like, the actual object is used to explain the object. Similarly, negative theology is a critical reasoning tool in Buddhism. The self is defined by what it is *not*, rather than what it is. This is also part of Daoist vocabulary (e.g., "The way that can be spoken is not the way; names that can be named are not names" [*dao ke dao, fei chang dao. Ming ke ming, fei chang ming* 道可道非常道，名可名非常名]).

58. Or, alternatively, "Having seen Mi Zhengping play the 'Yuyang Triple Rolls.'"

59. In Daoist cosmology there are thought to be eight grottoes in the upper spheres of Heaven, or Mount Penglai 蓬萊山, each inhabited by an immortal in the Daoist pantheon. Each of these immortals is based on a historical figure from the Tang or Song dynasty, and all of them are figures in popular culture as well. They are He Xiangu, Cao Guojiu, Li Tieguai, Lan Caihe, Lu Dongbin, Han Xiangzi, Zhang Guolao, and Zhongli Quan. They are thought to refer to the group of scholars named the "Eight Immortals of the Han" 淮南八仙 who gathered under the court of Liu An, king of Huainan, to compile the *Huainanzi* 淮南子 in the late Western Han. Although the Immortal Cao Guojiu is no relation to Cao Cao, the allusion serves to affirm the importance of witnessing the play; otherwise, people might mistakenly believe that Cao Cao went unpunished in the afterlife and may have even been rewarded.

II

Zen Master Yu Has a Dream of Cuixiang

Act I

(*A* sheng *playing Yutong enters*)

Yutong:

What must be prepared for with the lion constellation?
The shadowless monkey star should not be submitted to.
Consider how much water there is in West Lake:
Can I gulp the West River down in one mouthful?[1]

I am the monk Yutong.[2] My Elder Brother,[3] who has now been reborn and goes by the name Moonlight Monk, and I used to be two old Buddhas in the Western heaven; but because I did not cultivate myself enough to transcend to the next level, I stole a lodging in mortal form

---

1. This refers to the Zen anecdote: "Layman Pang asked Mazu, 'Who is the one who is not a companion to the ten thousand dharmas?' Mazu said, 'When you swallow all of the water in the West River in one gulp, then I'll tell you.' Hearing these words, Layman Pang fully realized the mystery. He then stayed and practiced under Mazu for two years. Pangyun wrote a verse that said: *A man unmarried, /A woman unbetrothed, /Happily they are brought together, /They both speak without saying words.*" Andrew Ferguson, *Zen's Chinese Heritage: The Masters and Their Teachings* (Somerville, MA: Wisdom, 2000) 93–94.

2. His name is homonymous with illicit desire.

3. The term he uses, *shixiong* 師兄, indicates the brotherhood they share as followers of the same teacher; they are disciples together, and Moonlight is apparently more advanced in his studies. The term is translated here as "Elder Brother" for simplicity's sake.

and traveled south. I ended up in Lin'an[4] and, seeing its natural beauty, chose to settle here to quietly practice Zen at the Water and Moon Monastery on Bamboo Forest Peak. I have lived here for more than twenty years. My days are limited, and still it is not easy to attain enlightenment; it is difficult to make the leap to the next level. I think that self-cultivation at the dharma gates[5] is rather like struggling up the ranks inside the bureaucracy, from eighth or ninth rank to first or second: there are countless worthies and unworthies. It is also like climbing the inner steps of a *stupa*;[6] when you climb from the first or second step to the eighth or ninth, there are countless ways to slip and hit your head.[7] If one meditates much and feels little, then bam! Suddenly, one's two feet are able to join in flight and levitation, along with the eighteenth highest heavenly spirit of the Purple Cloud Palace. If one meditates little and feels much, ah, no good! Likely you will—Crash! Bang!—fall down into that gaping nothingness of the Underworld's eighteenth level of hell, Avici.[8] Those highest heavenly immortals are not even at the ultimate height: one twist or slip, and before you know it you'll have fallen into the deepest pit of iniquity. If you've reached Avici, then it's like a needle without an eye; as much as you fight and drag, you will never be able to dredge yourself up from the longest rivers or deepest seas. Then, there are those who brandish their fists, railing against spirits and ghosts, and those who go on their knees, closing their eyes and lowering their brows,

---

4. Present-day Hangzhou in northern Zhejiang province. Although the region is to this day famous for its bamboo forests, this does not necessarily lend significance to the fact that the temple is located on "Bamboo Forest (*Zhulin* 竹林) Peak," as this is a fairly common name for a temple or monastery site. A bamboo grove was the site of the first temple to be built for Buddha and his disciples, given to him by King Vimbasara.

5. The dharma gate is a reference to the practice of studying the Buddha's teaching. Soothill defines it thus: "The doctrines, or wisdom of Buddha regarded as the door to enlightenment. A method. Any sect. As the living have 84,000 delusions, so the Buddha provides 84,000 methods 法門 of dealing with them. Hence the 法門海 ocean of Buddha's methods."

6. A *stupa* is a pagoda encrusted with jewels.

7. One of the reviewers of the manuscript points out the significance of the careful tabulation of numbers here, a process akin to the tallying of accumulated deeds and misdeeds in this play.

8. According to Soothill, Avici is the last and deepest of the eight hot hells, where the culprits suffer and die, only to be immediately reborn to more suffering. All of this takes place with no interruption. Edward Soothill, *A Dictionary of Buddhist Terms: With Sanskrit and English Equivalents and a Sanskrit-Pali Index* (New York: Routledge, 2004).

who talk of sudden enlightenment and of gradual enlightenment. They are like crazed bees in battle over two kinds of honey, each boasting about the sweet and sour qualities of the two. Those promoting Confucianism and those promoting Daoism are like lame elephants dragging a pair of carts: never steady on either side. They scoff at the Bodhidharma's ways of single transmission and wordlessness, facing the wall for nine years:[9] Is it not like meditating blindly and chanting lifelessly in silence, being unable to reach the state of a falling leaf returning to its roots? They laugh at Huike's singular pursuit of the Buddha mind and teaching the texts to the hordes: Is that not like getting all muddled up, mouths arguing, teeth bared, until at last resulting in a cover from showers of heaven's flowers?[10] True inklings are like yielding to the plum blossoms exuding their fragrance.[11] False kindness, weeping, and crying

---

9. Bodhidharma (達摩 in the text, an abbreviation of *Puti damo* 菩提達摩) is the Buddhist monk who came to China from India during the Northern and Southern dynasties and is credited with founding Zen Buddhism. He is thought to have first visited the southern Liu-Song court and, being met with the emperor's skepticism, to have gone further into the Northern Wei capital at Luoyang, where he "wall-faced" (meditated, facing a wall) for nine years. Afterward, he transmitted his teachings to his first disciple, Huike 慧可. Single transmission refers to the passing down of teachings from one teacher to the next, in a direct line of descent, a feature specific to Zen Buddhism. The doctrine of wordlessness describes the attainment of enlightenment through direct experience rather than through scriptural (and thus textually based) study.

10. This is an allusion to the section of the *Vimalakirti sutra* entitled "Observing Living Beings," in which a goddess showers the bodhisattvas and their disciples with flowers. The flowers fall off the bodies of the bodhisattvas, but they adhere to the bodies of the disciples. The disciples try desperately to brush the petals off, as monks are not supposed to adorn themselves with flowers or jewelry, but to no avail. The goddess proceeds to explain that only those who have eliminated thoughts of discriminations will be able to brush off the flowers. She then goes on to challenge the disciple Sariputra to a discourse on gender in which she switches genders with him to demonstrate the futility of discussing things as being fixed or changeable.

11. An allusion about how all essences can be contained in a small thing: "In the thirteenth century, the polymath Luo Dagang concluded his *Jade Dew from Crane Forest* (*Helin yulu*), an extensive collection of notes and essays on a wide range of subjects, with the following short entry: 'The master [Confucius] said: "The Way is not far from man." Mencius said: "The Way is near but people seek it in faraway places." There is a poem on the enlightenment of a nun, which goes: "All day long I searched for spring but nowhere did I find it—/ On sandals of straw I trekked through the clouds atop the hills. / When I returned, I smiled and plucked a spring of flowering plum, / One sniff and I found that all of spring was there on a twig!"' Wilt Idema and Beata Grant, eds., *The Red Brush: Writing Women of Imperial China* (Cambridge, MA: Harvard University Asia Center, 2004), 158.

will only deceive a rat. If one is enlightened by speech, it is like a fish's golden scales suddenly bursting with a loud splash through one's net from miles deep in the water. If one sticks the slightest bit to words, is it not like a strong man stepping into the emptiness from the end of a hundred foot pole?[12] We chant: "Stop your feet on the bright pearl:[13] one moment full, the next on the wane again. Collect treasures in mountainous heaps, and debts will only increase." All I have said means: take advantage of the lightning to thread the eye of a needle, truly hitting the mark. When a hungry king chews on wax, all flavors are empty. Yet I hope that we all can come around and that no one will blame an old monk for running at the mouth. Ai! There I go again, running at the mouth. Enough with this speech![14] I will now talk about a certain prefect, newly arrived in our prefecture: surnamed Liu, named Xuanjiao.[15] I have heard that he is short in years but long in talent. He seems to have the energy to carry things through. I fear, though, that he is like yet-unfiltered gold sand, and he will bring pollution in with him.[16] In the old days, we in the three teachings[17] followed protocol in our interactions, but these last twenty years I have spent behind closed doors; as such, I neither go along with everyone to gather at court, nor do I heed calls to act in an official capacity. Here in this pure place I will stay. It's best for

---

12. This is an allusion to a popular koan (*gongan* 公案) inquiring what one does after having completed a journey to the top of a hundred foot pole. The question of whether one should fear taking the next step into the emptiness should induce the listener to contemplate what he is still clinging to.

13. The ten thousand directions are one bright pearl. An anonymous reader of the manuscript notes that the characters 明珠 (*mingzhu*, meaning bright pearl) are also used for the Sanskrit word "mani," which means thusness or being.

14. This refers to the speech he has thus far been giving in a metatheatrical way, that is his introductory speech to the audience. As well, the term "critical word" or *huatou* 話頭, beyond simply meaning speech or terms, refers to a Zen method specific to the Ming of attaining enlightenment, similar to, or sometimes part of, a koan wherein a question is repeatedly asked of oneself, or pondered until enlightenment is suddenly reached.

15. The surname Liu 柳 means "willow," and the pun on the name recurs throughout the play.

16. "Golden Sands" (*jinsha* 金沙) is an imaginary river in the promised land of Nirvana. Xu Wei could also be confusing this with the Hiranyavati (*jinhe* 金河), the river at the site where Buddha attained the highest nirvana. Either way, the implication is that Liu Xuanjiao would be a polluting element, as he is too worldly for the monastery.

17. Confucianism, Daoism, and Buddhism.

me to sit here cross-legged, calming my mind. Lazybones, where are you?
(*A* chou *playing an acolyte enters and pays respects to Yutong*)
Yutong: Lazybones, enter this Buddha's shrine and light a stick of incense, then go and shut the doors and wait while I meditate. If any visitors come, tell them that this little shrine is separate from the main hall, and that there's nothing here good for sightseeing. If they want to sightsee, tell them to go to the main hall, and then you can report back to me.
(*The* chou *assents, then acts out lighting the incense and fastening the doors*)
(*The* sheng, *Yutong, acts out sitting in lotus position in order to meditate*)
(*A* tie *playing Red Lotus dressed in mourning clothes enters and says*)
Red Lotus:

> From the waist of powdered girls hangs a dagger coiled up.
> Not yet on the battlefield, one's blood runs cold in fear.
> Magistrate Liu, when it was hot you used this Lotus,[18]
> But I fear that after a frost it is hard to keep a Willow[19] from wilting.

I am Red Lotus, a registered courtesan.[20] Last night, His Honor the magistrate, offended that Yutong neglected to pay court to him, sought to use my body as a snare. I should do such and such, and if I should manage to carry it off smoothly, I should gather up that stuff and bring it to him to serve as proof.[21] I was thinking, this Yutong is a good elder, how can His Honor carry out this transgression against a boddhisatva? Ah, the law is as insistent as a hot cauldron; all I can do is as I am told. I've arrived at this door. I might as well knock.
(*Acts out knocking on the door*)
(*A* sheng *calls out to his acolyte*)
Lazybones, with this kind of wind and rain, and the sky turned almost all dark, who knocks at the door?[22] If it's someone you can handle, then go see to it.

---

18. This is a play on the lotus as bound foot as well as her name, Red Lotus.
19. "Willow" is capitalized to draw attention to the play on his name.
20. That is, on the official rolls as a courtesan.
21. That stuff (*na huar* 那話兒) is evidently physical proof (semen stains) of their tryst.
22. Note the pathetic fallacy here, as clouds and rain (*yunyu* 雲雨) bespeak sexual intercourse.

(*Acolyte assents, acts out going to ask*)
Serving Monk: Who is knocking on the door?
(*He asks this three times, then Red Lotus replies*)
Open up, and then I'll tell you!
(*Acolyte's speech takes on the Hangzhou dialect*)
Odd! That is some Missy's voice!
(*He acts out opening the door*)
Here in this heavy rain . . . and with the sky dark, too. You're all dressed in mourning, so why have you come to our temple?
Red Lotus: Today is Qingming,[23] and while coming here in order to make offerings and sweep the grave of my departed husband, I had stopped my sedan chair inside Qingbo gate. Not realizing how long the lane was, I walked until my feet ached. I dilly-dallied for a while, and thus delayed until the sky was dark, and then rain started to fall. I sent my servant girl back inside to call for my sedan chair, but then I saw that the city gates were already closed and that even she would not be able to come back outside, either. Before me there was no village; behind me, there was no inn. Thank heavens for your honorable temple. I wish to lodge here for one night, and tomorrow I will return home and send back a small gift to thank you.
Acolyte: I see. Wait here while I go to ask my master.
(*Acts out repeating the story*)
Yutong: That woman, is she old or young?
Acolyte: She's no more than seventeen or eighteen. And a fine specimen!
Yutong: This is no good. I would tell her to go, but there is no place for her to go. Here, take her this bedding to place beneath the window on the left wall, and tell her that she will have to squeeze in there.
(*Acolyte acts out spreading out the bed mat, then exits*)
(*Red Lotus acts out first sitting, then rushing forward and calling*)
Yutong: Quickly, no, no! Quickly, no, no! Quick, get out beyond the window!
(*Red Lotus acts as if her stomach hurts, and increasingly worsens. Acts out that she is deathly ill*)
(*Yutong calls to his acolyte*)

---

23. A traditional holiday, designated for ancestor worship, that takes place on the fifteenth day after the spring equinox. Descendants traditionally go to sweep the graves of their ancestors and make offerings to their spirits.

Lazybones, quick! Warm up a bit of ginger soup and give it to the young lady to drink. I think she suffers from a surfeit of cold.[24]
Acolyte: We haven't any ginger here. I will go to the main hall and ask if they have any there. In the middle of the night, at the third watch, black as can be, what is the rush?
(*Acolyte leaves again*)
(*Red Lotus acts as if she is dying of pain and then regains consciousness*)
(*Yutong calls out, and when his acolyte does not reply, he asks*)
Young lady, this affliction of yours: is it newly felt, or an old one?
Red Lotus: It's one I've had.
Yutong: Since it is an old one, usually on the occasion when it flares up, how do you treat it?
Red Lotus: I will not hide it from you, sir. In the past, when my illness surfaced, I tried every kind of cure, but none worked. Even to speak of it embarrasses me, but my husband would expose his warm belly and press it against my belly, and with one rubbing I would be better.
Yutong: So it seems that the potency of an infinity of herbs does not compare to that of a single person's body.
(*Red Lotus again acts as if she is dying of pain*)
(*Yutong again calls out, and when his acolyte again does not respond, he asks*)
This is no good! In the case of a person's life, what am I to do? When they investigate about the corpse and see that it is a woman's, the officials will ask, "What were you doing harboring a woman here in the temple?" I'd have a hard time explaining. My acolyte, too, does not respond when I call him. I have no choice.
(*Acts out hoisting Red Lotus inside*)
(*Yutong quickly jumps back onto the stage, Red Lotus follows him and comes up, and Yutong shouts loudly*)
Finished! Finished! I have fallen into this bitch's carnal trap and been ensnared!
[To the tune *Xinshuiling*]

I meditated twenty years on Bamboo Forest Peak,
Passion's Rivers blocked, not letting a trickle through.
Though I lived on earth,
It was as if I were already dead, wasn't it?

---

24. In this case not referring simply to temperature, but to humors, or an excess of *yin* that needs to be balanced by the warming tendencies of a "hot" food like ginger.

This kind of firmness, this kind of firmness . . .
And now a little bug bored a hole in the dikes that shored up my Yellow River.[25]

Red Lotus: Master, if a bug could breach the dike of your Yellow River, it cannot have been very firm. Master, Why didn't you make a Yellow River dike that could not be bored through and leak?
Yutong: Now I will ask you, are you not that official courtesan . . . that "Red Lotus" who always plays those dirty tricks?
Red Lotus: That's me, what's it to you?
Yutong: You, Red Lotus, are you here by orders of a Green Willow?
Red Lotus: Yes, that's it, what's it to you? Master, how did you figure it out?
Yutong: Under these brows are sunk knowing eyes of mental perception[26] like flashing lightning. How could I not know?
Red Lotus: Eyes of Perception, Eyes of Perception, how much have they let sneak by?
Yutong: [To the tune *Bubu jiao*]

Come to think of
That rotten Red Lotus, this cheating whore!

Red Lotus: Master, lay off a bit, you've got to take half of the blame, haven't you?
Yutong:

What enmity have I got with you
That among the pear blossoms on Cold Food[27] day,
You'd pretend to be on the way home from sweeping
and offering sacrifices,
And seek refuge in this monastery in wind and rain?

---

25. Presumably referring to the great amount of *yang* that he had been accumulating over the years through abstinence.

26. "Eyes of Perception" (*huiyan* 慧眼) is a Buddhist term used to describe eyes that see beyond the illusions of the flesh to underlying truths about existence.

27. Originally celebrated for three days before Qingming, Cold Food Day was later condensed to the day before Qingming. Qingming is also known in English as All Soul's Day and Grave Sweeping Day, as it is the day to honor and make offerings to one's ancestors at their gravesites.

Red Lotus: If not like that, how could I have trapped you?
Yutong: Then

> You put on an act about being sick,
> About to
> Rush off to the Yellow Springs,[28]
> Circling my meditation couch,
> You called on me to carry out expedient means.[29]

Red Lotus: Master, if you had paid no heed to my calls, I would not have been able to do it. Had you not, I would have failed. Who told you to practice your "expedient means" with me?
Yutong: [To the tune *Zhegui ling*]

> You told me that all your Cinnabar Field[30] was full of pain as if a snake was worming in,
> Telling me to bare my belly and rub against your navel,
> Lending warmth to drive out the cold.
> At the time, I was trying to save a life.
> I was determined to rescue you from suffering,
> I was fully devoted to saving you from your troubles,
> I simply lacked the means to drive you away,
> How could I have been moved by amorous thoughts?

Red Lotus: If you weren't moved, who told you to move the chess piece when it got to that point?
Yutong:

> Before I knew it, I was riding a horse, traveling in a boat,
> Once the wind rose to fill the sail, it was too hard to lower it;
> The bridle was rotten, and it was hard to rein in.

Red Lotus:

> Master,
> If you had not mounted the boat,

---

28. The Underworld.

29. The term here is *fangbian* 方便, which is from the Sanskrit term "upaya," the doctrine that one teach according to the capacity of the listener, by whatever means are most suitable, also known as the doctrine of expedient means.

30. Pubic area.

What need would you have had to lower your sail?
As you yourself raised the whip,
How dare you marvel that the horse was hard to rein in?

Yutong: Too bad about my twenty years of hard work: in one flash it is all cast aside.
[To the tune *Jiang'er shui*]

A few drops of Bodhi water,
Fell between two lotus petals.
Ai! Buddhas and bodhisattvas didn't protect me,
The foolish *vajra*[31] didn't heed the mountain gates, leaving them open,
And was tricked by that rotten misty flower whore, entering her little palace of pearls.
I hooked my precept robes on wanton pins and bangles,
Atop a hundred-foot long pole, it is hard to turn around.
One Māra,[32]
And I have lost hold of my original self.[33]

Red Lotus:
Do you fail to realize how you are blessed? You are a gourd[34] hooked on a peach flower face.
Yutong (hatefully): Red Lotus, you rotten whore!
Red Lotus: Master, don't curse me like that!
Yutong: [To the tune *De sheng ling*]

You are no Miss Qincao,[35] engaging in playful meditation,
Instead you were a wild fox spirit full of clever tricks.

---

31. A symbolic tool in Buddhism that is associated with the male principle. It is meant to be a physical reminder of the protection of Buddhist teachings.

32. The demon who tempted Buddha with visions of beautiful women.

33. The term used here is 本來之面.

34. The gourd (*hulu* 葫蘆) is a metaphor for unimpededness, as in a gourd floating on water, and represents the monk. Here I translate *gua* 掛 as "hooked," but the word also refers, according to a reader, to a term *guada* 掛搭, which refers to itinerant monks taking temporary lodging at temples and such, thus highlighting the irony of Yutong's predicament.

35. A Song dynasty courtesan from Lin'an. Su Dongpo would often have her as his companion when traveling in Hangzhou. When he introduced her to Zen Buddhism, she became a convert and later became a nun.

In the blink of an eye, you took my Bamboo Forest hall,[36]
And turned it into a Peach Blossom torrent.[37]
Red *yeme*[38] Lotus, for whom do you toil, to whom do you yield your sweetness?
On whose behalf did you vitiate your good heart?
Wielding a Dragon Spring lusty sword,[39]
Powdered skeleton, with a three-foot-long sword,
You trapped this mottled gourd within a circle.
Western *yeme* Heaven's
Five hundred arhats,
From what direction shall they appear?
Southern *yeme* Spring's
Twenty years as a steer:
What lured it away?

Red Lotus:

Yellow *yeme* Heaven's
Five hundred arhats,
You are ashamed to see any of them.
Clear *yeme* Spring's
Not reflecting the fisherman's hook,
You let yourself be led away by me.

---

36. A kenning for Yutong's Buddhist temple.

37. Peach Blossom Spring is the key site in two famous allusions that are sometimes conflated. The first version is Tao Yuanming's 陶淵明, also known as Tao Qian 陶潛 (365?–427) "Peach Blossom Spring," of a man leaving his village to meander into an idyllic world inhabited by people who, cut off from the rise and fall of dynasties, live peaceful agrarian lives. When he left to bring back more people, he could not find his way back. There is also the story associated with Mount Tiantai of two men, Liu Chen 劉晨 and Ruan Zhao 阮肇, who go to the mountains to pick medicinal herbs. There they come upon a grove of peach trees, beneath which lies a spring. They meet and are lured into marriage by two beautiful goddesses, and when after six months they try to head home to their village, they find that they have missed seven generations of descendants.

38. *Yeme* is a meaningless syllable that is inserted at intervals to create the rhythm of this song.

39. Dragon Spring sword is used here as a metaphor for Red Lotus' deadly skills of seduction. It is one of two mythical swords said to have been created in the Jin 晉 dynasty when Zhang Hua saw an auspicious moment in the skies. One was named Dragon Spring and the other "Tai'a." Dragon Spring is a kenning for a precious sword.

Yutong: That Western Heaven's Matangi[40] girl was a whore with magical powers who used her seductive charms to steal Ananda away in the blink of an eye, and he nearly destroyed his abstemious body. It was only thanks to the world-honored one[41] that he was rescued and returned. Now if that Ananda, a bodhisattva, could come to this, how much more so me?
[To the tune *Jiaojiao ling*]

Matangi's turbid sea of desire
And lewd charms will always seduce Heaven.
I want to find the Tathagatha, but how can I see him?
The precept-body of this old Ananda is destroyed,
The precept-body of this old Ananda is destroyed.[42]

Red Lotus: Master, I scoff at Matangi's lack of skills. If Ananda had run into me, Red Lotus, ah . . .
Even if he were an iron Ananda, I would have torn him apart.
An iron Ananda, I would have torn him apart.
Yutong:
[To the tune *Shou jiangnan*]

Let me tell you,
You'll be wearing a coat of fur when you are at the Six Domestics road,[43]
You'll become a grub for a hundred birds to swallow,
Your calculating, cheating heart will keep you in such a state until the sun and moon are together in the sky.[44]
This situation that I've now come to,

---

40. The Matangi 摩登伽 girl is a girl from a low caste who tries to seduce Ananda. Buddha steps in and rescues him.

41. Buddha.

42. The highest title for a Buddha, literally "one who [as all Buddhas] comes" (*rulai* 如來), is the Tathagatha, who comes (and also goes, *ruqu* 如去) into Nirvana.

43. The Six Domestics Road alludes to the Chinese Buddhist belief that after death, spirits come to an intersection of six roads to repay their mortal misdeeds through reincarnation. First is the road of heaven, second is the human road, third is the demon road, fourth is the ghost road, fifth is the domestic animal road, and the sixth and final one is the road to the underworld. The six domestics are the domestic animals: horse, cow, goat, chicken, dog, and pig. Yutong is saying that Red Lotus will be reborn as a domestic animal because of what she did to him.

44. In other words, not for a long time, if ever.

This situation that I've now come to,
Who knows how many more revolutions must be made before I pass through the eye of the needle,[45]
After I pass through the eye of the needle, when will the circle be complete?
I've faced the wall at Shaolin's north mountain.
Stopped my boat at Puto Temple's east banks,
Committed my fetus back onto the Brocade River's western banks.[46]
But now that I am back to one more karmic entanglement,
Why talk about Nirvana?
Ai! Now my spirit will first go into the Liu family's home.

Red Lotus: Mister, I have not sought to add another entanglement,
The truth is: both pounder and basin got polished.[47]
Ai! Now I will convey these few drops to report back at Master Liu's yamen.[48]

(*Yutong acts out pushing Red Lotus out the door*)
Red Lotus: You may shut the doors, and push out the moon from before your window, but I shall be like the plum tree and make decisions for myself.[49] (*Exits*)
Yutong: So this is my karma for refusing to pay the prefect a visit. What a pity that this should ruin twenty years of arduous work. Alas! How can I let him get away with it? I have no choice but to turn head over heels and be reborn into the womb of Liu Xuanjiao's sordid family. I'll be his daughter and grow up to be a base courtesan, and I will destroy their reputation. All this will happen in the blink of an eye, and will not stand in the way of the great cultivation that matters. It's just that this impudent Willow (Liu) seeks to use this to insult me. He will certainly send someone to inquire about me, and I must prepare a few sentences in

45. That is: How much longer on earth must he stay because of what has just happened?

46. Meaning back into the mortal world.

47. In pounding a basin to polish it, the pounder gets polished as well; that is, both parties benefit from the encounter. My thanks go to Wai-yee Li for this explanation.

48. She takes the evidence of "bodhi water" (semen) as proof for Liu Xuanjiao.

49. Her words are a composite of couplets from popular plays. I thank Wai-yee Li for pointing this out.

response. I shall write a few words to Lazybones to instruct him to prepare this and that. Then I shall sit upright and send off my spirit, where it will speed off on a trip to the Liu house.
(*Acts out writing a note, then acts out reading it*)
Since I entered these Zen gates, I was without a care.
For fifty-three years, my mind was centered.
Because of this single deviating thought,
I broke the Buddha's precept against lasciviousness.
You sent Red Lotus to destroy my chastity,
I now owe Red Lotus a payback for one night.
My body's moral behavior bore your harm,
Your household's reputation shall bear my destruction.
(*Again acts out writing a letter for his monk, and then acts out reading it*)
Left for my serving man, Lazybones: "If there should be a messenger come to the temple from the Willow's establishment, you can tell him that there is a letter of response at the foot of the incense burner."
(*Recites*)

> Red Lotus made a monkey out of me,
> So I shall hide for a springtime in the skin of a Green Willow.
> Waves beat the duckweed, there are none that aren't struck;
> But my only fear is that when I return you will not recognize my self of old.

(*Acts out leaving his body*)
(*Acolyte enters*)
Acolyte: Last night I went to ask for ginger, and the master of the main temple said, "A short time ago, at the foot of the hill, there was a tiger." Knowing this, I did not dare to come home. I wonder what happened to that Missy. Ai! The Missus isn't here. Ai! Master has left his body! Queer! What's this all about? I've got it! She was a Guanyin who came to transform Master away. Ai! There is a note under the incense burner.
(*Reads*)
So! That Missus was Red Lotus, the prostitute! It was Prefect Liu who sent her here to carry out his ensnarement. My master failed the rules of abstention. This letter is to serve as a response for Liu. Here is another letter. Ai! These are the instructions left to me.
(*Reads*) (*A* mo *acting the part of a messenger from Liu enters, and speaks*)

Following Prefect Liu's instructions, I was told to present this letter to the Elder Yutong, to inquire about the events with Red Lotus, to see if he has a response for me.

(*He looks at the monk, who replies*)

My master, as a result of these events, has given up his life. What use does he have for confrontation with you?

Liu Servant: Prefect Liu wanted me to personally return with his response. Now what should I do?

Monk: Let me take a look at your letter.

(*Reads*)

"To the monk called Yutong of Water and Moon Monastery,
For so long you never descended Bamboo Forest's peak,
What a shame that a few drops of *Bodhi* water
Poured into Red Lotus's two petals."

Well! I said that my master failed the rules of abstention, not a bit of what I said was wrong. Hey, old man, there is a response: it is under the incense burner. You can take that back. Hold on a moment! Old Man, let me ask you, how did this happen?

Liu Servant: How did this happen? Your master was extremely proud and high-minded, and didn't go to pay his respects to Prefect Liu, and that is why he sent the prostitute Red Lotus to do what she did. Your master reached out with bare hands to put out a fire, and so he got burned. There's your reason. Now I will take the papers as instructed, and go back to report it.[50] Old monk, I shall take my leave. (*Exits*)

Monk: Thus the work of fate. I will now report this to the community in the temple, and take the master's body for cremation. Or he may be put in a shrine; I will leave it up to them.

[To *Qing jiang yin*]

> In the temple I spent twenty years starving on vegetarian meals,
> Long did I steal glances at my master.
> He sat there, like a sculpted Amitabha,[51]

---

50. The papers are mounted on a horizontal scroll.

51. Amitabha is a celestial Buddha, and one of the highest-ranking. He is often depicted seated with hands held together in meditation (thumbs touching and fingers together), flanked by two followers. Often one of these followers is Guanyin.

Standing up, he was a living Luohan.[52]
Ai! Prefect Liu, beware! Yutong will not forget Red Lotus' scheme.
That shrew Red Lotus sold her poison as if it were honey,
The Zen monk Yu was defeated in his efforts to take a mercury flight,[53]
When even a Buddha or bodhisattva will seek revenge through reincarnation,
How can people of this world avoid repaying the debts they owe?

(*Monk turns his back and exits*)

Act II

(*A* wai *playing Moonlight Monk enters the stage, carrying a bag filled with a gauze cap, a woman's face mask, a monk's hat, and a coarse robe*)
When at the tip of a hundred-foot pole, you should not vaunt your strength,[54]
One slip and you will be the neighborhood laughingstock.
A pity that the stream flowing out from the opening of West Lake's waters
Would trick Master Ruan with its peach flowers.[55]
I am not going to speak about where I come from, but I will share a few words about my sect's wisdom. What is that wisdom like? It is like the

---

52. *Luohan* is the Chinese transliteration of the Sanskrit word *arhat*, or "worthy one." It is often used in reference to Buddha or his disciples.

53. It was believed that ingestion of mercury would lead to immortality by giving the soul flight. The basic meaning is that Yutong failed in his quest for enlightment.

54. See act 1, note 9.

55. This line alludes to Yuan Zheng: "Lazily I stir the water and send afloat a petal, flowing out beyond to fool Master Ruan." Master Ruan is Ruan Zhao, who was gathering herbs with Liu Chen on Mount Tiantai when they were led astray by two beautiful women (see act 1, note 96). This story is the subject of a painting by Zhao Cangyun 趙蒼云 (fl. late thirteenth–early fourteenth century) as well as a play in the *Yuanqu xuan* 元曲選 "Liu Chen and Ruan Zhao Mistakenly Enter Peach Blossom Spring" 劉晨阮肇誤入桃源 by the early Ming playwright Wang Ziyi 王子一. The handscroll painting is at the Metropolitan Museum of Art in New York and can be partially viewed at http://www.metmuseum.org/toah/works-of-art/2005.494.1. Tiantai is also home to the Mahayana sect of Buddhism called Lotus Buddhism (because of its emphasis on the Lotus Sutra) emphasizing scriptural study and practice.

pearl of dew on top of a lotus leaf: it wets the leaf, and it doesn't. It is like the white root in the dirty mud beneath the lotus leaf: it is not filthy, and it is. As to the rudiments of cultivation: just lower your antelope horns, and hang them upon the blessed Sala tree.[56] Though things do not adhere, as years deepen and days lengthen, there will be some traces on the bamboo's joints. To pay some attention to the process: it is like mixing a peacock's gall with amber wine. Once mixed, the bitterness is removed and it is sweet; but it is still better to spill it out of your golden cup.[57] If one thread is not secured, it will result in a mess of creeping tendrils and tangled vines. Myriad thoughts will be emptied in vain; look on them as piles and piles of fine mountains and rivers and great worlds. I do not understand how to free myself of the five defilements, and have completely divested myself of the One Vehicle of the Lotus Sutra.[58] I fart on the three lives and curse the four elements. One flower, five leaves: they all commit the crime of hollow affection. A hundred seductions, a thousand vanities: they are all the dharma root.[59] In stirring up the Milky Way, one must be hung with koumiss and ghee;[60] discussing the circle of Heaven,[61] one cannot avoid the tiles and shards, the piss

56. The antelope was believed to suspend itself from tree tops with its antlers so that it would not leave any tracks behind and thus would be protected from hunters. Zen masters compared the notion of awakening to enlightenment, saying that chasing after enlightenment by pursuing a master's words was equivalent to chasing after the invisble tracks of an antelope. The Sala tree is a teakwood tree, under which Sakyamuni reached Nirvana.

57. The gall of a peacock was thought to be poisonous. Even though the wine would mask the bitterness of the gall, it is still poisonous and would therefore be best poured out.

58. The five defilements (*Wuzhuo* 五濁) are the five *kasaya* periods of turbidity or decay, commencing when the earthly life begins to decrease below 20,000 years. They are marked by (1) decay, suffering of deterioration, giving rise to (2) deterioration of view, egoism, resulting in (3) passions and delusions of anger, desire, stupidity, pride, and doubt. The world sees (4) an increase of misery and decrease of happiness, and (5) human lifetime gradually diminishes to ten years (periods 2 and 3 are the actual *zhu* and 4 and 5 the results of the *zhu*). See Soothill, *A Dictionary of Buddhist Terms*.

59. That is, they are all things. The dharma root also means the truth, or law and order, of anything Buddhist.

60. Koumiss is a fermented milk product, somewhat like a watered down yogurt drink. The ghee is the essential and most clarified distillation of butter, and therefore is used as a metaphor for Mahayana.

61. Heaven was thought to be a circle, and earth a square, in traditional Chinese thought.

and shit.[62] You only have to kill the Tathagata and feed him to the dogs. Convulse with laughter and bare your feet, and you've saved a cat.[63] That is to say: creatures like myself, emerging with the stink of yellow leeks and plain rice, can still become like dried lion's dung, transformed into an aromatic.[64] The smallest drop of impurity expelled from dog and turtle meat is like brass, a good fake for a red gold Buddha face. What we have just seen is like a furnace fire of the wrench and mallet; it rolls over all: flesh both rotten and divine. Those who are unable to get it run every stretch of the road as if they are two. Those who are able to get it kick over the monkey and get rid of the ghost.[65] Those who are able to get it enter the fray wielding a blade, and are able to see. Those who are not able to get it face the mirror and then turn away, missing the opportunity that is right there. Ai! Mandarin ducks, already embroidered, are for all to see. Do not try to pass the golden needle to another.[66] Audience, ask me who I am. (*Answer from offstage*)

---

62. This is an allusion to Zhuangzi's explication of the *dao* as existing within all things, including the shards of tiles; when questioned about how it could be in something so low, Zhuangzi responds that the *dao* is also in our "piss and shit."

63. This refers to a koan about a conversation between the Tang dynasty Zen masters Nanquan 南泉普願 (748?–835?) and Zhaozho 趙州從諗 (778?–897?). Nanquan was telling Zhaozho how he came upon two monks fighting over a cat, and told them that if any of them could say a word of Zen he would not kill the cat. No one answered, so he slew the cat. Zhaozho, upon hearing this story, took off his straw sandals and put them on his head. Nanquan said that if he had answered this way, he would have saved the life of the cat, making the point that there is no answer. For a discussion (occasionally with the Japanese names Nansen for Nanquan and Joshu for Zhaozho), see Douglas Mikkelson, "'Who Is Arguing About the Cat?' Moral Action and Enlightenment According to Dogen," *Philosophy East and West* 47.3 (1997): 383–97.

64. This refers to storax, a kind of fragrant resin brought to China from Parthia for use as incense, thought by the Chinese to consist of dried lion's dung.

65. The mind monkey/gibbon appears again.

66. This is an allusion to the second couplet in the third of Yuan Haowen's 元好問 (1190–1257) "Three Poems on Poetry" (*lun shi sanshou* 論詩三首). The poem reads: Misty blue cuts through the red, the point bastes them equally/Every turn pulled through, every turn fresh/Mandarin ducks, already embroidered, are only for looking/Do not try to pass the golden needles to another. This is to say that the efforts in creating something are for the product, not for the mastery of the efforts in order to pass them on to another. The handiwork is what is passed on, not the skill. 暈碧裁紅點綴勻／一回拈出一回新／鴛鴦繡了徒教看／莫把金鍼度與人. For a discussion of the poems, see John Timothy Wixted, *Poems on Poetry: Literary Criticism by Yuan Hao-Wen (1190–1257)* (Wiesbaden: Steiner, 1982), 237.

Who are you?

Moonlight: I am an elder fellow disciple of the Monk Yutong of the Water Moon Monastery. I used to be a revered old Buddha from the Western Heavens, but now I have come again to earth, changing my name to Moonlight Monk. It is all because of my little brother, Yutong, who had not yet freed himself of the image of self and, snagged by the roots of desire, allowed Liu Xuanjiao to use Red Lotus to deceive him. In order to take revenge, he chose to be reborn. He has been reborn as a young girl named Liu Cui, now aged seventeen, who has toppled into prostitution. Our patriarch pities him for tarrying so long without enlightenment, and he specially sent me to direct him and turn his head.[67] Ah! Yet it is hard work. This, ah, what is it like? It is just like curing blindness: it is using a golden needle to push the membrane away from another's pupil;[68] you are fearful of pushing it over, but if you succeed in doing so, the bright vision of old will return. It is also like making a lion push over Mount Taihang; some may be able to do it, but in so doing, who knows how much effort I will have wasted? But as for this thing, it is not something that language can do. In my Zen faith, we have a tradition of "dumb riddles," a miraculous method of meeting one's opponent with the blade of wit. Now, all of a sudden, I see this Liu Cui. Today she is with that Huizhou merchant who often visits her, Feng Chaoyang; he has come to take in the sights of West Lake. That Liu Cui has come first to the Great Buddha Temple to wait for him, and I will wait until she comes: I have a plan.

(*Mimes assuming the lotus position in meditation*)

(*A* dan *playing Liu Cui enters*)

Ever since I fell from crimson gates[69] to the courtesans' rolls, I've lived all these years like Little Su in Qiantang.[70] I can't remember how many I've accompanied carousing on the painted boat; but whenever I see the

---

67. That is, to convert or awaken him.

68. The procedure for cataract removal.

69. A wealthy and respectable family.

70. A river in Zhejiang. Apparently in Qiantang there lived, during the Southern Qi as well as the Southern Song, famous courtesans by the name of Su Xiaoxiao 蘇小小, or Su Xiao 蘇小.

peach blossoms, they break my heart. I am Liu Cui. It was not long after my father's funeral that the purse of earnings from his post had emptied. Day after day I grew poorer, until I, his very own daughter,[71] began life as a courtesan, chasing pleasures and selling smiles. But thankfully, amidst this misfortune, I've recently hooked up with a merchant from Huizhou called Feng Chaoyang. He may be the type who mocks the breeze and enjoys the moon like a playboy, but he loves righteousness and is a spendthrift. Relying on him, I've just barely been able to make a living. Today he has planned to look at the peach blossoms with me on the lake, and he asked me to come first to this Great Buddha temple to wait for him. I am here now; why isn't he here yet?

(*A* jing *playing a servant*)

Servant: Sister, the boss had just reached Yongjin gate when a messenger came to report that his eldest son has taken ill of a sudden. The boss had to go back to see how things are; he will return shortly. He said that Sister should first take the boat on to the lake, or else stay at the temple and wait to get on the boat with him . . . either way would be fine.

Liu Cui: All right. Go on back and let him know I got the message.

(*The* jing *assents and goes*)

(*The* dan *mimes touring and then seeing Moonlight Monk*)

Liu Cui: Where did you come from, old man?

(*Thrice she asks, and thrice there is no reply*)

(*The* wai *holds up his hand and points west, then points to the sky*)

Liu Cui: One hand points west, one hand points to heaven, so you don't mean you are from the Western Heavens? What nonsense! All right, so tell me, what are you doing come down here to the world below from the Western Heavens?

(*The* wai *uses his hand to strike his head once. Using his hands, he forms a three cornered* si 厶 *character, then acts out a four-sided square, to make the character* kou 口, *then acts out a circle, to make a full moon*)

Liu Cui: That three-cornered thing is a *si* character, the four-sided one is a *kou*, putting them all together, it makes a *tai* 台 character. The round thing is a moon (*yue* 月) character, but since he first hit his head (*tou* 頭)

71. That is, born to the primary wife.

once, it must mean that this is a way of saying reincarnation.[72] Now I ask you this: you are a monk, so how does reincarnation concern you? You are fabricating this weird language. Ai! He is a crazy monk. (*turns and sings*)

Liu Cui:

[To the tune *Xinshuiling*]

> I was just
> Stopping the boat awaiting a customer, and walked around these corridors.
> Without any reason, I ran into this nutty monk.
> I asked him where he came from,
> He pointed to heaven with one hand,
> He boasted of coming from the West.
> He boasted of coming from the West
> And in the end,
> The two characters that he acted out were like "reincarnation" [*toutai*].

Ai! Though he is a mad monk, there's something strange about it. I don't know why, but suddenly my mind is roused. I certainly want to question him. Forget about that trip on the lake. So, master, this *huatou* "reincarnation" is somewhat bewildering. Could you be so kind as to explain it to me?

(*The* wai *takes the gauze hat and puts it on his head, then acts out Prefect Liu being angry. Then he takes the hat off and puts it on a table. He puts on the female mask and kneels own, facing the table. He kowtows, acts out a conversation, then rises*)

Liu Cui: This set piece[73] fills me with even more doubt . . . let me try to guess its meaning.

---

72. The characters for reincarnation (*toutai* 投胎) are created thus by Moonlight and guessed by Liu Cui: first he acts out the second character, *tai* 胎, by breaking it down into its component parts. First, he makes the triangle and square that comprise the right side of the character, using his hands, and then he describes roundness with his hands to imply a moon, because the left part of *tai* is the moon radical. The first character in the compound for reincarnation, *tou* 投, is evoked by Moonlight's playing on its homophone, *tou* 頭, by striking his head. This makes Liu Cui think of the homophonous *tou* 投, and she then combines it with *tai* to come up with the compound word for reincarnation.

73. *Taoshu* 套數.

[To the tune *Bubu jiao*]

He wears the black gauze, with his back to the north and facing south,
He seems like a local official, sitting in the yellow hall,[74]
Even if this countenance is not like my father's, these few steps at the end . . . that really is like my father's.
He turns his body in a few hurried steps,
If I observe this in detail,
It truly resembles my father's person.
And in the end he sends off the girl in red,
and she seems to be the general of whores who leads her troops lying in ambush.

Master, as I see it, that black gauze hat and woman's face mask must be an official who dispatches that woman on some kind of dirty business? How close is my guess? Just tell me!
(*The* wai *puts on the female mask and walks a few turns, then acts out knocking on a door. He drops on the floor and acts out a stomachache, miming rubbing. Then he takes off the female mask and puts it on the floor. He puts on the monk's cap, and drops down next to the female mask. He loosens his clothes and mimes rubbing the stomach*)
Liu Cui: This demonstration . . . it seems as if the woman had some sort of stomach trouble, and the monk is fussing over her. But what is the fuss leading up to? This is really tough to figure out.
[To the tune *Zheguiling*]

This shiny bald gourd, pressing on the girl in red,
Like two wooden sieves,
One pressing out the sauce, and,
Unavoidably, the more it presses, the more sauce it makes.
Naturally, the sieve urges, the husks speed,
How could one help but free oneself from the gibbon reins?[75]
He could not prevent the dragon from descending.[76]

---

74. The Prefect Yamen's Main Hall was plastered yellow.

75. The mind is like a gibbon that needs to be reined in by religious or moral teachings.

76. The dragon descending can stir up the clouds to cause rain; this of course suggests the euphemism of clouds and rain for sex.

The flame-scorched one asks the temple Vaira to further feed the fire with explosives,
Repentant, yet inviting a hungry ghost to come oversee her kitchen.[77]

Master, I can't guess the better part of this; please tell me clearly.
(*The* wai *vigorously grabs the* dan's *earring, then mimes a finger guessing game*)
Liu Cui: You're asking me to guess again.[78] All right, do your gestures once more.
(*The* wai *mimes pointing at the space between his eyebrows*)
Liu Cui: Again, a head.
(*The* wai *shakes his hand, then with angry eyes points again at the space between his eyebrows*)
Liu Cui: Not the head . . . then, it's anger.[79]
(*The* wai *puts on the female mask and points at the space between the brows*)
Liu Cui: Angry at this woman.
(*The* wai *takes off the female mask and exchanges it for the gauze cap. Again he points at the space between the brows*)
Liu Cui: Also angry at the official . . . but why?
(*The* wai *points at himself, then points to his own head*)
Liu Cui: Anger, again.
(*The* wai *shakes his hand*)
Liu Cui: It's not anger . . . then, it's the head.
(*The* wai *again uses his hands, as the first three times, to make the character* tai 胎)
Liu Cui: Reincarnation again, but I don't get it.
[To the tune *Jiang'er shui*]

He is not only angry at the black gauze guest,[80]
But also hates the glossy-haired girl.
Though he's angry at both, and wants to be reincarnated, how can one mortal frame split into two people's bodies?

---

77. Instead of remediating, the actions make the situation even worse.

78. He has used the homophones *huan* 環 for "earring" and *huan* 還 for "again." By grabbing her earring he draws her attention to the sound *huan*, for "doing over."

79. The word for anger, *nao* 惱, is homophonous with the word *nao* 腦 meaning "head" (brain) that could also be indicated by the monk's gestures.

80. Official.

How can one slingshot's pellet split to strike a pair of crows?
To whose house did the embryo go, in the end?
Further, the black gauzed guest is also a male's form,
Where can such a big round belly be found for all this?
This owing a debt, and repaying a debt,
Must be balanced in the woman's skirts and hairpins.

(*The* wai *takes a willow branch out of the altar vase, and again uses his hands to make the* tai 胎 (*"mortal frame," of* toutai) *character, then both hands emphatically beat the willow branch*)
(*The* dan *acts surprised*)
Liu Cui: Ah! It can't be that this reincarnation is in my body, is it? I've got it: it must be that I, too, am a part of this grievance and enmity!
[To the tune *Deshengling*]

How could I help it, as I plied this trade in a building of green,[81]
Unavoidably burying men in a mountain of rouge.
I remember that year I plucked some profit off Monk Huang,
I've only ever brought that single bridge down.
I did once let the little baldy penetrate my pants crotch:
On the ledger's face, a pair of names,
In the lotus wrap, a warm ooze.
As for sour flavors, very soon my melon-seed teeth will be nibbling on sour plum sauce.[82]
As for medicine, soon enough it will be carp broth and musk incense.[83]

(*The* wai *laughs and says*)
Moonlight: All for naught! A waste of energy! A waste of energy! (*In a loud voice he reads out*)

Red Lotus made a monkey out of me,
So I shall hide for a while in the spring in the skin of a green willow.

---

81. Signifying the Pleasure District, the equivalent of a "Red-Light District."
82. Thinking she is pregnant, she predicts that she will be craving sour foods soon.
83. It is unclear whether these are abortion aids (musk was an ingredient in a contraceptive) or certain types of food that aid in pregnancy or in a woman's recovery during the post-delivery confinement period (milky-colored fish soup is thought to encourage milk production).

Waves beat the duckweed, every one of them gets struck;
But my only fear is that when I return you will not recognize my self of old.

Ppft!

(*He spits a full mouth violently at the* dan)

Liu Cui (*shouting*): I get it! I get it![84] Had I known earlier that the lamp was a fire, the rice would have been cooked a long time ago.

(*She throws down her hair bun and takes off her women's clothes*)

(*The* wai *hurriedly assists her by retrieving from offstage a monk's hat and a coarse gown, and gives them to the* dan *to put on. The* wai *and* dan *kowtow to each other several dozen times*)

Liu Cui:

[To the tune *Yuanlinhao*]

Thank you, Elder Brother, for making this trip from the Western Heavens.
You used the golden needle to uncover the pupils on both my eyes,
Only pinch the tip of the *liuli*[85] lamp,
A little fire will cook the Yellow Millet,
A little fire will cook the Yellow Millet.[86]

[To the tune *Shou Jiangnan*]

Liu Cui: Elder Brother, what a separation of forty years it has been!
Moonlight: Younger Brother, it was only for a brief moment that you performed on this stage.
Both: We count this reincarnation of snatching an abode as lasting only long enough to burn an inch of incense.

---

84. Liu Cui's sudden realization comes here, either by the letter or by the loud sound from his spitting.

85. *Liuli* 琉璃 is a precious crystal-like substance that has more brilliance than glass, due to its higher lead content; here it is used as a metaphor for the mind.

86. An allusion to the Yellow Millet, or Handan, dream, which is the subject of a deliverance play ascribed to Ma Zhiyuan in the Yuan dynasty. The story takes place in the Tang dynasty and is the subject of Shen Jiji's 沈既濟 (ca. 740–ca. 780) tale "Record Within a Pillow" ("Zhenzhong ji" 枕中記). It is also the subject of Tang Xianzu's play, *The Handan Dream* (*Handan ji* 邯鄲記). See chapter 2, page 40, for a summary of this story.

Liu Cui: Elder Brother, at this time I would like to move on.

Moonlight: Younger Brother, at this time I am not moving on.

Both: Put going and not going together and they make one way.

Moonlight: In Little Lin'an, it shone through my black winds and waves.

Liu Cui: This Red Lotus showed up through my powders and rouge pastes.

Both: The womb of the Liu family leaked out my coiled blood and circumstances.

(*From here onward, the* wai *and* dan *sing together, alternating lines*)

Moonlight: Now I change the tune[87] and change costumes,

Liu Cui: Now I change the whore into a girl.

Moonlight: The little brother helped a tiger-ghost[88] trap a goat,

Liu Cui: The elder brother took the horse's reins and tied up the roebuck deer.

Moonlight: This tastes like sugarcane juice mixed with sugar,

Liu Cui: Those taste like garlic shoots pounded with ginger.

Moonlight: Now I flee the flaming road, pursuing the sun's early coolness,

Liu Cui: Then I cooked up crafty schemes, measuring the ocean in ounces.

Moonlight: Winnow and pound again the white millet and rice chaff,

Liu Cui: Do not laugh at Mister Guo's long sleeves.[89]

Moonlight: Ah-hah-hah! Emperor's and hegemon's strength,

---

87. *Gai qiang* 改腔 means to change the tune, or put a new face on it.

88. It was believed that a person killed by a tiger would become a wild (*chang* 倀) ghost that urges on other beasts to wildness and brutality. It is a metaphor used for an accomplice to acts of violence, or, in this case, revenge.

89. Mister Guo 郭郎 was a famous comic actor. Long sleeves are part of the actor's costume. That is, play-acting was used to sort out right from wrong, although the reader should remember that Moonlight ultimately had to resort to reading Yutong's letter out loud for Liu Cui to reach enlightenment.

Liu Cui: What a mixup! Even Ping and Liang's[90] valor was hidden.[91]

Moonlight: Heroes and leaders accept submission or bow to the strong,

Liu Cui: As for lucky and unlucky affairs, one mourns the deceased and celebrates a son's birth in turn.

Moonlight: Giving free rein to perversity by lusting after calamus[92] and eating scabs,[93]

Liu Cui: Managing merit by digging an embankment and rescuing those suffering famine.

Moonlight: Assisting at the palace with three bonds[94] to correct the Way.

Liu Cui: Illuminating a fine family reputation with gold tablets and jade pendants.

Moonlight: False immortals dressed in clouds at a moon door.[95]

Liu Cui: True companions: the mandarin ducks, the phoenix and its hen.

---

90. Chen Ping 陳平 (d. 178 BCE) and Zhang Liang 張良 (262–189 BCE) were among Liu Bang's most valued retainers and strategists, aiding him in the establishment of the Han before retiring into Daoist reclusion. Zhang Liang advised Liu Bang and protected him from the hegemon king Xiang Yu 項羽 (232–202 BCE) by allying with his uncle, Xiang Bo 項伯 (fl. 209–202 BCE). Together with Chen Ping, he advised Liu in his assault on Xiang Yu at Chu and helped Liu Bang win the five-year war.

91. The original line translates approximately as "like a horse, hidden." This line could refer to the fact that Chen and Ping were good suppliers for Liu Bang whereas Xiang Yu did not, at the end, have even a good horse to rely upon. In his notes to this section, Zhou Zhongming notes that the horse's penis is retractable, which is also the case with the Buddha's penis. The interpretation, if read in this way, would be that Ping and Liang's valor and wisdom were hidden, though present.

92. This plant, *chang* 菖, is from the Acoraceae family and was long associated with male love, perhaps because of the phallic shape of its leaves and reed. The rhizome was used as an aphrodisiac.

93. Liu Yong 劉邕 of the Southern Song (420–79) was so dissolute that he enjoyed eating the scabs that formed on skin ulcers, claiming that they tasted like abalone. He was said to have liked the taste so much that he would routinely have the men under his command whipped, so that he could partake of the scabs that formed on their body.

94. The three bonds are of retainer to his lord, of child to father, and of wife to husband.

95. A large hole in a grotto. These references to cloud garments and grottoes indicate the life of a recluse.

Moonlight: The ruined wayfarers strike the gong and beat the clappers,

Liu Cui: The ascetics chop wood and hull grain.

Moonlight: In this one moment: ten thousand affairs, a hundred anxieties,

Liu Cui: All stand in for Impermanence's pasteboard clothes.[96]

Moonlight: Nimble and agile knives of wit clash like spears and compete in flashes,

Liu Cui: Blunt roots and shoots are like the dung beetle trying to jump across the wall.

Moonlight: With stomach pains, the false-widow cherry apple,

Liu Cui: Avenging enmity, the frosty colored crane.[97]

Moonlight: How many magpies can fill up this lake with their load?[98]

Liu Cui: Almost like a bustard roosting on the mulberry trees at this hall.[99]

Moonlight: All spent is the chatter and dissembling, and seductive ways,

Liu Cui: Just now was accomplished a roiling broth to smelt.

Moonlight: The two brothers going together like a pair of geese,

Liu Cui: Two old bodhidharmas take their provisions and cross the river.[100]

Moonlight: The heels of our feet on rushes and reeds, their leaves yellow,[101]

---

96. Impermanence, *wuchang* 無常, is the Chinese translation of Anitya, the notion that everything is constantly in flux and only temporary. Pasteboard, *bei* 褙, is a kind of material made from gluing layers of cloth or paper together. It was used to form the base of shoe soles. Drama costumes, props, and puppets would likely have also been constructed of pasteboard.

97. The frosty colored crane alludes to the color of monks' robes. The couplet here refers to Red Lotus' (the cherry apple) seduction and Yutong's (the monk dressed in robes the color of the frosty crane) vengeance plot.

98. A happy portent.

99. An unlucky omen.

100. It is said that when the bodhidharma did not manage to win over the emperor, he packed dry provisions and took a boat from Jinling to Luoyang.

101. In one version of the bodhidharma's journey, he rides on leaves to cross the water to Luoyang.

Liu Cui: In a moment we have reached our old home in the west.
Moonlight: As we did before, we return to our Buddha forms,
Liu Cui: Looking to treasured pennants on the raft of enlightenment.
Moonlight: We have cast away a sack of stolen property,
Liu Cui: Exchanged it for cleaned entrails that give off light.
Together: Ai! Now we place together the palms of our hands,
And report on our mission at our Teacher's cell.

(*A gong and drums are sounded from offstage, and Liu Cui and Moonlight quickly exit*)

In Great Lin'an one third of an official,
Old Yutong's single strand of self-image.
Making use of Red Lotus: a couple of dew and water:
Delivering Liu Cui: the Moonlight Monk.

III

The Female Mulan Joins the Army in Place of Her Father

Act I

(*A* dan *playing the girl Mulan enters*)

My surname is Hua, my given name is Mulan. Generations ago, in the time of the Western Han, my ancestors, being among those descended from good families of the six prefectures,[1] settled here in Wei.[2] My father's name is Hu, and he is also called Sangzhi. All his life he has been skilled both in literature and martial arts, and he was at one time a famous "commander of a thousand." He married my mother, of the Jia family, and then she gave birth to me.[3] This year, I am barely seventeen years old. Neither my little sister, Munan, nor my little brother, Yao'er, has reached adulthood. Yesterday I heard that Black Mountain's bandit chief, Leopard Skin, led hundreds of thousands of men on horseback in rebellion and is now calling himself king. Our great Wei's Tuoba Khan[4] has sent down to our district, calling up troops. The army rolls have been

---

1. The six prefectures are Longxi 隴西, Tianshui 天水, Anding 安定, Beidi 北地, Shangjun 上郡, and Xihe 西河, located in present day Gansu, Inner Mongolia.

2. The Wei district was founded in 195 BCE by Han Gaozu, in the Ye jurisdiction, in what is now southwest Linzhang in modern-day Hebei.

3. That is to say, Mulan is the daughter of her father's first wife, not of a concubine.

4. The version of this story from the *Historical Romance of the Sui and Tang* places it in the Tang dynasty, but Xu Wei sets it in a non-Han setting, during the Northern Wei period. The rulers during this period were from the Tuoba 拓跋 family, which was ethnically part of the non-Han nomadic Xianbei 鮮卑 tribe federation. They used their word "khan" for Emperor, and Mulan is here referring to the emperor when she references the Tuoba Khan.

arriving, twelve in a row, scroll after scroll bearing my father's name. As I think of it, not only is my father old, but he has no one in the next generation who can carry on for him. When I was young, I was the strong one, and had a bit of smarts, too, so I followed my father in studying books and martial arts. Now this is my opportunity to repay him. Just take a look at what it says in the books about Qin Xiu[5] and Tiying,[6] one of them willing to die, the other one willing to go to court to be a slave, both for their fathers' sake. But, weren't those two still putting their buns in hairnets instead of wearing male caps? Didn't they go on wearing their girls' skirts and jackets? There's just one thing: if I were to stand in for him, I must have a new set of a bow, horse, spear, sword, gown, and boots—all prepared from scratch. And I'd better go over my martial arts once or twice. Only then can I tell my family about my aim to take dad's place. They will know that there is no alternative and certainly should not take pains to keep me. Where is Xiaohuan?
(*A* chou *playing Xiaohuan enters*)
Xiaohuan! Don't let Father and Mother find out: we're going shopping!
(*Mulan turns offstage and mimes buying things*)
(*She comes back leading Xiaohuan, carrying her packages*)
Xiaohuan: Miss, where should I tie up the horse?
Mulan: Stable it at Wang San's home, across the way!
[To the tune *Dianjiangchun*]

> The Xiu girl braved death,
> Tiying faced judgment,
> They were both my female companions, in skirts and hairpins.
> Standing on the ground, holding up heaven,
> What's all this about male heroes?

---

5. Qin Xiu 秦休 is a girl who avenges the death of her father by killing his murderers in the marketplace. She is incarcerated and sentenced to death, although she is later pardoned.

6. Tiying 缇萦 of the Western Han. Her father was convicted of embezzling government funds and sent to the capital for death by mutilation. Tiying submitted a memorial to Han Wendi 漢文帝 (Emperor Wen of the Han dynasty, 180–157 BCE), begging him to allow her to be her father's substitute and pay off his debt as a slave at court. Moved by her devotion, Wendi abolished corporal punishment, which was a significant reform of existing Qin law.

[To the tune *Hunjianglong*]

Army scrolls by the dozen,
Roll upon roll, scroll upon scroll, listing my father's name.
He is already aged,
And plagued by debilitating illness.
To think, how
In earlier times,
He fit an arrow to hunt the hawk, piercing it with its white-feathered shaft.
Now, ah,
He leans on a staff to watch the wild geese, counting them against the blue sky.
He calls in the chickens and feeds the dog,
He stays in the village and minds the fields.
For training falcons, his wrist is too weak,
For chasing hares, his back is too bent.
He leads us sisters by the hand,
He combs the hair of us little girls.
Seeing us in front of mirrors touching up rouge, he laughs out loud,
Hearing about swords raised in battle, his brow furrows in frowns.
With a long sigh, he says:
"For us parents, North Mang Hill[7] is rearing,
For our girls, the 'Bared Belly of the East' has yet to come."[8]

---

7. This hill north of Luoyang in Henan province is the burial site of royals from the Eastern Han and the Wei, and it thus functions as a metaphor for death.

8. The "bared belly" refers to an anecdote about the famous calligrapher of the Eastern Jin dynasty (217–420) Wang Xizhi 王羲之 (303–61). In the *New Account of Tales of the World* it is recorded: "While [Chih Jian] was in [Jingkou (Jiangsu)], he dispatched a retainer with a letter to Chancellor Wang [D]ao, requesting a son-in-law from among Wang's nephews for his daughter, [Chih Xuan]. The chancellor said to [Chih]'s messenger, 'Go to the eastern apartment and follow your own wishes in making a choice.' After the retainer had returned, he reported to Ch'ih, 'The sons of the Wang family are all of them admirable, each in his own way. When they heard that someone had come to spy out a son-in-law, they all conducted themselves with circumspection. There was just one son, who was lying sprawled out on the eastern bed with his belly exposed, as though he hadn't heard about it.' [Chih] said, 'He's just the one I want.' When he went to visit him, it turned out to be Wang [Xizhi]. So he gave his daughter to him in marriage." Liu I-ch'ing, *Shih-shuo Hsin-Yü*, 197.

> If I want to practice martial arts, I've got to first let out these feet[9] and change to this pair of boots. Only then will I manage!

(*As she changes footwear, she acts out pain*)
[To the tune *Youhulu*]

> Just-removed, the half-folded "tiny ripple socks" bindings,[10]
> How it hurts!
> It took me several years to bind together these phoenix-head points.[11]
> Now I quickly turn them into floating boats.[12]
> How will I now fill up these boots?

When I return, I'll still want to get married. So what can I do? Well, no need to mope about that! My family has a method for shrinking golden lotuses:[13] just take a bit of saltpeter, boil it, and use it to wash the feet. In this way, we make them even smaller!
(*Sings*)

> Take the raw saltpeter,
> Boil it so it is white like snowflakes,
> And in a moment, you've shrunk them back into golden lotus petals.

In these boots, I'm pretty much steady. Now I'll put on these clothes!
(*She changes clothes and puts on a man's felt military cap*)
[To the tune *Tianxiale*]

> Dressed up, I daresay I *am* a senior campaigning officer,
> Among their ranks, it will be easy to hide.
> Hook the belt tightly—
> I shall hang my sword on the plates,
> The chain mail is pliant and supple,
> Its quilted lining is comfy and warm.
> I'll bring this armor back, and it will still be good enough for my brother to wear.

---

9. She is referring to her bound feet—an anachronism, as discussed in ch. 3.
10. "Tiny ripple socks" is a metaphor for bound feet.
11. "Phoenix-head points" is another metaphor for bound feet.
12. That is, her feet have become big and flat.
13. "Golden lotuses" is another metaphor for bound feet.

Clothes and boots are all changed, and now I've got to practice some swordplay for a bit.[14]
(*Performs swordplay*)
[To the tune *Nezhaling*]

This sword!
How long it's been since I've drawn it,
I've got to say, I thought it wouldn't be easy.
But hoisting it up and giving it a whirl,
Well, it's just like old times.
Why aren't my hands sore with pain,
Used as they are to threading the loom's shuttle?
The girl of Yue still needed the instruction of the white ape.[15]
If I take dad's place in the army, how can I not grasp this green serpent[16]
So fast that round my red skirt I grip this frosty blast![17]

Now I am finished performing with the sword, I had better practice the lance.
(*Acts out practicing with lance*)
[To *Queta zhi*]

Whetted until fresh as a leaf of green,
Fixed onto this fine wood staff,
It is as good as any number of rounds of Pear Petals Dancing in Moonlight,
And Ten-Foot Snake Creeping.[18]

---

14. The earliest printed edition of the play includes this additional note that does not appear in later editions: "Let the changing of clothes and shoes be performed slowly for viewing" 衣鞋都換了試演一會看. See Xu Wei, *Sishengyuan*, in *Guben xiqu congkan chuji* 古本戲曲叢刊初集, vol. 77 (Shanghai: Shanghai yinshuguan, 1954), 30.

15. A legendary heroine, the girl of Yue was a peasant girl who was taught swordplay by a white ape from the mountains.

16. The green serpent refers to her sword.

17. Her swordplay will be so swift that the glints around her will blend into a whirl of frost-like silver, set off by her red skirt.

18. These are names of various fighting methods involving lances.

Wait, wait, until my feet have unfolded,
And with big steps I can stride again.
And then, with one turn of my body, I will push over the tip of Black Mountain.

Ah, arrows! I can't practice them here. I'll just have to try pulling on the bowstring. I will see how my way with the bow and string compares to the old days.
(*Acts pulling on bow*)
[To the tune *Jishengcao*]

The thumb ring is thin,
The frame's ends are rounded.
With one fist closed tight, I grasp the "Yellow Snake."[19]
For a single arrow, I plucked a full eagle's tail.[20]
One outstretched arm holds forth with the strength of the white ape.
Singing drawn-out songs, the hero enters the pass,
Then, only then, shall I reveal my Tianshan arrow.[21]

As for riding a donkey or a horse, it is familiar enough to me. Even so, I've got to get the posture of jumping astride a saddle.
(*She assumes the posture of sitting astride a horse*)
[To the tune *Yao*]

Embroidered front and back, my horse-riding vest,
Inlaid with coral, my horse-urging whip.
This costume is not army issue,
So with these

---

19. The character *cuan* 攛 used for grasping the "Yellow Snake" bow is the same character used for casting a shuttle (as in weaving), subtly underscoring how textile arts have been exchanged for martial arts.

20. Arrows were traditionally made with eagle tail feathers as fletchings.

21. During Tang Taizong's 唐太宗 (599–649) reign, one of his generals, Xue Rengui 薛仁貴 (614–83), was under siege on Tian Mountain (Tianshan). He was challenged to fight ten members of the opposing Tiele cavalry. The three arrows he shot killed their three top generals, and this show of skill caused the rest of the Tiele to surrender.

Two leather reins I'll firmly work my *qilin*,[22]
Through millions of mountains I'll catch alive a monkey companion,[23]
With this one bit and bridle, I'll trample out the foxes from their den.
I will only reveal that a beautiful girl was the one in the saddle when I return home.[24]
Everyone shall call me a great hero!

Everything is taken care of now. I have to call Father and Mother to come out so I can talk to them.
(*Calling backstage, she asks her father, mother, younger brother, and sister to come out*)
(*A* wai *playing her father, a* lao *playing her mother, a* xiaosheng *playing her brother, and a* tie *playing her younger sister enter. They are surprised to see her.*)
Mother: Child! Why are you dressed up like this today? You have unbound your feet! How strange! How strange!
Mulan: Mother! Father is supposed to join the army, how can he not go?
Mother: He is old already, how *can* he go?
Mulan: Could little sister or little brother be made to go?
Mother: You're mad! How can two as young as they are be able to go?
Mulan: Things being that way, then no one will go.
Mother: That's precisely why we are at our wits' end. Your father is ready to hang himself from worry!
Mulan: As I am now . . . would I be able to go?
Mother: Child! I know well your abilities. You could indeed go. (*Crying*) It's just that . . . how can two old folks like us bear to let you go? And

---

22. *Qilin* refers to her horse. The mythical *qilin* 麒麟 (also known by its Japanese name *kirin*) is sometimes translated as the "unicorn of China," as it is in Jorge Luis Borges' *Book of Imaginary Beings*, perhaps because it is thought to have horns. The deer-like creature has a light and fleet tread. The *qilin* was later identified with the giraffes brought back to China by Zheng He (鄭和 1371–1433) from Africa.

23. It was thought that exhausted horses, if allowed to sleep for too long, would become severely ill; therefore, the horse's keeper would house a monkey in the stables with the horse to distract it and keep it awake, making a monkey part of one's riding paraphernalia.

24. The Chinese lines play on words and sounds here. The word for "beautiful," which is a feminine adjective (*jiao* 嬌), sounds similar (indicated by the shared sound radical) to the word for saddle (*jiao* 驕).

another thing, if you go, you are still, after all, a girl. Through a thousand provinces and a million miles, you'll be marching with men and keeping their constant company—breakfasting together in the morning, lodging together at night—how can you keep your you-know-what from showing? Don't you think that this will create problems?

Mulan: Mom! Don't worry. I will return to you as a virgin.

(*They weep together*)

(*Two soldiers enter*)

Soldier: Is this the Hua residence?

Father: Why do you ask?

Soldier: We are also recruits. Our home office said that in this ward there is a Hua Hu; he told us to come and hasten him along so that we can all travel together, so hurry up.

Mulan: Brothers, sit for a while! Allow me to prepare a few things, and then I'll be all set to go. Xiaohuan, go fetch my horse!

(*Mulan readies her military equipment*)

(*Everyone watches*)

Parents: Fine horse! Fine arms! You'll certainly be a success, returning to hurrahs. No matter what, you must regularly write to us, and spare us both from worrying. Now, we'd like to drink a toast to you, but things are so helter-skelter. I've sent Xiaohuan to go buy you some hot buns. Bring them with you for munching on the road. I'll put these needles and thread in your bag, and you'll be prepared if you get a rip in your clothes, or a break in your armor!

Two soldiers: Hurry up!

(*Family members weep in parting, then exit the stage*)

(*Mulan goes to meet the soldiers*)

Mulan: Elder brothers, thanks for waiting such a long while! Let's mount our horses and be off.

(*The soldiers secretly confer*)

Soldiers: This Hua Hu doesn't look bad at all. He doesn't look like a senior officer, but he'd be a nice morsel. Tomorrow we can take him to meet our needs.

Mulan:

[To the tune *Yao*]

> I'm no further from home than a shot from an arrow,
> But I hear the sputtering Yellow River's flow.

The horse lowers his head, and I point far off to where the goose drops into the reeds.
My iron armor is unlined—suddenly there appears a fleck of frosty crystal,
From the intensity of the sorrows of parting, my peach-flower face has become drawn.
If for a moment I think of these tightly-stitched clothes[25]
Two rows of tears drip from their pearl strings.

[To the tune *Liu yao xu*]

Ai!
The smell of face powder still lingers on my face,
I try to wash off the mark left by my hair ornament.
It still isn't gone even after a whole day.
But I have been twisted into a veritable man, and
In great haste, I mount my horse, astride the saddle.
In my boots are planted a golden whip,
My feet push against the bronze rings,
Dropping the needle's point,
I've slung on my strung bow.[26]
Before I meet anyone, I first prepare to bow to him with a bend at the waist,
No more of curtsying like I did in women's skirts.
I don't fear the mandarin ducks becoming a pair and asking for marriage,
I'm only concerned about the bother of needing to pee and poop.[27]
I need a ruse.

---

25. An allusion to Meng Jiao's 孟郊 (751–814) "Song for the traveler" (*Youzi yin* 遊子吟): "慈母手中線，遊子身上衣。臨行密密縫，意恐遲遲歸。誰言寸草心，報得三春暉。" A. C. Graham translates this classic exposition on a mother's love in *Poems of the Late T'ang* (New York: New York Review Books Classics: 2008), 63: "The thread in the hand of a kind mother / Is the coat on the wanderer's back. / Before he left she stitched it close / In secret fear that he would be slow to return. / Who will say that the inch of grass in his heart / Is gratitude enough for all the sunshine of spring?"

26. Here Mulan observes that she is replacing one kind of "needle" and "thread" for another.

27. This is because of the risk of revealing her sex to fellow soldiers.

[To the tune *Yao*]

Brothers! While we've been talking,
And without urging the whip,
We've crossed ten thousand green mountains like dots, and
Neared the "Five Zhang"[28] Red Pass.
Where the sunlight rests on the city wall's parapets,
Several banner flags are raised.
In tattered caps and worn shirts,
They are not very intimidating,
This must be an officer of the guard!
Is he not like us, one of the same kind?
Relying on our youth,
Relying on Blue Heaven,
Not fearing hardship,
Not loving money,
Yet our portraits shall hang up in Lingyan Tower.[29]
Isn't this better than scheming to rob someone of his command, stealing another's glory?
It is worth much more than wealth and position, which is after all dispensed by Heaven.
Even if the crimes of the Black Mountain bandits are broad as heaven.
They began as nothing more than mere thoughts in the mind.

(*Acts out asking*)
[To the tune *Yao*]

Where are we now?
Feet and inches away, but
Seeming halfway to heaven,
The long slope ahead winds like a coiled snake.
It must be that the commander-in-chief is seated atop the platform,

28. A *zhang* is a Chinese measurement equivalent to 11 feet 9 inches.

29. This refers to portraits commissioned by Tang Taizong of twenty-four meritorious officials. Here, Mulan says that she and the other soldiers are not looking for glory, but only want to serve their ruler.

A little Tiying is about to meet a great officer.
By now my heart is shaken,
In time I will get comfortable with a warrior's heart.
Commanding a thousand men and horses,
I will sweep across Black Mountain in battle,
I shall sweep away the traces of old rouge from my flower cheeks
with my sable cap.

All: While we were talking, we happily arrived at the commander's camp. We will first set up camp, and tomorrow we will all go together to see our leader. (*Exeunt*)

Act II

(*A* wai *playing the commanding general enters*)
Xin Ping: I am the "Subduing the East" commanding general, Xin Ping. Our ruler ordered me to lead 100,000 brave troops to kill the Black Mountain bandits, and I have been victorious in every battle. But we can't do anything about the chief bandit, Leopard Skin, who has hidden himself behind high, steep cliffs, and won't come out from behind their walls. The other day, three thousand braves arrived, and I will take their names and try out their martial skills. There is a Hua Hu who seems capable. Now I am about to roll out this catapult, to fire on those steep cliffs above. This bandit chief will have no choice but to come out and fight. When the troops are drawn up against each other in battle formation, I will have Hua Hu cut through in the middle on horseback, and we are bound to capture Leopard Skin at the first roll of the drum. Where are Hua Hu and the new soldiers?
(*Mulan and the group of soldiers enter, and kneel*)
Xin Ping: Hua Hu! Tomorrow I will attack Black Mountain. After two rounds of battle, you have to give your horse his head, and dash into the troops. You will be sure to capture the bandit chief alive. Then I will recommend you to the emperor, and your reward will be generous. If you disobey, you will be beheaded.
Mulan: Yes, sir!
Xin Ping: Then let's raise the troops and go forth!
[To the tune *Qingjiang yin*]

Black Mountain's little bandit is truly shortsighted!
He continues to hide himself—what can he accomplish?

When the flower opens, butterflies fill the branches.
When the tree falls, the monkeys scatter off.
The more you hide, the more I'll seek the sight of you.

Chorus of soldiers:
[To the same tune]

Black Mountain's little bandit is truly farsighted!
Left or right, he's used to defeat.
All day long he feels no shame,
And at all three meals, gobbles his fill.
The more you seek him out, the more he hides and watches what will happen.

Your Lordship! We have arrived at the bandit hideout.
Xin Ping: Tell the troops to raise the catapult and fire!
(*They fire the catapult. A* jing *playing the bandit chief thrice comes out in front of the ranks to fight. Mulan rushes out in front and captures him*)
Xin Ping: Call back the troops to return!
Chorus of soldiers:
[To the same tune]

Our great leader is truly farsighted,
Only after careful calculation did he act.
This bandit was a false case of:
When the flower opens, butterflies fill the branches,
In truth, he was like:
When the tree falls, the monkeys scatter off.
Returning with a victory song, we share in his pride.

Xin Ping:
[To the same tune]

My gathered soldiers,
The great sight that you witnessed a moment ago,
Means we'll have an extra string of cash every month.
No more of
"All day long he feels no shame";
I'll make sure
Each man shall have three meals to gobble his fill.
When it comes to weighing merits, Hua Hu claims the greatest share of credit.

(*Arriving at the capital, there is the sound of bells and drums. They act out an audience at court*)

Xin Ping (*memorializing to the throne*): The humble "Subduing the East" commanding general, Xin Ping, respectfully reports: By Your Majesty's grace, we were sent to march against the bandits from Black Mountain, and we have fully pacified them. The Bandit Chief, Leopard Skin, was indeed captured by my soldier, Hua Hu, in front of the ranks; he has been brought here for your disposal. As for the other worthy men, I have put down their names on the registers and made distinctions according to their merits, and I hope you will make your decisions accordingly.

(*A* chou *playing a eunuch presents the khan's edict*)

Eunuch: His Majesty commands: you have gained great merit in eradicating the bandits, and we have specially enfeoffed you as the marquis of Changshan.[30] We present you with a tablet of office for perpetual inheritance. Hua Hu shall be the secretarial court officer in the Imperial Secretariat. Bearing in mind his many years of laboring in military service, we order that he return home posthaste to rest for three months, then await his new appointment. He will be given official cap and girdle, and, following this, he and Xin Ping may give thanks for our imperial grace. Leopard Skin will be beheaded. As for the other worthies, we will act once their cases are verified.

(*Mulan puts on official cap and girdle*)

(*Xin Ping and Mulan give thanks, and receive the decree. The* chou *exits*)

Mulan: I, Hua Hu, am grateful to Your Honor for raising me up with this recommendation to receive imperial glory and grace beyond my due. But as I am anxious about visiting my parents, I cannot go to your office to give thanks. Allow me first to kowtow to you here, and allow me to one day repay you as a dog or horse would its master.

Xin Ping: What you achieved you did on your own. What does it have to do with me? Because we are in such haste, I, too, cannot send you gifts to congratulate you properly.

Mulan: Today you have helped me greatly.

Xin Ping: I have done no more than lend wind to the sail of a boat going along with the current.

(*Xin Ping exits first*)

---

30. In other words, Xin Ping has been given a title and stipend.

Mulan:
[To the same tune]

> Everything is—when I think of it—an illusion, after all;
> Why should I boast that I succeeded in this scheme?
> The "I" who killed bandits, and captured their king,
> Was a female officer who switched to a man.
> After all, these successes did not cost me a drop of sweat.

(*Two soldiers hurry onstage*)
Soldiers: Sir Hua! How well you have done!
Mulan: Why are you two so late in coming?
Soldiers: We were awaiting successful investigations, and now we have acquired centurion positions. We hope that you will look out for us!
Mulan: Happy news! Let us travel together.
Soldiers:
[To the same tune]

> When you think of it, Big Brother Hua is really queer!
> Whether he's pissing or shitting, he won't allow anyone to watch.
> (*The companions say to each other*)
> That's a mark of gentility for you!
> If Heaven gives birth to a worthy man,
> It brings luck to his three companions.
> The two of us, with offices puny as sesame seeds, raised our eyes to take a look at him.

Mulan:
[To the same tune]

> How am I, Hua Hu, so queer?
> Of queer things, I only know of one!
> Right next to my home, in a temple,
> There is a *jingang* statue whose face
> Suddenly changed into Chang E's!

Two soldiers: Truly?
Mulan: If you don't believe me, when we reach my home I will take you to see it.
(*Exit*)
(*Father, mother, and Xiaohuan enter*)

Parents: Since the time our child Mulan left, there hasn't been a bit of news. The good thing is that during the New Year's festival, Minister Wang's son, Mr. Wang, was impressed that Mulan was so filial as to take her father's place, and sought to be affianced with her. Who would have thought that Mr. Wang would go on to succeed in the "Wise and Good" and "Literary Scholarship" categories?[31] Now he is at home, visiting his parents with the title "Collator of the Imperial Library." Mulan, too, has been gone for more than ten years. With the two of them each grown into man and woman, and of marrying age, this is no light matter! But how do we get her to come home, so that we can conclude this betrothal and depart this world with a clear conscience?

(*Two soldiers enter with Mulan*)

Soldiers: Sir Hua! We have arrived at your home! We shall take our leave and go!

Mulan: What kind of talk is this? Please have a seat in the left chamber, and wait until noon to continue on.

(*The soldiers assent, stepping aside so as to indicate leaving room*)

(*Mulan advances and sees her parents*)

Mother (*to maid*): Girl! Quick, call Second Sister and Third Brother to come out, tell them that Big Sister has come back!

(*The maid calls for younger sister and brother, who enter*)

(*Mulan, facing her mirror, changes back to female makeup, then bows in greeting to her parents*)

Mulan:

[To the tune *Shua haier*]

> Your child left, cutting down bandits with martial sword,
> Like the wind scattering clouds, with a blow;
> I captured the bandit chief alive, then left the capital:
> This black gauze cap came from the khan himself.

Mother: What is your position?

Mulan:

> It is "Secretarial Gentleman." Mother!
> I have been bound up tightly so many years in a hall with the nightly
> rain of pear-blossom petals,

---

31. The modern equivalents to these categories would be "Civics" and "Composition."

But I return to you
As before, a little box of dogwood bud in spring winds.[32]
How could I shame my parents?

Mother: My child, to think of what you have done!
Mulan:

I don't mean to boast that
True gold withstands fire,
Or that it can compare to
The red lotus emerging from the mud.[33]

(*She bows in greeting to her brother and sister*)
[To the tune *Er sha*]

When I left, you were just a little thing,
When I return, your shoulders reach mine.
It seems you are now quite ready to go to battle on Father's behalf.
Sister,
Thank you for supporting our two elderly parents,
Brother,
All of our generation should consider you its number one.
When I left the city,
I hadn't the time to buy perfume or handkerchiefs.[34]
For sister:
just a package of face powder,
And for brother:
two boxes of pine soot ink.

(*The two soldiers hurry on*)
Soldiers: Sir Hua! You were a girl all along! We lived with you for a dozen years, and none of us found you out. So! It turns out that this was the riddle of the *jingang* who turned into Chang'e that you spoke of on the road! You are a great wonder for all time, and your story will be known the world over. Everyone will remember you!

---

32. That is, she is still a virgin after all these years.

33. The lotus is prized because it blooms pure and unblemished, although it grows in the mud.

34. Other editions have handkerchief (*juan* 絹) or, alternatively, light silks, as fan (*shan* 扇).

Mulan:
[To the tune *San sha*]

It is said that between men and women, even their mats shouldn't touch,
But when there's no other option, one must use expedient means.
The clever blossom hid securely from the butterflies' ardor.
In Father's place, I, ah!
Was like the younger brother-in-law for whom
It's impossible to let go of his sister-in-law's hand, to save her from drowning.[35]
Towards you men, ah!
You were like fire lusting for dry tinder, how could I but deceive you?
I was like the heron, which is seen only when it soars from the snow.[36]
All in all,
We were together for ten years,
That makes for
Half of a marriage.

Soldiers: With them so busy, we should make ourselves scarce. So we won't take our leave, but just go!
(*Exit*)
Xiaohuan: Mr. Wang has come to offer congratulations.
Mother: This is the son-in-law that I wrote to you about the other day. I was about to invite him over, so that you could have your wedding. What perfect timing!
(*A* sheng *in official cap and girdle playing* Mr. Wang *enters and greets them*)
Mother: Mr. Wang . . . please hold your greetings! I have just looked at the almanac for an auspicious day. You two are as old as cast bronze

35. Mulan refers to Mencius' clarification that while men and women should keep a distance from each other, extreme circumstances (such as a woman's risk of drowning!) could cause a man to extend his hand to even his sister-in-law: "Man and woman should not touch each other, but in stretching out a helping hand to the drowning sister-in-law one uses one's discretion." See Book IV, Part A, 17 in D.C. Lau's translation of *Mencius* (London: Penguin, 1970), 124.

36. See note 29 in the translation of *Mi Heng*.

elephants,[37] so let's make ourselves a family today! Quick, quick, bow and greet each other!

(*Mulan turns her back, shyly*)

Mother: Child! After a dozen years as an officer, what do you need to be shy about?

(*Mulan turns and bows*)

Mulan:

[To the tune *Si sha*]

Barely reunited with my family,
How could I have dreamed of a wedding?
Now meeting this way, I can't help but perspire with embarrassment.
I've long known of your honors in literature at court,
I'm ashamed that I've returned from the din of battle.
I cannot pair with this "Eastern Couch" mate.
I shall serve you
As the Divine Immortal flutist,[38]
Don't fear that I'll
Be like Sun Quan's little sister.[39]

[To the tune *Wei*]

I was a woman till I was seventeen,
Was a man another twelve years.
I passed under thousands of glances,
Who among them could tell cock from hen?

---

37. This is a contemporary turn of phrase indicating that they are already past marrying age.

38. Xiao Shi 簫史 (the Divine Immortal) is a legendary figure skilled in playing the *xiao* (簫) flute, she is said to be able to imitate a phoenix cry on the flute. Nongyu 弄玉, the daughter of Duke Mu of Qin 秦穆公, was also a skilled *xiao* player, and the duke gave his daughter in marriage to Xiao Shi. One morning, Nongyu mounted a phoenix and Xiao Shi mounted a dragon, and they flew off together.

39. During the Three Kingdoms period, the ruler of the Wu kingdom, Sun Quan, had a younger sister who was skilled in martial arts. She was given by Sun Quan to Liu Bei in marriage. On their wedding night, Liu Bei found their bridal chamber filled with weapons, which he asked her to remove. In spite of this rocky beginning, the two had a loving marriage.

Only now do I believe that to tell cock from hen, you can't rely on
your eyes.
Who was it that really occupied Black Mountain top?
The girl Mulan went to war for her Pa.
The affairs of the world are all such a mess,
Muddling boy and girl is what this play did best.

IV

The Girl Graduate Rejects the Female Phoenix and Gains the Male Phoenix

Act I

(*A* dan *enters*)
[To the tune *Nü guanzi*]

A girl's pointed headscarf, I, since sending off my parents, whose flames were snuffed,[1]
Have long been a tenant in an empty valley.
Bright pearls were entrusted to a servant to sell, so as to repair this thatched hut.
Auntie Huang and I spent these nights together,
For so many nights, with a single lamp,
We sped on the years, eating rice porridge.
Wasting away, this jade-like body,
Colorful sleeves, in winter's cold,
At dusk I lean against the bamboo.[2]

---

1. Huang Chuntao identifies herself not as a girl, but rather by a girl's costume.
2. This song alludes to a poem by Du Fu 杜甫 (712–70) entitled "Beautiful Lady" (*jiaren* 佳人), about a woman who has fallen upon hard times and been cast off by her husband. This aria borrows images of the empty valley, selling pearls for thatch, and the final couplet from "Beautiful Lady." Widely anthologized, the poem is the tenth poem in the collection *Three Hundred Chinese Poems* (*Tangshi sanbai shou* 唐詩三百首). *Tang shi sanbai shou xin zhu* 唐詩三百首新注. Ann. Jin Xingyao 金性堯 (Shanghai: Shanghai guji chubanshe, 1980).

[Recites, to *Jiangchengzi*]

I still vaguely recall my mother and father.
They loved me like a pearl in the hand;
Since those two elms were ravaged by the fifth watch's winds,
Now who will care for the bereft cherry apple tree?
Red azalea!
Since I was born, I have been wrongly saddled with a daughter's chores.
When it comes to talent and learning,
I aim to grasp the dragon of success.
I would definitely have my name on the golden plaque, placed at the top among gentlemen in my class.
As for things like getting married,
That can be dealt with later.

I am surnamed Huang, my milk name is Chuntao.[3] I am Prefect Huang's daughter, and my family had lived in Western Shu's Linqiong for generations.[4] When I was twelve years old, my father and mother died, one after the other; and I had no brothers, nor had I been betrothed to any family. On top of that, when my father was alive, he served in office in an upright and diligent manner, and thus his official purse was thoroughly empty. I am but a woman, lacking any kind of trade, and over time fell into dire straits. Along with my old wet nurse, Auntie Huang, we leased, temporarily, a small room on Mount Huacheng in the western township of our district. Now, before we knew it, eight years have passed. Fortunately, in this place the valleys are dark and deep, and the wooded peaks are elegant and refined, imposingly rising beyond my study table's window. The silence helped my soul pinch the brush tip: I mastered writing, painting, playing the *qin*, and chess, and also devoted myself to drawing *luan*[5] birds and doing embroidery.

---

3. Name given by a family to the baby until a formal name is chosen.

4. Lingqiong is in Sichuan, near Chengdu. Shu 蜀 is the ancient name for Sichuan.

5. The *luan* (鸞) is a divine bird of the phoenix type, second only to the *feng* bird and the *fenghuang* bird (the male and female phoenixes referenced in the title). See Richard Strassberg, ed. and trans., *A Chinese Bestiary: Strange Creatures from the Guideways through Mountains and Seas* (*Shanhai jing*) (Berkeley: University of California Press, 2002), 102.

Although I had to sell all the pearls, we still have enough to keep these rooms in good repair. Being paid for our labor according to how much thread we spin, we have had enough food to survive. But if I carefully consider our situation, it is not a long-term strategy. It may be sufficient for the present, but it is only just scraping by. Ai! I don't mean to brag about myself, but if I, Chuntao, could change my costume for just one battle, I could easily take first place in the examinations. Then my "eating emoluments" would be a thousand *zhong* of grain, and that would be much better than our present willfull starvation. Thus, one must act as the younger brother helping his sister-in-law:[6] in a crisis, one does not follow the canonical rules. With false mandates, I will defeat the Qiang, rebelling against the classics to conform to the Way.[7] Even so, I still have to talk it over carefully with Auntie Huang. If we can do it, then we will. If we have to stop, well, then we will stop.
(*Acts out calling Auntie Huang*)
Dear Auntie Huang, please come out, I have something to tell you.
(*A* jing *playing Auntie Huang enters*)
Auntie Huang:
[To a half-measure of the tune *Nuguanzi*]

Age came, not fortune.
Night after night, I sleep alone with Chang E for companionship.[8]
A female water buffalo,
A red leaf on her back,
A few notes tremble from the flute,
As the child shepherds it home.

(*They act out greeting each other*)
Auntie Huang: Miss, what are you calling me about?
Chuntao: Auntie Huang, these last few days I have been thinking constantly. We can't go on living the way we've been living here. You know full well that with my kind of talent and education, if I were to take

6. This is a reference to Mencius' explanation of how extenuating circumstances might require someone to step beyond social proprieties; even though men and women should not touch, a man may break those rules to rescue a sister-in-law from drowning. See note 35 in appendix 3.

7. This line refers to the periodic settlements of the western regions by the Han Chinese that resulted in subsequent "rebellions" by the nomadic Qiang 羌.

8. That is, the moon.

part in the exams, I would be guaranteed absolute success and, lickety-split, become an official. Once I become an official, I'll have an official's emoluments, and so I gradually will be able to accumulate a fortune and make a good plan to retire into reclusion. Then, when I sneak away to return, you and I can live together as we did before, but we will also make a good living. Isn't that much better than our situation at present: eating when there's a meal to eat, forgoing a meal when there isn't any? What do you think?

Auntie Huang: Great! Great! If you go and take the exams, you will certainly make it, but what are you going to do about changing your girlish face?

Chuntao: What difficulty is there with that? I will take my father's old clothes, shoes, head-wrap, and hat and put them on in exchange for my own skirt, jacket, and coiled-up chignon. Anyone seeing me would never be able to tell that I am a girl and not a man!

Auntie Huang: This really makes sense.

(*Auntie Huang acts out clowning around*)

Chuntao: Let's not talk nonsense anymore. Quickly go and prepare father's old clothes and bring them out. I will change costume. And you also need to be ready to impersonate an older servant. We will call you Huang Ke, and I will take the name Huang Chonggu, and that's how we will go together. Command your son, Number Two, to take care of the house, and that should do it.

Auntie Huang: I've served you for all my life, so this old slave complies with a happy heart. But I want the emoluments and whatever you scrape together to be shared equally with me.

Chuntao: Naturally.

(*Auntie Huang leaves and collects the clothes, then re-enters. The two of them mime changing their costumes, and Auntie Huang faces offstage and says*)

Number Two! I am going to accompany the young lady into the city to visit relatives. We won't be back for several days. Take good care of the place, and cut firewood and herd the cows every day. If there is no grain, then go over to Old Lady Zhang's house to borrow a little to eat. Don't go around with ruffians looking for trouble. When I come back, I'll be bringing all kinds of food we've never had before, I certainly will! I only fear that you won't have a mouth left to eat them with, you daredevil!

(*Acts out getting on the road*)

Chuntao: [To the tune *Furong deng*]

Facing the mirror, I wipe off the red rouge,
Take off the lotus ornament, and from now on wear green robes.
A sail full of wind helps one a little,
Brushing the rosy clouds, a solitary duck.
My source of words will overturn in Qutang's waters,[9]
My literary style is wholly free of the vulgar habits of rouge and powder.
My cloth-wrapped bundle is tied up tightly, my chignon fastened into a snood,
I will come back wearing gold flowers of success stuck into my cap.

Auntie Huang: [To the same tune]

I used to be the wet nurse,
Now I'll serve a while as a long-bearded servant.
I only help the oar and assist the boat,
Relying on one person's fortune.
With the old head-wrap, she is so disguised she could pass before her own mother,
My ordination may be fake, but who would check to see if this monk is bald?
In our luggage we only have a few measures of stripped millet,
But once she accedes to office, I'll get half of all her emoluments.

The talented poet, the beautiful woman—surely they exist,
But when have they ever been combined in one body?
Chuntao: Yanping[10] does have a pair of matched male and female steels,[11]
But that will only become known later when they have become dragons.

---

9. This is an allusion to a poem by Du Fu entitled "Drunken Song" ("Zui ge xing" 醉歌行) with the line "The source of words is overturned in the Three Gorges' waters" (*ciyuan daoliu sanxia shui* 詞源倒流三峽水).

10. Yanping 延平 is in Fujian province.

11. The "male and female steels" (*cixiongtie* 雌雄鐵) are the names of legendary swords. One is named *Longquan* and the other is named *Tai'a.* In two-handed sword combat, the sword in the right hand is considered the male sword: it is longer and used for cutting and slashing. The "female" sword in the left hand is shorter and used for stabbing. Both *Longquan* and *Tai'a* turn into dragons in the legend, so neither can be distinguished by gender. Chuntao implies that her accomplishment will likewise be the equalizer that nullifies gender distinctions.

Act II

(*A* wai *playing Prime Minister Zhou enters, leading a group on stage*)
Prime Minister Pingjin opened the Eastern Pavilion,
And the "peaches and plums" were all transplanted.[12]
As I have received orders to catch unicorn and phoenix,[13]
How could I not capture the elusive goose in my nets?[14]

I am Zhou Xiang, and I used to work in Qiongnan's auxiliary office of the Secretariat. I was summoned and selected by my lord, the King of Shu, and was given various positions until I became the Prime Minister. My lord supports scholarship and promotes literature. This year we are vetting and selecting *jinshi*[15] scholars, and it is my turn to preside over the exams. Last month, I sent dispatches to be posted on boards, announcing that we would collect the students today to hold the examinations. I expect that everyone will already be there waiting. Runners! Open the doors and take this plaque out to summon in the *xiucai* scholars.

(*Runners assent and mime summoning*)

(*A* dan *playing Chonggu, a* mo *playing Jia Lu, and a* chou *playing Balderdash*[16] *enter stage, and act out presenting their credentials*)

Zhou Xiang: Gentlemen, in earlier years, in the exam halls, when the examiners issued a theme, they were generally in accord with past precedents. When you students replied in an itemized way, you all complied with the old conventions. Moreover, at court, scholar candidates have always been chosen according to their ability to compose verse,[17] but nowadays song is the descendant of verse.[18] I would like to wipe clean our former scholastic pedantry, and I will therefore select an anecdote from Shu history as our theme. You will each compose a song and then

---

12. This is an allusion to Han Wudi's Prime Minister, Gongsun Hong 公孫弘, who was enfeoffed as the Marquis Pingjin in 124 BCE. One of his accomplishments was opening the Eastern Cabinet to invite talented men to apply as retainers. The peaches and plums are the scholars being transplanted into the center.

13. That is, to gather talent.

14. That is, he cannot fail in finding the talented scholar.

15. Scholars who have passed the metropolitan exams attain *jinshi* 進士 status.

16. The candidate's name, Balderdash (Hu Yan 胡顏), is a homonym for the word for nonsense, or balderdash (*huyan* 胡言).

17. Respectively, *ci* 詞 and *fu* 賦.

18. I translate *yuefu* (樂府) as "song." This use of the term *yuefu* reflects later usage as a general descriptive name for popular song, which was certainly never an official exam requirement in the history of imperial exams.

recite it for me; I will critique you on the spot. I will first provide the first line; each of you will complete it. The opening line that I provide will end with the word *chai* 柴 (firewood). In the the following line you will supply rhymes using the word *cai* 纔 (then) and end with a rhyme on *zhai* 債 (debt). Since the waters of the Yangtze River emerge from Western Shu's Min Mountains, this song's tune will follow "Northern Song of the River's Waters" (*Bei jiang'er shui* 北江兒水). You all must try your best: do not fail to live up to the magnanimity of the Emperor's sagacity in seeking worthies, and consider the trouble taken by me, your examiner, who has undergone this search. First step aside and listen, and when you hear me intone your name, come and receive your theme.
(*Acts out intoning names from their portfolios*)
Huang Chonggu, your topic is "Xiangru removes his kingfisher robe and buys wine to dispel Wenjun's sorrow."[19] Jia Lu, your topic is "The peasant sends cherries to Du Fu."[20] Balderdash, yours is "Du Fu allows his western neighbor's wife to beat down dates."[21] Huang Chonggu! Come forward and listen to my opening lines.
[To the tune *Bei jiang'er shui*]

Kingfisher robe and sash,
Quickly, he unfastened his kingfisher robe and sash,
He came to Apricot Village.
He faced the wine house and pitched in the coat, saying
"Anything but low quality wine."[22]

---

19. Sima Xiangru 司馬相如 (179–117 BCE) was a scholar who eloped with Zhuo Wenjun 卓文君, the daughter of a wealthy man. Wenjun was disowned, and the lovers were penniless. Xiangru sold his kingfisher coat so that they could have enough capital to open a wineshop. When Wenjun's father saw their state of affairs, he forgave his daughter.

20. The subject is taken from one of Du Fu's poems, "A Peasant Sends Red Cherries" ("Yeren song zhuying" 野人送朱櫻), written on the occasion of the poet's receiving cherries from a peasant and reminiscing about how he used to receive them at court. See pages 220–21 of David McMullen, "Recollection Without Tranquility: Du Fu, the Imperial Gardens, and the State," *Asia Major* 14.2 (2001): 189–252; for a translation and brief analysis, see David McCraw's *Du Fu's Laments from the South* (Honolulu: University of Hawaii Press, 1992), 90–92.

21. This topic alludes to a line in Du Fu's poem "Presenting Again to the Man from Wu" ("You cheng Wu lang" 又呈吳郎), in which he describes himself allowing an impoverished neighbor to gather dates from his tree.

22. The term thatch kindling (*maochai* 茅柴) is a description of bad wine, thus providing the sound *chai* required here for the end rhyme.

Continue using the *cai* rhyme, here.
Chonggu:

> In this way he bought one jug of "Surpassing Pearls" just [*cai*] dripped from the press.
> Why was he running so fast that he got holes in his shoes?
> In order to make the beauty smile with parted lips,
> He feared only that a frown would damage those peaked jet black eyebrows.[23]
> How amazing that she should go with the poor scholar,
> Accompanying him to heaven's edge.
> He also had to give this pheasant-head gown to the wine boss,
> In exchange for a wine house's debt [*zhai*].

Zhou Xiang: Carefully I savor this song. It is truly rich and heavenly, like the words of some divine immortals. Further, these two difficult rhymes were put together subtly. I don't believe that on this examination stage there could be another rival! Jia Lu, come over. Yours is: "The peasant sends cherries to Du Fu."
[To the tune *Bei jiang'er shui*]

> Beyond Washing Flowers Stream,[24]
> The thatched hut on the path encircled by Washing Flowers Stream,
> Is the house of the poet Du Fu.
> From whence this local peasant leaning on his staff,
> Knocking on the bare brushwood door?

Continue it with a rhyme on *cai*.
Jia Lu:

> Bringing the cherries that were plucked just [*cai*] then,
> Like a basketful of beauties' cheeks,
> Whose rouged lips are pulled askew,
> Cursing the parrot for its treachery.[25]
> It happened that the poem's well had just run dry, and

---

23. Zhuo Wenjun was famed for her jet black eyebrows, which were said to look like distant mountains.

24. This is the place where Du Fu lived, outside Chengdu in Sichuan province.

25. Parrots announce a visitor, thus breaking a rendezvous.

He was moved by the old one's concern.
How good to eat his fill of bright pearls,
And then spit out a crimson-colored poetic debt [*zhai*].

Zhou Xiang: The *cai* character was inserted quite properly, two or three sentences in the middle, and the conclusion also seemed to have been divinely guided. Balderdash, come forward. What is yours?
Balderdash: It is "Du Fu allows his western neighbor's wife to beat down dates."
Zhou Xiang: Listen to me recite.
[To *Bei jiang'er shui*]

The neighbor to the west was abjectly poor,
It happened that the neighbor to the west was abjectly poor.

Balderdash: Sir, Main Examiner, the other opening sentences were all about such things as kingfisher robes and Washing Flowers Stream, things that were lucky because they are rich and luxurious, flowery and elaborate! Then for me, it's a sentence full of "abjectly poor, abjectly poor"! Examiner, you must protect me like an infant.
Zhou Xiang: What do you mean protect you like an infant?
Balderdash: To protect like an infant ... even if you do not hit it exactly ...[26]
Zhou Xiang: Now your example gets even farther from the mark.
Balderdash: Yet not so far.
Zhou Xiang: Balderdash, you truly are talking nonsense [*huyan*].[27]

---

26. The joke, as Wai-yee Li pointed out on an earlier draft, plays on this passage from "The Great Learning" ("Daxue" 大學): "What is meant by 'In order rightly to govern the state, it is necessary first to regulate the family,' is this: It is not possible for one to teach others, while he cannot teach his own family. Therefore, the ruler, without going beyond his family, completes the lessons for the state. There is filial piety—therewith the sovereign should be served. There is fraternal submission—therewith elders and superiors should be served. There is kindness—therewith the multitude should be treated. In the Announcement to Kang, it is said, 'Act as if you were watching over an infant.' If a mother is really anxious about it, though she may not hit exactly the wants of her infant, she will not be far from doing so" (Legge's translation, accessed on the "Chinese Text Project" http://ctext.org/liji/da-xue).

27. This is a play on the homonym to Balderdash's 胡顏 name (see note 16). The similar-sounding compound, *huyan* 胡言, means nonsensical talk.

The old widow had a thorn as her only hairpin,
And on top of that, the soldiers razed the land year after year,
There was little rice, and no firewood.

Continue with the rhyme of *cai.*
Balderdash: This omen about little rice and no firewood is an even worse example. This woman is poor to the extreme. My inability to hit it exactly may also be to the extreme.
Zhou Xiang: Hurry it up!
Balderdash:

There was little rice, and no firewood,
This old lady, ah,
Just like me, one and the same in suffering, then [*cai*].
It wasn't my fault that the date tree was planted near her.
The dates, too, grew quite perversely,
They all hung on the side over her home,
So that in the end they fell down on to her steps,
I didn't even get to do her the honor [*de*].

Zhou Xiang: This last word is not the assigned rhyme.[28]
Balderdash: What is so absolute about rhymes? Poetry rhymes are just like fates.[29] If the examiner says that it rhymes well, then even if the rhyme doesn't rhyme, it will rhyme! If the examiner says that the rhyme is no good, even if the rhyme rhymes it won't rhyme. My fate resides with the examiner, not with me.[30] That is why it is said: "Essays of the past cannot be relied on; one only relies on the nod of the red-robed examiner."[31]
Zhou Xiang: It also has to correspond with the universally agreed-upon public standards.

---

28. Balderdash ends the line with "*de*" instead of the assigned "*zhai.*"

29. Poetry rhymes (*shiyun* 詩韻) are just like fates (*mingyun* 命運) plays on the *yun* homonym.

30. Or, my rhyme resides with the examiner. The play on the name "Balderdash" continues here, because he refers to himself by the name Hu Yan throughout these exchanges.

31. When Ouyang Xiu 歐陽修 (1007–72) was an official grading examinations, he imagined that there was a red-robed person behind him. If the man nodded his head, then the candidate would pass. "Red-robed" is a kenning for the official examiner.

Balderdash: Ah! Sir, you are mistaken! If you emphasize the public standards, then there'd be no need to say: "I don't care if the essays hit it exactly with everyone. I only care that the essays hit it exactly with the examiner."[32]

Zhou Xiang: Ai! You people! I don't have time to listen to this kind of idle chatter. Hurry it up, now!

Balderdash:

> They fell down on to her steps,
> I didn't even get to do her the honor,
> How hard it is to relinquish one's love!
> Next year, ah, I'll take all the fruit,
> And bring it myself to sell,
> Including those that are still unripe,
> For now, I will suffer the pain, and
> Then exchange my flesh for a debt [*zhai*] of Buddha light.[33]

Zhou Xiang: The style of Balderdash's lyrics is unbridled, but it is too far out there, and the errors are so numerous. What I like about him is that he doesn't conceal from me his true nature, which is quite unlike those who, though they are arrogant and stingy in their hearts, act magnanimous through their mouths. He too can be made into something. I'll take him. Balderdash, I've passed you, but still I have changed a few sentences on your behalf, in accordance with the old regulations. Recite the opening lines for me.

Balderdash:

[To the tune *Bei jiang'er shui*]

> The neighbor to the west was abjectly poor,
> It happened that the neighbor to the west was abjectly poor.
> The old widow had a thorn as her only hairpin,
> And on top of that, the soldiers razed the land year after year,
> There was little rice, and no firewood.

---

32. This line appears in two of Feng Menglong's short stories.

33. One pays a debt to Buddha by lighting oneself, like lighting a candle. On lighting parts of one's body, such as fingers, see James A. Benn, *Burning for the Buddha: Self-Immolation in Chinese Buddhism* (Honolulu: University of Hawaii, 2007); or James A. Benn, "Where Text Meets Flesh: Burning the Body as an Apocryphal Practice in Chinese Buddhism," *History of Religions* 37.4 (1998): 295–322.

Now the *xiucai* shall continue it.
Zhou Xiang:

> For a long time, they relied upon each other, and not just now [*cai*].

Balderdash: Yours is clearly just like mine.
Zhou Xiang:

> Fortunately, the fence dates ripened at the frosty studio,
> What I planted is as if you planted it, too:
> Feel free to take a long staff and coarse sack.

Balderdash: That makes it seem like they are all hers! With them all knocked down, what good is that?
Zhou Xiang:

> Beating the tree repeatedly,
> For a while it serves as a banquet,
> I regret without end that I cannot fill up all the world's hungers in a debt of hunger [*zhai*].

Balderdash: Rather! Yours is better than mine! And if we went by me (Balderdash), we would pass you.
Zhou Xiang: This guy really is too unbridled with the rules!
Balderdash: A little joke [*nüe*] is not going too far [*nüe*].[34]
Zhou Xiang: What's that?
Balderdash: Tyrannical [*nüe* 虐]!
Zhou Xiang: This scholar talks nonsense! Can you think of another *nüe* from the *Book of Odes*?
Balderdash: Got it! They sport with [*nüe*] each other, and he gives her a peony [*mudan*].[35]
Zhou Xiang: Now how are you reading that line?

---

34. Balderdash plays on the homophones *nüe* 謔 and *nüe* 瘧; the first compound, *xinüe* 戲謔, means jokes or banter, and Balderdash follows this through with the comment on how this is not like *nüe* 瘧, meaning a fever.

35. From the Odes of Zheng 鄭, the poem is "The Zhen and the Wei" ("Zhen Wei" 溱洧): "They sport with each other, and she gives him her peony" (*yi qi xiang nue, zeng zhi yi shaoyao* 伊其相謔，贈之以芍藥). Balderdash substitutes the more common word for peony (*mudan* 牡丹) accidentally.

Balderdash: Oh, peony [*shaoyao*].

Zhou Xiang: Thank heavens he remembers! As for the ranks among the members on the stage, clearly Huang Chonggu is the first, Jia Lu is the second, and Balderdash is the third. I will announce this to his majesty. Gentlemen! Tomorrow you will all come outside the palace gates to view the signboards and prepare yourselves for parading the streets and going to a feast. Chonggu, you will be presented a title by the king tomorrow, and you should ready a fitting hat for the top of your head. You should not err with the proper ceremonies of gratitude.

> The woodsman and the buffalo driver return so many times,
> But hardest of all is dredging out timbers to make pillars.[36]
> This morning I carefully established Mr. Huang.
> Among the flowers, the plum is certainly the chief.

(*He exits stage first*)
(*Those left on stage perform a "wrapping up scene"*)
(*The three students each act out making introductions, asking about where they are from, regional customs, and where they are lodging. They make plans to view the signboards and go to the feasts*)
(*The* mo *and* chou *both mime congratulating Huang*)

(*Exeunt*).

Act III

(*The* dan *wearing the official's cap and belt and the* wai *playing her assistant enter stage*)
[To the tune *Xi qian ying*]

> Since my name was at the head of the golden board,
> I reckoned I would be close to the Heavenly Face,
> to discourse at leisure every day on the principles of government.
> But suddenly I was appointed as merely an assistant,
> And put in charge of the records and documents as Regional Administrator.
> Black curtains and blue gowns are easy to put on,

36. In other words, dredging out scholars to make into officials.

Clear waters and red lotus are difficult to emulate.[37]
The court ranks now are far off:
Though when raising my head, I can still see the sun,[38]
my sleeves chill the censer's incense.[39]

[To the tune of the *ci* lyric *Pusa man*]

Now local official and government official are basically the same,
So the Red Lotus is temporarily lodged for three years at the local administration.
In the mirror of water[40] all is illuminated,
As every morning I focus on court cases.
Even though the Postmaster General is haughty,
If I have to seek an audience with him, what harm is there in doing so?[41]
I only consider it a play on a stage,
And bend my waist as if it were soft cotton.[42]

Since I attained the top graduate position, I encountered this new rule: everybody who has passed the examination has to be tested in civil affairs and administration, and so I have been posted in Chengdu prefecture as a regional administrator. Although this office deals with documents, and petty difficulties abound, it has really allowed me to

---

37. This is an allusion to a comment made by Yu Gao 庾杲 to the official Wang Jian 王儉 (452–89) on the difficulty of finding worthy assistants: "I float on clear river waters and trust the fairies, what is the beauty in that?" 庾景行泛淥水，依芙蓉，何其麗也？ From this, the phrase "clear water and red lotus" 綠水紅蓮 came to mean a secretary to a high official.

38. That is, the king.

39. She had hoped to serve the king but was positioned in a low administrative post. Dressing is easy, but acting the part is difficult.

40. The mirror of water is a symbol of the transparency of ideal official life, where nothing is hidden.

41. This alludes to Tao Qian 陶潛 (365–427) or Tao Yuanming (see appendix 2, note 37), who was not willing to bow down for three pecks of rice and left his post. Contrast the poet with Chonggu, who hoped to gain a high position but was appointed to a lowly one. See Xiaofei Tian, *Tao Yuanming and Manuscript Culture: The Record of a Dusty Table* (Seattle: University of Washington Press, 2005), 77.

42. A male actor playing a woman impersonating a man is comparing the life of officialdom to a play.

exercise my talents in helping the people and reining in the government runners. In the blink of an eye, three years have passed, but I still make hardly enough to eat in this sinecure. His Majesty saw the many talents of my examiner, Prime Minister Zhou, and appointed him to serve concurrently as Prefect of the City and Prime Minister. Yesterday he sent me three felons, all in a row, each convincted long ago, each claiming that justice was miscarried. Last night I looked into their cases, and truly there is something suspicious in each. However, the witnesses are either already dead or have been released, and I don't know who will be able to vouch for the convicted. All right, I'll bring them out and rule on their cases. Runners! Go bring out the three memorialized convicts that Prime Minister Zhou sent yesterday to be interviewed.

(*Runners leave, and mime bringing back a* xiaosheng, tie, *and* mo *on stage, and chant out their names*)

Huang Tianzhi! Madam Wu! Zhen Kexiao!

Chonggu: You three convicts have all been imprisoned for a long time now. Two of you are meant to be wearing the cangue, so who freed you?

(*The* xiaosheng *and* tie *reply*)

Yesterday, when we brought our cases forth, Prime Minister Zhou was so good as to look briefly into them, order the cangues removed, and have us sent here.

Chonggu: Huang Tianzhi! Come forward. At the time when this Butcher Mao first brought forth the accusation that you forged seals, what was the cause? Speak the truth.

Tianzhi: Sir! I lived in front of Cockcrow post station. I observed that those post station officers' seals of office were so colorful and amusing, and, against my better judgment, asked someone who knew how to engrave seals to make a little personal seal for me in the model of an official seal's carving.

Chonggu: Where is that seal engraver now?

Tianzhi: Dead and gone. I often went to Butcher Mao's place, bringing my seal with me to use on chits to buy pork. Later, I got into a dispute over property with a wealthy man named Xia Ge. Xia Ge bribed Butcher Mao to inform on me, saying that I had forged seals with the intent to impersonate a post station officer. Later, another rascal named Chang Duoxin, said: "that little seal of his is not incriminating enough against him. He already has this history, he could easily forge large ones to sell." Xia Ge knew how to get things done, and he had a lot of helpers, so I

had no way to fight it. Sir! These are false charges!
Chonggu: How big was your seal?
Tianzhi: It was about half the length of my pinkie finger.
Chonggu: Was that seal character purely like that of the post station's seal, or did it also have your own name carved on its face?
Tianzhi: It had my own name and surname on it.
Chonggu: Your accounts for meat must have been summed up at some point. Who kept most of these receipts for the orders?
Tianzhi: Most of us were his customers. When he and I would settle the bill, I never asked him for a receipt.
Chonggu: Runner, go to Butcher Mao's place, and tell his wife: "there is a group of robbers who told us that you had an affair with one of them. They said that the jewelry and head dresses that they took were all hidden in your house's walls, and the judge has sent us to come and investigate you." Don't bother with the large cases; take the smallest cases and small caskets to inspect, and bring the woman back with you, too.
(*Runners assent and leave*)
Chonggu: Madam Wu, come forward and tell the truth.
Madam Wu: Sir, in the northern section of the ward where I live there is a rich landowner named Gu Shiyue. He is someone who thinks less of money than of being good. He became close friends with my husband Jia Da. There is also a certain Jiang Song, who was also a rich landowner. However, he is a bad man who was always trying to seduce me, and I made the mistake of reviling him for it. Later, Jiang Song oversaw the spring festival gathering. My husband returned from drinking at his house, and around the middle of the night, all five of his orifices began spurting blood.[43] We tried everything to save him, but we failed, and he died. Jiang Song then bribed neighbors to falsely accuse me of having an affair with Gu Shiyue and plotting the murder of my husband. This is how I came to be imprisoned.
Chonggu: Awful! Cases of a vassal plotting to murder his lord, a son plotting to murder his father, or a wife plotting to murder her husband are unpardonable. You should not have had any relations with Gu Shiyue. This situation must be true: why have we allowed such a wicked person here! Tell the executioner to come here, take this woman and

43. The bleeding is caused by poisoning.

bind her, and take her out and finish her off!

(*A* sheng *playing the executioner comes and binds the* tie. *The* tie *cries as she is escorted out*)

Chonggu: Sound the clappers! Call my Huang Ke to come out.

(*The* jing *enters*)

Huang Ke: Sir, how ferocious you are in condemning that woman to death! What have you summoned me for?

Chonggu: Huang Ke! Go quickly to where that woman is going to be finished off, and listen to see if anyone says that she is innocent, then quietly ask about the particulars. When you have heard the truth, then pass on the message, "My master says to let the woman go for now," and bring her back with the person who said she was innocent. Hurry! Go![44]

(*The* jing *agrees and exits*)

Chonggu: Now Zhen Kexiao, what have you to say?

Kexiao (*Mo*): Sir! I am from Jiangnan. I played a drum and sang in the streets as a busker, and sang my way right up to Linqiong. In Linqiong, the Zhuo family had just been robbed.[45] The police agents had no way of capturing the real booty and culprit. They listened to a habitual liar named Qiao Bushi (False Eyes), who said that I was not a singer but someone who had commited crimes before and was now hiding in Linqiong pretending to be a singer. If I were to meet up with a band of rogues, he claimed, I would go back to my old tricks. That bunch of police officers pretended to be thieves and tried harassing me to join them, but I refused to go at any price. Later, because the yamen was trying to show its toughness on crime, I was arrested as a thief. Still under pressure from its superiors, the yamen panicked and was all too happy to brand me the actual thief. That's how it happened.

Chonggu: What you said makes sense. The officers caused all this, but if I try to seize them right away, there are so many of them that they would be able to escape. I'll set you free now, and in the dark of the night you will go to each particular officer's house and make a small circle with a piece of chalk at the top of his door as a sign. Then I will be able to send

---

44. If the judgments are made during the morning session, then executions are carried out in the third quarter of the noon hour.

45. Wilt Idema pointed out to me that the use of the surname Zhuo recalls Zhuo Wenjun's family, which implies to the audience that they are the richest family in town.

men out at dawn to bring in everyone whose door is marked with chalk, and I will have them beaten to death. How about that?

Kexiao: I would not recognize their houses.

Chonggu: Nonsense! They tried to harass you into joining them. Do you mean they never invited you into their houses to have a meal or a drink?

Kexiao: They definitely made an effort to invite me, but I was steadfast in my refusal to go.

Chonggu: Well, in that case, we cannot arrest anyone or further investigate this case. You will have to put your cangue back on and go on back to prison.

(*Kexiao weeps loudly*)

Kexiao: Had I known it would end this way, I would have just eaten at their table.

Chonggu: You still haven't gone, yet, then?

(*Kexiao leaves in tears, and Chonggu addresses clerk*)

Chonggu: Now how could a person who would not even enter their homes also be the kind of person capable of the acts of a hardened man who consorts with criminals?

I have just tricked him by saying: "Since you don't recognize those officers' residences, we cannot let you go." He would rather go to prison. Doesn't this show the truth of his story?

Wai: You, sir, have true prescience.

Chonggu: Bring this Zhen Kexiao back in.

(*Runners mime calling him back*)

Chonggu: Take this Zhen Kexiao and open his cangue. I ought to free you immediately, but instead why don't you wait here at the red steps for a bit. Wait until the other two cases have been cleared, and then I will release all of you at once.

(*Kexiao kowtows and speaks*)

Sir, you are as the clear sky.

(*Runners bring an old* dan *carrying a casket; a* jing *[still playing Huang Ke] brings a* tie *and a* chou *playing a little servant on stage. Runners speak*)

Your Honor commanded us to go to the Mao household and search through their caskets, and we return bringing this woman with them in response.

Huang Ke: After hearing Your Honor's commands, I hurried to the execution grounds where there were thousands of onlookers. They all said that this was a huge miscarriage of justice, but there was one servant in particular who instead held his hands together in prayer chanting, "Amidha Buddha! Her death is a wrongful death! This evil karma is my doing!" When I saw him speak in this peculiar manner, I pulled him over to a quiet place, and carefully questioned him. But of course he refused to say anything. At that moment, the bound woman had just arrived, and I shouted loudly to the executioner: "His Honor says to release the woman, and ordered that this servant be bound up and executed!" He was immediately scared silly, and proceeded to tell me the whole true story.

Chonggu: Very well done.

(*Huang Ke indicates* chou)

Sir, question him and you will learn all.

Chonggu: You, servant boy, in whose house do you serve?

Boy: I am a servant in Jiang Song's household.

Chonggu: Is Jiang Song at home?

Boy: Yes.

Chonggu: Two of you runners, quickly go and bring Jiang Song here. If he gets away, then it will be your heads instead.

(*Runners assent and exit. Chonggu questions the servant*)

You have more or less given up the case, so out with the truth, and your life may be spared.

Boy: My master always wanted to seduce this Madam Wu, and was only reviled by her. He blamed it on the fact that she must be having relations with Gu Shiyue, and this caused a hatred in his heart.

Chonggu: So was she having an affair with Gu Shiyue, then?

Boy: This was another injustice against her. Later, when he was overseeing the spring festival gathering, after all of the guests had left, my master retained only Madam Wu's husband Jia Da to drink one more cup. He told me to get the large goblet of wine, put some arsenic into it, and serve it to Jia, then he told me to bring him home to Madam Wu. This is how this court case arose. Now that I have spoken to you, I might as well just die today, as there is nothing left to say.

Chonggu: Step down!

(*Chonggu looks at the casket and with a smile addresses the deputies*)

Huang Tianzhi's receipts are all in here, each and every one. And they are certainly the size of half a pinkie finger, and his real name and characters are certainly carved on the top. How could he want to impersonate a post

station official, and further, forge a seal, yet not try to conceal his name and surname, and then go on to use it at the butcher's? Huang Tianzhi, did you use chits like these to vouch for goods at other stores?
Tianzhi: Yes, sir!
Chonggu: The case against him makes less and less sense. This is clearly a case of a small child making a muddy cap and sash from clay, and pretending that he is a Prime Minister or general, or something. Everyone knows it's just make-believe. But to take it as the real thing would be inconceivable even to babies not old enough for solid food! Piteous! Piteous! What a shame that this Butcher Mao and Xia Ke and that Chang Duoxin are all dead. Lucky for them! Runners, free Huang Tianzhi and Madam Wu from their cangues.[46] Take Butcher Mao's wife and have her fingers pressed.
(*Runners bring in a* zhongjing *playing Jiang Song*)
Chonggu: Jiang Song, come forward.
(*Chonggu indicates the boy and says*)
Take a careful look. Who is this?
Jiang Song: That is my servant, named Jiang Bang. Say no more. I deserve to die.
Chonggu: Runners, take Jiang Song and give him a hundred strokes, and Jiang Bang fifty.
(*Beating enacted*)
Chonggu: Now hammer down the cangues and take them to prison.
(*They enact putting the two in prison*)
Chonggu: Huang Tianzhi, Madam Wu, we still need to discuss your guarantees. Wait until I memorialize your cases, and then I will close them. Zhen Kexiao's case is lighter, so we can just release him.
(*Addresses the deputies*)
Make up three documents: tomorrow we will report this to Master Zhou. You three, listen:
[To the tune *Hong na ao*]

> Huang Tianzhi, the honeybee that occupies the flower's core is called king,

46. Xu Wei was well acquainted with the cangue, having worn it for five years and written two *fu* on the subject of being released from it.

The supernatural turtle that arranges fake battle arrays is called a general.[47]
Ai! These are all false.
How could there be legal chits only an inch long?
How could they be taken for real bronze seals of the ninth rank?
Furthermore, his true name was not concealed
Like one playing a large toad while hiding that he was a little tadpole!
In the past there have been cases like these,
If it is not a case of forcibly appointing Tang Shuyu,
Then it's a play about cutting a pawlonia branch to serve as a jade tablet.[48]

[To the tune *Hong na ao*]

That Madam Wu,
Even though you, by your stylish dress,
Incited the lust of Old Jiang.
It is also the case that
Gu Shiyue got involved in this karmic retribution.
Nowadays
When people want love, they do not spare the house for love of the crow.[49]
You were responsible for a fire that raged to the point of killing all the fish.[50]

---

47. The Daoist deity of the underworld, Xuanwudi 玄武帝, is served by two generals, a turtle and a snake.

48. Tang Shuyu 唐叔虞 of the Early Zhou dynasty (1046–771 BCE), or King Shuyu of Tang, was the son of the first king of Zhou, King Wu 周武, 王 and the brother of King Cheng of Zhou 周成王人 (r.ca. 1042–1021 BCE). According to the *Records of the Historian*, when Cheng and Shuyu were playing, Cheng pretended to hand his younger brother a tablet and appointed him King of Tang. The scribe made preparations to give the title to Shuyu, and King Cheng said, "I was just joking [*xi* 戲], that's all." To this, the scribe replied: "The son of heaven does not speak words in jest [*xi*]. His words are the culmination of the *Rites*, *Documents*, *Music*, and *Songs*." He then appointed Shuyu as the King of Tang. The moral of the story is that one cannot fool around when one is emperor.

49. In *The Book of Documents* (*Shujing* 書經), it is recorded that those who love people also love even the crows on the roof of their house. Hence the play on the surname *Wu* 烏, which also means "crow."

50. The *Extensive Records of the Taiping Reign*, or *Taiping Guangji* 太平廣記, contains a story about emptying a lake to put out a fire, leaving all the fish in the drained lake to die, just as Gu Shiyue is made to suffer because Jiang Song wishes to punish Madam Wu.

Madam Wu, you owe thanks to Jiang Bang,
If not for the Jiang household's Jiang Bang,
Even I, Lord Huang,
Would not have been able to prevail.
Ai!
I see how time and again human affairs are like a game of chess,
Where you lose a pawn to save the general!
[to the tune *Hong na ao*]
This Zhen Kexiao,
Even though you beat the drums and sang out tunes at thousands of doors,[51]
Still it was a case of
The helmsman pitying you from afar.
You followed them into seas churned by wind and wave,
Holding fast to your little leaf of a boat, you went to face them.
Those hoodlums, ah,
They tried to trick you into joining their gang,
But you never even entered their gates.
If you ever had the slightest wickedness or hardened heart,
You would eagerly find some rogue chief; how would you be willing to leave Taihang mountain?[52]

(*The* xiaosheng, tie, *and* mo *together kowtow and sing*[53])
[To the tune *Hong na ao*]

My lord,
You are a pitch-black sky hung with a bright moon,[54]
Able to pick out three kinds of fish from the muddiest waters.
Why speak of
Blossoms that will open again on the shriveled iron tree?
You are truly
the tonic of resurrection that saves life in Ksitigrarbha's hell.[55]

---

51. I.e., Zhen Kexiao, like Mi Heng, spoke freely of whatever was on his mind.

52. Taihang is associated with the bandits of the *Shuihu* (*Outlaws of the Marsh*) tradition.

53. This never happens in *zaju*.

54. Judge Bao, the epitome of wise and fair court decisions, had a black face with a crescent moon mark on his forehead.

55. Ksitigrarbha is the bodhisattva of all beings in hell, since his vow is not to enter Nirvana until all others have transcended as well. In some tellings, Ksitigarbha was originally a girl.

How can this secret virtue be weighed?
We three little ants, ah,
What can we do to repay your virtue?
It is so hard to
Live in a world that is like the ocean wildly roiling with waves,
Yet still be like you, Our Lord,
Who resembles Dizhu rock,[56] a pillar in the rush; or the rock of Yanyu.[57]

Chonggu: Runners, bail out those who need to be bailed, release those who need to be released. (*The three kowtow together in parting and shout together*)
All three: May he remain a high official for an eternity of service: a hundred years of long life! Five sons! Two daughters! May you live happily with seven children.
(*The* wai *kowtows and speaks*)
I have never seen such divine judgment as Your Honor's.
Chonggu: All laugh at the regional administrator who hurriedly ties his sash, shouting loudly on hot summer days, a stickler for books. If at the time he had not done his real job, he would only have sat and observed midsummer snow atop Emei.[58]

Act IV

(*A* wai *playing Prime Minister Zhou enters*)
[To the tune *Chuanyan yunü*]

Wanting to select a riderless dragon mount,
I find by chance a Song Yu among the top graduates.[59]
If this one were to wait on King Xiang,[60]

56. A rock island formation in the Yellow River in Henan, Dizhu is famed for its fixity in spite of the rushing waters around it.

57. Yanyu is another rock in the Three Gorges, also an example of firm stability.

58. Legend has it that snow will fall in June in sympathy for the unjustly convicted, an allusion to Guan Hanqing's 關漢卿 (ca. 1225–1302) play *The Injustice to Dou E* (*Dou E yuan*) or *Snow in Midsummer*.

59. A Chu poet from the third century BCE, Song Yu 宋玉 is thought to carry on Qu Yuan's 屈原 (339–278 BCE) poetic style, contributing several works to the *Chuci* 楚辭.

60. That is, King Xiang of Chu.

He would produce just as good a *fu* on his Gaotang dream.[61]
For a Nongyu from the house of Qin,[62]
Who could best accompany her as she rides her phoenix?
Look carefully: only this one is fit to share the perch.

Long ago, I lost my wife, and as I now only have thoughts of Xiang Ping's Five Great Mountains,[63] I have sworn not to remarry. As my wife left me with my firstborn, a son named Fengyu, and a daughter, named Fengchu, who are both yet unmarried, my mind is troubled. Several years ago, when I happened to supervise the exam candidates, I selected Huang Chonggu to be the top scholar. Currently, he is a regional administrator. His learning truly stands out from the crowd, and his administrative abilities, too, are completely sharp. One day, he will be an instrument of vast talent. As chance would have it, he is not yet engaged. My daughter, Fengchu, is just 20 years old, younger than Chonggu by three years. Luckily she is smart and proper, too. The ancients emphasized the choice of a suitable son-in-law. Who would be a more suitable son-in-law than Mr. Huang? The day before yesterday, I sent over three suspicious and difficult cases to test him. I have discovered that he has reached a verdict in each. Today he will certainly come to report to me, and I will also be able to test his literary abilities by having him do some writing on my behalf. I can then select him personally.
(*Mimes looking at the plaque marking the hours*)
It is already the *chen*[64] hour; why isn't he here yet? Call for my clerk.

---

61. Song Yu authored the "Rhapsody on Gaotang" (*Gaotang fu* 高唐賦), about a dream King Xiang of Chu had while traveling in Gaotang. In the dream, an immortal visits and shares a pillow with him. King Xiang asked Song Yu to compose a *fu* on this topic.

62. See p. 186 note 38.

63. Xiang Ping 向平 was a recluse of the Eastern Han (220–225 CE) named Xiang Chang 向長, with the style name Ziping 子平. It is said that after retiring from public life, he sought only to see his sons and daughters married; having achieved that, he set off on a pilgrimage to the Five Great Mountains, never to be heard of again. The Five Great Mountains (Wuyue 五岳) is a collective name for the five famous mountains in China, as defined in the Daoist tradition. Each of the five mountains corresponds to the five directions in Daoist geomancy and is therefore a site for pilgrimage. They are Taishan 泰山 to the east, in Shandong province; Huashan 華山 to the west, in Shaanxi province; Hengshan 衡山 to the south in Hunan province; Hengshan 恆山 to the north in Shanxi province; and Songshan 嵩山 in the center, in Henan province.

64. This is the block of time between seven and nine in the morning.

(*A* mo *playing the clerk enters*)
Zhou Xiang: Go to my study and get Regional Administrator Huang's reports from the day before. He wanted to arrest that bunch of policemen, but he said that as they were special yamen he was not at liberty to act, so he requested that a memorial be submitted. Once you finish the draft, let me have a look. (*A* mo *mimes assenting and exiting, and then returning to present to Zhou Xiang*)(*A* wai *mimes studying the report*)(*The* dan *and* jing *enter*)
[To the tune *Chuanyan yunü*]

> As the sun sets, I finish my work;
> It is a good time to go chant amidst the pines.
> But a red invitation sheet
> Has just passed between my gates.
> Today, horses face this statesman's residence, crowding the sand-covered dike,
> Hurriedly I return with the reports from yesterday morning.

The day before yesterday, I received three cases from Zhou Xiang's prefecture. Everything has been resolved now, and I have come to present my response. Huang Ke, this report has some confidential material in it: carry it personally for me, and follow me in.
(*Huang Chonggu enters and, with two kneels and a bow, hands over the report*)
Chonggu: The day before yesterday, Your Honor sent three cases concerning Huang Tianzhi and others. I have reached my verdict and have come to hand over the reports for your perusal.
Zhou Xiang: All resolved? Very good! Bring them over. Rise! Runners, close the doors. Come to the rear hall and have a seat, Regional Administrator.
(*Chonggu again kneels twice and bows once, then sits*)
(*Zhou Xiang looks at the reports*)
Zhou: You have reached the perfect judgment in all three cases: investigating subtly, redressing grievances, and plucking out the hidden. That is heavenly! The day before yesterday, I had my doubts, too; so, even before the judgment in the first case had been made, I had the prisoners released from their cangues. But this cannot compare to your finessing: marvelous things like binding that widow, and using accusations of robbery to frighten Butcher Mo's wife to allow you to search for the receipts! What

ingenuity! None could sort out Zhen Kexiao's background, but you found out from his own actions, producing the truth that he had not joined the gang. What quick-wittedness! When Zhang Shizhi presided over cases, none under heaven were falsely accused.[65] Later, under Yu Dingguo, the people felt themselves protected from false accusations.[66] Now we have you.

(*Zhou rises and bows*)

I am respectfully humbled! Respectfully humbled! Let's do as you adjudicated, dear friend. I will give my approval, and it is settled.

Chonggu: I cannot presume to do so! You have promoted me to this position. I only do my duty.

Zhou: As to your proposal to arrest those runners and Qiao Bushi, I have already written a memorial based on it. Have your old man Huang come in, take off the round-collared official gown, and bring in a cushion from inside so that we can sit together. Presuming upon your kindness, there are a few more things that I would like for you to do.

Chonggu: I cannot presume to do so! As you please.

Zhou: I had built an ancestral hall for Wen Weng[67] and Zhuge Liang,[68] and on the plaque above the gates I have selected the inscription: "Twin Pillars of Shu."[69] I still require a couplet to flank the gates. Yang Xiong,[70]

---

65. Zhang Shizhi 張釋知 (ca. second century BCE) was a Western Han figure who was Governor of Gaol (*tingwei* 廷尉) to Han Wendi 漢文帝 (202–157 BCE). Known for following the word of the law, Zhang allowed no one to be unjustly convicted under his watch. He famously interceded when Han Wendi sought to sentence a man to death for frightening his horse, advising that the punishment should not exceed the letter of the law. *Hanshu* 50: 2310.

66. Huang Chonggu is being compared to Zhang Shizhi (see above note) and Yu Dingguo 于定國 (fl. 74 BCE) who was Chamberlain for Law Enforcement to Han Xuandi 漢宣帝 (91–49 BCE). Like Zhang Shizhi, he is an exemplar of good judgment and wisdom in matters of criminal law. *Hanshu* 71: 3043.

67. Wen Weng 文翁 was a Western Han governor of Sichuan who founded schools under Han Jingdi 漢景帝 (181–141 BCE).

68. Zhuge Liang 諸葛亮 (181–234) was the famous and learned Three Kingdoms strategist.

69. Shu 蜀 is the ancient name for Sichuan, and Wen Weng and Zhuge Liang are famous local heroes.

70. Yang Xiong 揚雄 (ca. 53–18 BCE) was a Western Han scholar and poet from Chengdu.

Wang Bao,[71] Sima Xiangru, Qiao Zhou,[72] Chen Zi'ang,[73] Li Bai,[74] and Du Fu[75] were all sojourners in Shu, and the seven geniuses will share one hall of worship. The plaque there reads: "The Temple of the Seven Geniuses," and also requires a couplet for the doors. Lying further to the front, the "Zither Pavilion of Zhuo Wenjun"[76] lacks a poetic inscription. There is also the matter of a long-standing debt of mine: neighbors of my ancestors recently erected a temple to Mulan, and my friends are requesting a "Raising the Beam" text for it.[77]

(*Gets up and bows*)

For these matters, I would like to "borrow your light." Servants, bring in the brush and ink.

Chonggu: As you have asked, I cannot refuse. But acting so foolishly in your presence is truly like flourishing an axe at Lu Ban's door.[78] Allow me to follow your orders, and I shall draw up a draft copy for your consideration.

---

71. Also from Sichuan, Wang Bao 王褒 was a scholar and writer employed by Han Xuandi (r. 74–49 BCE).

72. Qiao Zhou 譙周 (201–70) served in Shu during the Three Kingdoms and was said to have been an astrologer whose readings helped Zhuge Liang strategize.

73. Chen Zi'ang 陳子昂 (656?–702) was an early Tang poet and a native of Sichuan, known for his poem cycle called the *Ganyu* 感遇.

74. The great Tang poet Li Bo (Bai) 李白 lived in Sichuan for a time as a young child.

75. Du Fu, on fleeing the An Lushan rebellion, settled in Chengdu and wrote many poems on his life there in his "thatched cottage."

76. Sima Xiangru played the zither (*qin* 琴) to woo Zhuo Wenjun, and after they were married, the two would play the zither together to dispel their sorrows at having been disowned.

77. This refers to a ceremony of thanks to Lu Ban 魯班 (507–440 BCE) (see the following note) performed when raising the final ridge pole, or beam, of a building. See Klaas Ruitenbeek, *Carpentry and Building in Late Imperial China: A Study of the Fifteenth-Century Carpenter's Manual* Lu Ban Jing (Leiden: Brill, 1996).

78. The historical carpenter and strategist Lu Ban was and continues to be revered as the patron saint of carpenters and builders in China, so to challenge him with an axe would be an act of supreme conceit.

Zhou: You have the talent to do it propped against your horse,[79] so you should certainly display your talent here on the spot. Don't be so modest. Servant, rub the ink. Write the big characters first. Bring a large cup over and pour three cups to give him some inspiration.
(*Chonggu writes "The Two Pillars of Shu," and Zhou examines it carefully*)
[To the tune *Liangzhou xu*]

The rock inscribes the crane's tomb,[80]
These silver hooks are like a curved scorpion's tail.[81]
When comparing the two,
Then definitely, it is standard style[82] that is more difficult.
A single character of Ziyun's[83]
Was taken to a special pavilion to be hung in Xiao Studio.[84]
No one compares to you, whose inscriptions are like those on bronze vessels,
Or coral curled up in iron nets,[85]
The rustling leaf blades of the Wuguang script.

---

79. "When Huan Wen went on his northern expedition in 369 CE, [Yüan Hong (Yüan Hu)] was his companion, but after being reprimanded for some fault, Yüan was relieved of his post. It happened that Huan needed a conspicuous sign proclaiming his victory. Summoning Yüan, he ordered him to write one, propped against the front of his horse. Yüan's hand did not break from writing until in one dash he had filled seven sheets of paper, all extremely beautiful to behold. Wang Hsün, who was by his side, sighed with the greatest admiration for his ability. Yüan said to him, 'This ought to let us win a verbal victory, anyway.'" From the "Letters and Scholarship" (*wenxue*) section of *SSXY*, translation by Richard Mather. Liu I-ch'ing, *Shih-shuo Hsin-Yü*, 149.

80. This is the carving known as "Crane tomb engraving" (*yihe ming* 瘞鶴銘). Found on a cliffside in Jiangsu, it is of unknown hand and time period. The style of carving is the standard, or straight, style of writing Chinese (*kaishu* 楷書), which remains the modern-day script. The Song dynasty poet Huang Tingjian (黃庭堅 1045–1105) praised it for its unsurpassed beauty.

81. He is describing the cursive, or "grass," script (*caoshu* 草書), which is the most abstract of the calligraphic styles.

82. By "standard style," he means the *kaishu* style described in note 80 above.

83. Xiao Ziyun 蕭子雲 was a famous calligrapher of the Southern Dynasties (Southern Liang, 502–57) who favored the cursive and clerical scripts (*caolishu* 草隸書), the cursive *cao* script, and the older *li* script that was used for display writing.

84. Liang Wudi 梁武帝 (464–549) had built a temple and commissioned Xiao Ziyun to paint the character for his family name, "Xiao" 蕭, on it. The temple was renamed "Xiao Studio."

85. Still referring to Chonggu's calligraphy, the metaphor is that of rare quality and exquisite beauty.

(*Chonggu writes "The Ancestral Hall of the Seven Geniuses"*)
(*Zhou Xiang looks at it*)
Zhou: Those fingertips have an exceptional force that could carve into cliff sides, so it really fits the formal green-black plaque flecked with gold.
Chonggu: A Wei Dan suspended in a basket, hair turned white,[86] how dare I imitate Wang Huizhi's eccentricity?[87] To make it into a *qilin* study, one must still repay the prime minister.[88]
Zhou: Well done!
Chonggu: I look to you to educate me.
Zhou: What's there to improve! Servants: another three cups! Pour for my companion, who still has to write the couplets for the doorways of the two halls.
(*Chonggu does this, and writes*) (*Zhou Xiang examines them before reading them aloud*)
Zhou: "Civil virtue and military merit illuminate and reflect on Brocade River's jade battlements.[89] In the divided realm of Shu, the worthies are widely distributed; lingering, I contemplate the green grass and yellow orioles."[90]
(*Continues to read the couplet for the "Seven Geniuses"*)

"Writers seven, gathered stars in letters like dragons and tigers of literature,

---

86. Wei Dan 韋誕, styled Chongjiang 重將, was a Three Kingdoms calligrapher from the state of Wei 魏. He was ordered by Wei Mingdi 魏明帝 (or Cao Rui 曹叡, 204–39) to inscribe, while suspended in a basket, a plaque for the emperor on a cliff overhanging the ocean. By the time he was finished, his hair had turned white.

87. Wang Huizhi 王徽之 (d. 388) was one of the seven sons of Wang Xizhi, who was known for his eccentric behavior. This eccentricity is exemplified in a famous anecdote about him in which he undertakes an all-night journey in a boat through the snow to visit a friend and, upon arriving at the doors, immediately turns back without visiting, saying that he followed a whim in going and, the whim having passed, did not need to stay.

88. The *qilin* (麒麟) study was established by Xiao He 蕭何 (d. 193 BCE) for the gathering of talents and documents. Xiao He was Prime Minister of the Han dynasty and the ultimate model ruler and statesman.

89. Brocade River is located in Sichuan. This is a reference to Du Fu's poetry from his time in Sichuan.

90. This line is borrowed from a poem by Du Fu and expresses the sentiment, "Being at this site makes one think of all the worthies who have been there before."

Standing out above all eternity, clouds stretch over Emei's half of the sky."

Good as well! It really is on the level of the seven geniuses.

[To the tune *Liangzhou xu*]

Two wise men still beloved, seven heroes steeped in learning,
Their merits stand out beyond the age.
All these heroes are justly praised in these four inscribed lines;
Further illuminating the sparrows and swallows amidst the beams,
And the turtle and dragon carvings at the stone stele's bottom,
That encircle and protect the spirits within.
The four lines, in gilt and many colors,
Will certainly sprout auspicious mushrooms.

Have the servants count how many words are on these two couplets.
(A *Chou* answers): Forty characters.
Zhou: You have stolen away forty bright pearls to ornament these walls.[91]
Chonggu:

This image of moon dew,
This form of wind and clouds,
Crooked couplets like mine, they are nothing but
The amusements of a small child at night, scheming to finish schoolwork as quickly as possible.
My dear teacher, today
You are like Golden Valley's owner[92] having to borrow from a beggar.

Zhou: Servants, another three cups for Mr. Huang, and we shall wait for him to get the inspiration to compose the poems. Quatrains will do. (*Chonggu writes the poem on Zhuo Wenjun's Zither Terrace. Zhou Xiang reads it*)

---

91. He compares the hangings of poems to hairpins (metaphors for women's beauty) that are used to embellish hair arrangements.

92. The wealthy Shi Chong 石崇 (249–300) of the Jin dynasty (265–420) was a favorite of Emperor Jin Wudi 晉武帝 (r. 265–90). He used his immense wealth to construct a garden in the Golden Valley that hosted poetry composition, music composition, and feasts. His ill-fated romance with the flautist Lüzhu 綠珠 is commemorated in a Yuan dynasty *zaju* by Guan Hanqing entitled *Lüzhu Falls from the Tower* (*Lüzhu zhui lou*).

Zhou:

The orphaned swan could not restrain her virtuous heart,
The old affair of pursuing a phoenix wife is long cold.[93]
On the *qin* pavilion, one night, the mountain flowers bloodied,[94]
The moon rises over Mount Emei as the cuckoo cries.
(*Zhou claps his hands and cries out*)
Matchless beauty! Young brother, you really are one rowing a boat of pearls; each and every pearl a treasure.

Zhou:
[To the tune *Liangzhou xu*]

The thick amber is still not at the third cup,
But the boat of pearls arrives once more.
The strings and wood[95] send off a tone,
That seems to come from among the yellowed grasses in the graveyard.
Those plaintive notes, ah,
Are truly like a Du Yu bird's[96] calls at Qingming[97]
Or a birchleaf pear at Cold Food festival.[98]
Saddening her blackened spring mountain brows:
a pile of red petals.

---

93. This refers to Zhuo Wenjun, now cast off by Sima Xiangru, whose pursuit of Zhuo is long past.

94. The "mountain flowers bloodied" refers to red azaleas (*dujuan*) in bloom. Sichuan's mountains are famous for the azaleas that bloom through the months of spring and summer. The cuckoo bird (also called *dujuan*) is tied to the azaleas because it is thought to cry so plaintively and bitterly that its tears would run with blood, thus lending the azaleas their color. For more lore on the cuckoo, see note 96 below.

95. The strings and wood are the *qin* 琴.

96. The cuckoo bird, or *dujuan* 杜鵑, is said in Shu 蜀 folklore to derive its name from the Zhou dynasty (1122?–221 BCE) statesman Du Yu 杜宇 (222–85 BCE). He seduced his prime minister's wife and was made to abdicate. Upon his death, his remorseful soul was transformed into a cuckoo, hence the name "*dujuan*." See C.M. Lai, "Messenger of Spring and Morality: Cuckoo Lore in Chinese Sources," *Journal of the American Oriental Society* 118.4 (1998): 531.

97 Qingming is the day known as "All Souls Day" or "Grave Sweeping Day" or "Clear and Bright Festival." It takes place on the 104th day after the winter solstice and is the day designated for making offerings to departed ancestors and sweeping their graves.

98. The birchleaf pear (*tangli* 棠梨) is a Chinese pear tree.

Having received your poems, I hate that I am not
Buried at the Qin Pavilion,
Why talk of
Reminiscing about the ancient genius on the banks of Spotted Stone Jetty?[99]
Chonggu:
Examiner, you ordered your student to write in your place,
And moreover Wenjun herself fittingly recited the song of white hair.[100]
Therefore it was
Difficult to use the brush,
And I almost
Failed to pay back this poetry debt,
But here is my "Raising the Beam" text.

Zhou: A parallel prose piece plays even more to your strengths.
(*Chonggu writes*)(*Zhou looks at it, and then reads aloud*)
Zhou:

Now, as a young lady, beautiful and talented,
A beauty of brows painted in the moon-shaped mirror.
Suddenly, dressed in martial array,
Hung with armor, in Tianshan's dangerous passes.
Substituting for your father, heart as firm as steel,
You held to the form of tiger and leopard.
Ashamed of your female appearance;
You joined the army, brave to the heavens.
With the changing of the *mingjie* leaves,[101]
And twelve years passed.
Displaying filial piety for loyalty,

---

99. Spotted Stone Jetty (Caishiji 采石磯) is in Jin'an 今安, where Li Bai died.

100. Zhuo Wenjun wrote the poem "A Song of White Hair" ("Baitou yin" 白頭吟) to protest her husband's suggestion that he take a concubine.

101. According to *Matthews' Chinese English Dictionary*, "The *mingjie* 蓂莢 is an auspicious plant said to have grown in the palace of Emperor Yao. It produced a leaf on the first of the lunar month, and one each day till the full moon, after which it lost a leaf each day till the end of the month." This way, the plant could be used to mark time based on the number of leaves it gained or lost (entry no. 4532).

You emerged pure from the mud.
A pair of rabbits, side by side on the ground,
It is hard to tell apart male from female.[102]
When the swift horse surprised people,
It transcended male and female, black and yellow.[103]
Your heroic soul stirs up the ages,
So your altars and temples should be renewed.
Your pure form is cast in cold,
Your cloudy top-knot and misty temples ride purple mists.[104]
Behind the red banner, your fragrant soul,
Must adhere to the army of women.
From the River Xiang to the mountain altar,
There is no need to feel inferior to the Wives' temple.[105]
As the highest beam is now raised,[106]
May the incense fires burn forever.

(*Zhou Xiang finishes reading*)
Excellent! Excellent!

---

102. This refers to the "Ballad of Mulan."

103. This line alludes to a story in the *Liezi* 列子 about the horse expert Bole 伯樂, who was thought to be the greatest judge of horses and their physiognomy. He was summoned by Duke Mu to suggest a successor whose skill would equal his own. The man he chose was named Jiufang Gao 九方皋, who was sent to find the finest horse. Jiufang Gao reported back after three months, saying that he had found such a horse, and when asked to describe it, he called it "a yellow mare." When the horse was led in, people saw that it was, in fact, a black stallion. When Duke Mu summoned Bole to explain this, Bole replied that what Jiufang Gao looked at was the essential essence of the horse, focusing on the inside of the horse rather than its outer appearance. The horse turned out to be a great horse. Clearly this and the mention of Mulan is meant to resonate with Chonggu's own situation.

104. Purple mist marks the arrival of a divinity.

105. The faithful wives of the legendary Emperor Shun 舜 were thought to be buried on a mountain, where the eponymous temple stands. In one version of the story, they throw themselves into the Xiang river upon learning that their husband had died. Their loyalty earned them first place in Liu Xiang's 劉向 (77?–6? BCE) *Biographies of Eminent Women* (*Lienü zhuan* 列女傳). Continuing the tradition of tears of blood, the strain of bamboo called "Xiang Consorts Bamboo" (Xiangfei zhu 湘妃竹) is thought to be spotted from the blood-stained tears that his wives cried upon his death. The comparison here is between Mulan's loyalty to country and that of Emperor Shun's faithful wives to their husband.

106. "Beam" suggests pillars of state (Matthews entry no. 6607).

[To the tune *Liangzhou xu*]

Serving with fellow soldiers, when in her previous life it was skirts and hairpins,
Her heroic bearing is precisely described in your "Raising the Beam" text.
Compared to the filial girl, Cao'e,[107]
She added a bit of
Leading the attacks and raiding forts.
When we see these characters in red lines, and,
On yellow pongee silk, and the engraved backs of steles,
She will receive the admiration of a man like Courtier Cai Yong.[108]

Zhou: To take on the disguise that she did was all good luck for her old man.
Chonggu: Have I sullied your reputation?
Zhou Xiang:

Where the red gauze is newly hung with your inscription,
Everyone would say the material of *zhen* or camphor wood
Should be used to build a hundred foot tall tower to raise a "Five Phoenix Tower."

Chonggu:

How drunk I am! Hopelessly confused,
Still riding a sickly nag towards the heavenly road,[109]
When will Mulan's debt be repaid!

Zhou Xiang: What do you mean by this?
Chonggu: I got drunk, and my "Raising the Beam" text is missing six "Er lang weis."[110] Doesn't that mean that the debt is not yet fully paid?

---

107. Cao E 曹娥 was a filial daughter of the Eastern Han. After her father drowned in a river, she wept beside the river for seventeen days before throwing herself into the river as well. Her temple stands in Shaoxing.

108. Cai Yong 蔡邕 (c. 135–92) was so inspired by the story of Cao E that he wrote lines commemorating her.

109. Toward the khan.

110. "Er lang weis" are formulaic words of unknown meaning that are supposed to be inserted into "Raising the Beam" texts (these do not show up in such texts after the Song dynasty).

Zhou Xiang: Each character of your "Raising the Beam" is worth a thousand ounces of silver; forget about the lack of "Er lang weis."
(*Chonggu turns to the audience, acting out dismay*)
Chonggu: I almost gave myself away!
(*Facing the* wai, *she recites*)
As I am very drunk, I should give up.
Zhou: Why do you have to be such a wet blanket? Do you think me so coarse? Do you look down on me because I failed to "moisten your brush"? Am I like those people who ask for free poems and essays? I have plenty to offer you: I have already got nearly four rolls of grape brocade, four rolls of lantern brocade, four jade-handled brushes, and several dozen Xue Tao slips.[111] I also have a big box of Moung Qing snow grubs,[112] all readied for when your cup is dry after the poetry. Let's not have you write any more; just relax and have something to eat and drink.
Chonggu: When you put it that way, I would rather drink myself to the ground than to take my leave.
Zhou: If you really are drunk, then let's go into my little studio. There is a very small flower garden there where we can stroll together. Servants, tell the chef that we don't want any regular rich food, just prepare some bamboo shoots to go with the wine.
(*Chonggu goes to the studio and looks at the flowers, feeling better*)
(*From inside comes the sound of the* qin, *and Chonggu listens*)
Chonggu: Teacher, is there someone inside playing the *qin*?
Zhou: Yes! That is my young daughter, Fengchu. Since she was a little girl, she has been clever: she could read many books, could play several songs on the *qin*, and knew a few moves in chess.[113] She does not know that we are here. (*Calls out*) Servants, go in and tell her that we have a guest in the studio. Young friend, perhaps it was because my Fengchu was embroidering various kinds of flowers that she gradually learned how to paint several floral genres in the ink-wash style.

---

111. Xue Tao 薛濤 (768–831) was a Tang dynasty poet who wrote her poems on red slips of paper. Eight-line poems came to be called "Xue Tao slips" (*Xue Tao jian* 薛濤箋) as a result.

112. A delicacy of fine flavor. Mount Qing (Qingcheng shan 青城山) is located in Sichuan and is also called Zhangren shan 丈人山.

113. Zhou's understatement here and elsewhere to his guest is his polite way of boasting about her many talents. It would be unseemly to speak frankly about her gifts, so he couches his praise mildly.

Chonggu: Hearing you talk, she must truly be like a Ban Zhao[114] or a Xie Daoyun.[115]
Zhou: You embarrass me. Really, I hear that these three things are your own great talents.
Chonggu: I am just a dabbler. Actually, I'm not very good.
Zhou: Servants, go inside and bring out Fengchu's *qin*, and also bring one of her paintings out to let Mr. Huang take a look.
(*A* chou *brings them out for Chonggu to look at*)
(*Chonggu looks, and says*)
Marvelous! Truly, it is expressive art! Nowhere in it is there a whiff of the inner chambers.[116]
Zhou: Bring the paper here, and let Mr. Huang paint a bit so that my girl can use it as a template.
Chonggu: This too would be flourishing an axe at Lu Ban's door.
Zhou: Servants, pour out a cup and kneel. If Mr. Huang does not paint, then you must not rise.
Chonggu: Quick, get up. I will paint.
(*Chonggu paints. Zhou watches and says*)
Really extraordinary! Your reputation does not betray you. Send this in to the young lady and bring the *qin* over here. That will even more fulfill my long-standing desire.
Servants, bring the wine forward, kneel, and present it.
Chonggu: No need! I will play.
(*Chonggu plays the* qin, *while Zhou watches and says*)
Zhou: These notes resemble the song "Male Phoenix seeking the Female Phoenix."
Chonggu: Indeed. How do you know it?
Zhou: Why speak of Sima Xiangru? It is a pity that in my yamen there is no Zhuo Wenjun.
(*Chonggu acts startled and remorseful, and says*)
Chonggu: I really am drunk. If there were to be another competition of bets, I would have to force myself to drink a few more cups. What if we,

---

114. Ban Zhao 班昭 (45–116) of the Eastern Han was Ban Gu's 班固 (32–92) younger sister and a talented writer thought to have helped him write the *History of the Han* (*Hanshu* 漢書).

115. Xie Daoyun 謝道韞 (ca. fourth century) was an Eastern Jin poet from the literary Xie family. The poet Xie An 謝安 (320–85) was her uncle, and her father-in-law was the calligrapher Wang Xizhi.

116. That is, the weak and feminine.

after tallying up the moves, have you accept the drinking forfeits on my behalf?
Zhou: Preposterous! You've already decided that you will not lose, eh?
Chonggu: I am drunk and misspoke. If I offended you, penalize me.
Zhou: That's all right. Bring the chess board over, let's just play one game; each one of us will not exceed forty moves, so quickly plan your strategy.
(They play qi, *or chess)*
(*Zhou Xiang loses*)
Chonggu: You owe me five cups, and I will take two of them.
Zhou: Prodigy! Prodigy! In everything he excels above the highest order!
[To the tune *Jiejie gao*]

This clearly is like Chuyang terrace,
With its nine levels of stairways,
At every level that goes higher, he still wins.
Playing the *qin* with heaven-made tones,
Painting pictures of lifelike moss,
In his game of chess, I lost.
When it comes to the titles of master and pupil,
It is up to you to deny them.
In my reckoning, I should be staying outside the gate and wall.

Chonggu: Teacher, how can you make jokes like this?
Zhou: You are both cloud and dragon united in one body,[117]
How can I, like Meng Jiao, accept obeisances from Han Yu?[118]
(*Chonggu again tries to take leave*)
It's late.
Zhou: Pour more wine to present to Master Huang.
[To the tune *Jiejie gao*]

Don't refuse because the light of the sun is low,
Don't come up with excuses again and again.
Even if you return to your office, you cannot fulfill your debt of
documents.

---

117. Dragons are thought to create clouds, so to be both dragon and cloud combined is to be the epitome of magnificence.

118. Meng Jiao 孟郊 (751–814) was part of Han Yu's 韓愈 (768–824) circle. Although Han Yu went on to pass the examinations, Meng Jiao did not. Zhou Xiang thus uses the allusion to compare himself to Meng Jiao and Chonggu to Han Yu, to emphasize his unworthiness.

Our garden's celery and scallions, and
Our fish cheeks and brains,
Were mean fare to serve to you.
Now these rolls of grape brocade,
Would only be fit to make pouches to carry your poems,
Ten thousand pieces of treasure would not be enough to account
for your innumerable pearls.

Chonggu: My teacher, you praise your student too highly. What is the exceptional quality of an unmarvelous rock of Sichuan, to be, in a moment of good luck, worshipped by Nangong?[119] I really must call it quits this time.
Zhou: Fine, I will keep you no longer.
[To the tune *Wei sheng*]

Whenever you have leisure from your books,
And when flowers and moon are here again,
When your spirits are high, spur on your horse and come.
I too will try to get black bird and yellow fish,[120]
And we can finish this fine amber wine.

(*Chonggu gives thanks and takes leave*)
Zhou: Servant, take the rewards for the writing assignments that we just spoke about and send them over to Master Huang's yamen.
(*The* mo *holds them up*)(*Zhou lowers his voice and commands*)
I will await the response in the library; just beat the board before you come in.
(*The official assents*)(*The* wai *leaves without fanfare*) (*The official mimes escorting Chonggu to the gates*)
Official: I have been ordered to see if you understood my master's offerings of wine.
Chonggu: That was just to receive me as a guest for composing poems; what else is there to understand?
Official: Not so. My master has a daughter, Fengchu, who is still unmarried. His Excellency admires you, Regional Administrator, as a preeminent star in letters who would also make a charming son-in-law,

---

119. Nangong 南宮 was a Song dynasty figure so enamored of rocks that he made obeisances to one that he called older brother. This would be an anachronism.
120. Meat and fish.

and he very much would like to attach himself to you. He ordered me to transmit this to you not too bluntly, and says that he awaits your response in his studio. He entreats you to honor his request at this very moment.
(*Chonggu laughs loudly*)
Chonggu: How can this be? How can this be? Fine, as you say my teacher awaits my answer, I have no choice but to write a few words in response here in my chambers. I will trouble you to bring this message back for me.
Official: Yes, as you wish.
(*Chonggu gets off horse and enters a room, and writes*)(*The official calls to the* jing *playing Huang Ke*)
Official: Official Huang, please take all of these writing gifts and keep them. I still have to go in to take the response.
(*Huang Ke accepts them*)
(*Chonggu folds a poem and seals it and says to the official*)
Chonggu: Sorry to trouble you!
Official: Not at all.
Chonggu: I, Chonggu, have hitherto been able to hide myself like a broken halberd, half-rusted in the sand.[121] Teacher, you have to clean it to recognize the marks of a past dynasty. As for me, heaven chose not to make me a man: this is a case of the eastern wind not helping Zhou Yu along. Young lady, I'm afraid that I will betray you and lock you up in spring, like the two Qiao sisters in Copperbird Terrace.[122]
(*Chonggu and Huang Ke leave together*) (*The official knocks on clappers*)

---

121. This is an allusion to the late Tang poet Du Mu 杜牧 (803–52) and his poem "Red Cliff" ("Chibi" 赤壁), on finding a sword half buried in the sand and yet unrusted (Xu Wei changes the wording to "half-rusted," still bearing engravings of a former dynasty, the Three Kingdoms period). The halberd is a reminder of the glories of the past and the happenstance of fortune. In the case of Red Cliff, it is a wind that spreads the fire over Cao Cao's team of boats, causing him to lose a crucial battle.

122. See note above. These sentences all follow the allusion to the Du Mu poem, which reads "On the broken spear still unrusted in the sand/is burnished the marks of a past dynasty/Had the east wind not helped Zhou Yu/the Qiao sisters would still be locked in Copperbird Terrace in the spring" 折戟深沙鐵未銷，自將磨洗認前朝。東風不與周郎便，銅雀春深鎖二喬。Zhou Yu was a strategist under Sun Quan of the Wu Kingdom during the Three Kingdoms period. The two Qiao sisters were married to Zhou Yu and Sun Quan's younger brother, and Cao Cao sought to capture them and keep them in his Copperbird Terrace. This news unified Zhou Yu and Sun Quan in taking action against Cao Cao.

Zhou: What did he say?
(*The official hands over the letter and speaks*)
Official: About the thing that your honor ordered me to carry out, I did follow your orders and transmitted all that information to Master Huang. He wrote his reply in the office outside his gates and told me to present it to you.
(*Zhou takes the letter and reads it*)
(*Zhou recites*) Ever since I stopped collecting kingfisher feathers at Brocade River's edge,
Poor and keeping a humble thatched hut, I composed *fu* and poems.
Since I donned the blue gown of a graduate to take on official duties,
I had long cast away the *luan* bird mirror used to paint eyebrows.
Establishing myself with the bearing of the green pines,
I willfully maintained the carriage of tinkling white jade.
Now, minister, if you seek me to be your son-in-law with bared belly,[123]
I beg Heaven to quickly change me into a man.
(*Zhou is shocked*)
Ai! So he has always been a girl! Has there ever been such a wonder in this world? This case of a lover's match really is like Princess Huyang's:[124] it will never be. All right, my son Fengyu is trying for the exams, tomorrow the winning names will be announced. If Fengyu gets a lucky break, I will force him, Huang Chonggu, to become a wife, and make it something she can't refuse. I will now go to sleep on it, and wait to hear the morning's examination results.
(*Exits with his official*)

Act V[125]

(*Chonggu enters and speaks*)
Chonggu: Yesterday I hadn't thought such things would occur. I tried to conceal it but was not able to; I had to face the God of Spring and let the

---

123. See note 8 in appendix 3.

124. The sister of Eastern Han emperor Guang Wudi 光武帝 (5–57), Princess Huyang 湖陽公主 was newly widowed when she told her brother that she wanted to be married to the high official Song Hong 宋弘. Song Hong was unwilling to leave his first wife, so the match was broken.

125. Act 5 is the only act with a full set of songs.

plum fragrance leak out. The older son of the Zhou family was just rewarded the top graduate position, and today I will have to go make thanks for the wine of last night and also offer my congratulations. How should I present myself to see my teacher?[126] Have my servant ready my horse. I must go to Master Zhou's house.
(*Sits on horse*)
[To the tune *Banjiao zhegu*]

This horse is hasty,
My heart is lingering,
All because the plum blossom allowed out too much news.

(*Runner shouts out loudly to clear the road*)
Chonggu: Clerk, you are startling the country people beyond the forest,
You need not shout so loudly here in front of the horse.
Runner: Got it.
(*Chonggu dismounts horse and enters the back of the government office to wait*)
(*Zhou Xiang enters his office*)
Zhou: Now that my son Fengyu has been happily reported top graduate, Master Huang must be my daughter-in-law.
[To the tune *Banjiao zhegu*]

This news was hasty,
My smile is lingering,
Happy events, one after another, come in quick succession.
My son and that Chonggu, ah,
Are like two identical pearls, wept by a mermaid:
They would sell for a thousand ounces of gold at the southern market's Persian merchants' stalls.
Call my majordomo; go summon Regional Administrator Huang for me.

Official: Regional Administrator Huang came to present wine and gifts; he has been waiting outside the gates for a while.
Zhou: Why didn't you say so earlier? Quick, invite Huang in!
(*Official goes to invite the* dan *[Chonggu] in*)

---

126. Literally, "what 'face and mouth' should I take (*ba shenme zuilian* 把甚麼嘴臉) to go see him?"

(*Zhou looks at the* dan *and says in a teasing way*)
Wonderful! Yesterday in your "Raising the Beam" text, you said it was not enough to redeem Mulan's debt. Those words raised my suspicions; and, all this time *you* were Mulan! I shall report your misdeeds as a wicked official to the emperor!
(*Chonggu hurriedly kneels and says*)
Chonggu: I hope that teacher will forgive, and let grace and virtue last for an eternity, as heaven and earth.
Zhou: I was teasing you. Get up and bow. Administrator Huang, now there is another topic I would like you to undertake, which you cannot refuse.
Chonggu: I wouldn't dare!
Zhou: Because I loved you for your way with words and your character, I made that proposal. As you now cannot be my son-in-law, could you be my daughter-in-law? As Fengyu has had the happy coincidence of being a male top graduate, and you are the girl top graduate; and, as you are his top graduate superior, and he is your top graduate junior, you roughly match up with each other. If you wish to criticize me and say that I am an incapable Prime Minister, or that father and son's literary talents are not up to par, and therefore not deserving to be called "father-in-law" or "husband" by you, well, that is up to you.
(*Chonggu continues kneeling and says*)
Chonggu: When you speak this way, I have no ground to stand on. It's just that with my act of deceit, I now feel unbearably ashamed standing before you for a moment. If I were to be your daughter-in-law, and were to spend my whole life serving you as my father-in-law, how could I bear that shame?
Zhou: You yourself spoke of Mulan's situation as something for heroes alone, as glorious rather than shameful. How can you see things so topsy-turvy now? Now I would like to submit a memorial and order someone to take your place as Regional Administrator. Everyone must hear about this now, and from me, the father-in-law. Call my scribe!
(*A* xiaosheng *playing the scribe enters*)
Zhou: You, write up a memorial, beginning with Regional Administrator Huang's situation, as well as my desire to take her as my daughter-in-law. I reckon His Majesty will sanction it. Bring it to Mister Li to have him make a fair copy after inspection, and then present it to the Emperor.

I am very busy, so you will not need to show it to me to look over.
(*Chonggu acts embarrassed, and kneels again*)
Chonggu: I don't know what to say. I will obey your command.
Zhou: If you say this . . . you and my daughter are sisters-in-law!
(*Calls in a young girl*)
Wuye! Quickly call the young lady of the house to bring in new ceremonial robes and a bun extension and tell her to help dress up her sister-in-law. When you return, you can be married.
Chonggu (*kneeling again*): Teacher, this is so hurried and frenetic. Let us choose another day, please!
Zhou: Today is the day that the names of the successful are hung up; what else could you want? Take advantage of today and decide on this affair, lest you leave and have second thoughts.
(*The* tie *and* chou *bring in the costumes and greet her*)
(*Chonggu changes her costume*)
(*A musical band blows the flute and plays the drum to welcome the* sheng, *who enters*)
Fengyu:
[To the tune *Banjiao zhegu*]

> See, those with posted names are hasty,
> Those whose names were left off are lingering,
> The horse neighs against its golden bridle: how exceptional is its pride.
> In the apricot garden I broke off the top graduate's red,[127]
> Let them sell this apricot flower at every crossroads.[128]

(*Fengyu* [sheng] *sees Zhou Xiang* [wai] *and Fengchu* [tie])
(*The* dan *[Chonggu] has her back turned to him. Fengyu asks*)
Fengyu: Who is this?
Zhou: All this time you were in the examination quarters, I didn't want to embarrass anyone by sending word to tell you of these matters. This

---

127. The apricot garden (*xingyuan* 杏園) was an attraction to the west of Chang'an where, during the Tang dynasty, successful exam graduates would be feasted and where candidates would sightsee. As a result, it becames a kenning for a successful scholar. The graduates were festooned with a ribbon sash resembling a large red blossom, which is what Fengyu refers to in this line.

128. Only his is the *true* red of the *zhuangyuan*.

person is your brother from your generation of students, Regional Administrator Huang, who, it turns out, is a girl. Just yesterday I wished to make your sister Chonggu's wife. Once exposed, she came out with everything.
Fengyu (startled): How on earth could this happen! And why has she changed dress now!
Zhou: As she cannot be my son-in-law, I have changed my topic[129] and sought to make her my daughter-in-law, to be married to you. She could not refuse, so I called on your sister to help her change clothes, and we have been waiting for you to come to get married. The ancients say: "The names are inscribed on the golden placard; then it is on to the flowery candle in the nuptial chamber."[130] Is this not a wonderful opportunity? Daughter, invite your sister-in-law to come pay respects to her family and to stop being shy.
Fengyu: Father, this is all too hurried and frenetic. Let's change the date.
Zhou: So, the two of you are both alike with this fake propriety! Quick, do your obeisances! Call the Master of Ceremonies to perform the rites.
(*A* zhongjing *playing the Master of Ceremonies (M.C.) enters and officiates at the wedding*)
M.C.: The girl top graduate harmonizes with the male top graduate, and heaven commands them to join these two mandarin ducks in the minister's office. Just see how, with paired wings, they soar beyond the clouds and how their equal brilliance flutters about like embroidered brocade.
(*Chonggu and Fengyu bow together*)
M.C. (*recites*):
The wind-blown candle's shadows are deep in the mica screen.
As the Heavenly River slowly sinks, the morning star disappears.
Chang E must regret stealing the spirit elixir of immortality,
In the indigo sky like the azure sea, night after night this longing.[131]
(*Fengyu, Chonggu, and Fengchu bow to each other*)
The gauze skirt, all of green leaves, all cut of the same color,

129. This line keeps the vocabulary of essay writing.
130. That is, then on to the wedding festivities.
131. The Master of Ceremonies is quoting from Li Shangyin's 李賞隱 (ca. 813–58) poem, "Chang E" 常娥. This poem is translated by A.C. Graham in *Poems of the Late T'ang*, 155.

The lotus color on both cheeks,
When these lovebirds fall into the lake, they become unseen,
Hearing a song, I then realize someone is coming.[132]
Zhou:
[To the tune *Huamei xun*]

On that day I led the literary examinations,
My son and Master Huang, ah,
Became brothers like geese following one another to the same examiner.
Today, ah,
Happily he became like the head of the tortoise,
Making a companion for the phoenix, all in accord.
Who could have hoped that the plum and peach trees growing within these walls,
Would change and serve us old folks, a bride's father and mother-in-law?

Together:

Among top graduates there are scarcely coupled pairs,
Heaven's command gave a woman's appearance and a man's talents.

Fengyu:
[To the tune *Huamei xu*]

The Associate Judge and I were of equal rank,
In the beginning, ah,
We called each other as older and younger brother of connected families.
Who would have expected that this would be a false dragon officer with sharp tail-feathers,
And it would turn out to be a mother oyster with a pearl hidden in her womb?
Only now I know you as a beautiful woman like Chang E in the moonlight,
whereas I had mistaken you as a cohort in the previous exam class.

---

132. This is quoted from Wang Changling's 王昌齡 (698–765) "Song of Picking Lotuses" ("Cai lian qu" 采蓮曲).

Fengyu and Chonggu (together):

> Where else have top graduates come in a male and female pair?
> The only difference is between gauze cap and golden hairpin.

Chonggu:
[To the tune *Huamei xu*]

> It's not that I made a show of falseness,
> But only that my poor existence was too forlorn.
> I guessed that if in a palace gown I could steal the brocade,
> I would not have to live behind a twig and bracken door.
> I am humbled that the Prime Minister saw me as an immortal talent fit to ride the phoenix,
> And invited Xiao Shi to be the fine man mounting the dragon with his bride.[133]

Fengyu and Chonggu (together):

> Top graduates, you and I, are male and female companions,
> Both of us, chanting of the willow floss,[134] the finest of flowers.

Fengchu:
[To the tune *Huamei xu*]

> This fine son-in-law pleases father,
> Who would have thought you, Regional Administrator, would be of my kind.
> To sum up, the teacher set out a banquet,
> But alas the guest turned out to wear curled shoes![135]
> Changed anew from man to my sister-in-law, entering the kitchen,
> Sending me off to taste the soup vegetables for her mother-in-law.

---

133. See p. 186 note 38.

134. The willow floss refers to Xie Daoyun, the archetypal talented woman. She was a favorite niece of the great poet Xie An. When he asked her to describe a snowy day, she compared the snow to willow catkins on the wind. He was so pleased with the comparison that she was thenceforth called the "talent that praises willow catkins," and her name, linked with catkins, used to mean literary talent. She was unhappily married to Wang Ningzhi, son of the famous calligrapher Wang Xizhi.

135. That is, for bound feet.

Chonggu and everyone (together):

> My being top graduate almost interfered with our becoming male and female companions,
> Isn't this something to make the butterfly messenger and bee matchmaker die with laughter?

(*A* zhongjing *playing a eunuch enters bearing an imperial decree and gifts*)
Eunuch: I issue the king of Shu's royal decree, which by proclamation gives the female top graduate and Prime Minister Zhou's newly minted top graduate son permission to marry. I sped my horse on over here, and as this is the Prime Minister's studio, I come in to read the edict.
(*Mimes announcing*)
(*Lines up an incense table on which the edict will be placed, bowed to, and then read aloud*)
(*The* zhongjing *enters, and everyone kneels to hear the imperial decree*)
His Majesty decrees: Upon considering our officer's memorial, these circumstances are deemed especially wondrous, and we have also learned that the wedding date is to be exactly this evening. We have transmitted this news to the two palaces, and all are thrilled.[136] Therefore, by imperial decree I give to both parties twenty bolts of mandarin duck brocade dyed and washed in the Brocade River's waters, ten pints of real pearls, one purple jade hair ornament bearing a phoenix mother leading nine phoenix chicks, two hairpins of eight-treasure gold, and a thousand southern Yue kingfisher feathers as contribution to your festive occasion. As to the position that Chonggu previously filled, she will be replaced by your son, Fengyu. As to Chonggu, we admire her extraordinary behavior and commend her for serving most properly for the last three years. She should therefore be ennobled as a Lady of the third rank, in memory of the example from antiquity, and as the "Woman Preserving Purity" she will be called "Lord of Miraculous Purity." She is presented with a hundred stones of fine maize. Wonderful. Felicities! Your learning is abundant, your service as administrator excellent. For a long time, you took your position in the local administration and held it for its tenure. In choosing a horse, the horseman Jiufang Gao[137] valued little whether a

136. The "two palaces" are the queen and crown prince's palaces.

137. Jiufang Gao worked for Duke Mu of Qin choosing fine horses based on their internal qualities rather than their looks; see note 103 above.

horse was male or female. Guarding your chastity for ten years, who could tell whether the bird was male or female? On the seventh day of the seventh month, when the shepherd meets the weaving maid, all is well in the world. Both have occupied the position of top graduate. Here are two of them, which is unheard of. A good lord and fine guest: the two are difficult to get. You have achieved it all.
(*The eunuch stops reading, faces Zhou Xiang, and says*)
His Majesty ordered me to tell you, Prime Minister: the two top graduates becoming two regional administrators makes for four blessings.
(*Continues reading the decree*)
Thus decreed, all of Our thoughts have been declared. Thanks to His Majesty!
(*All make thanks*)(*All greet the eunuch. Eunuch performs unseemly jokes. Chonggu takes leave. Zhou Xiang retains the eunuch.*)
Eunuch: His Majesty wished for me to watch the marriage take place and awaits my response. You will not delay me?
Zhou: In that case, tomorrow I will prepare a small meal to thank you for your trouble.
Eunuch: What need is there for thanks! I would just like to know if they can provide a top graduate poem, that is all. (*Laughs, eunuch exits*)
(*The* chou *[Wuye] and* jing *[Auntie Huang] start making obscene jokes*)
Wuye:
[To the tune *Diliu zi*]

Who could believe that a girl could dress up as a man and go out in the world,
And at the tender age of twenty years
Manage not to damage her virginity in the slightest?
Servant Huang,
You closely followed her everywhere; would you deceive us, knowing the basic facts?
I ask of you, is the crab-apple still the same color red?

Auntie Huang (jests): Shut up! I fart at that!
[To the tune *Baolao cui*]

You, Meixiang, are no good,
Judging Chang E by your own standards,
How can she be like you,

Mixed up in the kitchen surrounded by fruits and vegetables.
Sister Meixiang!

Chou: I am not called Meixiang, I am called Wuye.[138]
Jing (Auntie Huang): Sister Wuye, take a look at this old man. Do you still say that I am really a man?
(Jing *tears open top and shows breasts to the* chou]

I have pulled open my collar, and dragged out nipples to rival yours,
That young lady—
I nursed her myself until she was three years old,
Needless to say
I was her constant companion at home,
And on the road, would never have allowed a man to be her companion![139]

Zhou: What are you two talking about in that room, gesticulating with hands and feet?
Chou: Your honor, this Huang is actually a Nanny. As I just saw her big breasts, I questioned her carefully, and only then did she tell all.
Zhou: Even more oddities come out! Tell me what was said.
Chou:
[To the tune *Didi jin*]

I, Wuye, ah,
Felt up the protuberances of her old oyster shell's paired pearls,
So large like plums added atop pig's bladders.
Her chest covering could not encase the two hanging shriveled tips like liquid-filled sacks of leather.
She said the young lady
Has no weaknesses,

138. Female servant roles are frequently generically called "Meixiang," but this maid claims her individuality.

139. Since Chonggu was dressed as a man, who could not travel with a woman, she should have had a male companion to keep her company. However, since Chonggu was actually a woman, Auntie Huang argues that she would never have allowed an actual man to accompany her ward, and therefore adopted a male disguise as well to keep up the ruse.

And in their home and on the road, she has always been her chaperone.
She is like a mandarin duck,
Occupying the highest position of us slaves.

Zhou: Daughter-in-law, come in, and tell me the story in detail again carefully. I didn't understand Wuye.
Chonggu: This Nanny's origins . . .
[To the tune *Baolao cui*]

She was a neighbor to the west, a "powder and jet" young woman,
Who came to be my wet nurse until the time I began school.
Who knew that my parents would both depart for the next world?

Zhou: I meant to ask you, who was your father?
Chonggu: He was Prefect Huang, his name was Huang Yan.
Zhou: Ah! He was an eminent official of my generation. How did you and your nanny survive after his death? And how did you get to where you are now?
Chonggu: This Nanny was also surnamed Huang, and so I called her Auntie Huang;

Auntie Huang and I entered faraway mountains like monks and nuns in austerity,
For ten years I paid back my debt of poetry and prose,
All this time I had no one for company but her,
How could I have replaced her with an old male servant?

Zhou: For more than twenty years, she was accompanied by this old woman. This makes me view her as absolutely pure. She is also a famous official's descendant. When I heard these words, I nearly danced with joy.
(*The* zhou *and chorus sing to Chonggu*)
All (*except Chonggu*):
[To the tune *Shuang shengzi*]

Mulan went for her father to the outposts at the northern frontier pass,
She is this young daughter Huang.

(*All sing to Auntie Huang*)

The peony would be burnt by the sun if not for the green leaf's cover,

Such was Auntie Huang's doting care.
Our young daughter became a champion of literature like an immortal banished to earth,[140]
And this Auntie Huang was serving the Weaving Maid in the Milky Way.[141]

Together:
[To the tune *Wei sheng*]

This marriage really is not bad.
We paltry ones
Have called forth an expression of joy on the dragon's countenance.[142]
Who would know that the embroidered chambers and golden needles,
Would change into the talent to mend the ceremonial gown?[143]

Zhou: Now it's rejecting the male phoenix and gaining the female phoenix,
Fengchu: Baring his belly and playing the *xiao*: these things are natural,[144]
Fengyu and Chonggu: On whom do the good deeds of the world depend?
Auntie Huang and Wuye: If not a man, then a girl!
(*Exeunt*)

---

140. The "banished immortal" trope is always taken as a compliment.

141. Huanggu is another name for the Cowherd (the Weaving Maid's companion) asterism.

142. The "dragon's countenance" refers to the ruler, in this case the King of Shu.

143. Mending the ceremonial gown means being able to govern, as the ruler wore dragon robes.

144. The bare belly allusion is again a reference to Wang Xizhi.

Reference Matter

Notes

Introduction

1. "欲知猿啼腸堪斷，除是儂身自作猿." Xu Wei, *Xu Wenchang yigao* (Shanghai: Shanghai zazhi gongsi, 1936), 133.

2. On Xu Wei's contemporary Li Zhi 李贄 (1527–1602) and his similar preoccupations with authenticity, see Ray Huang, "Li Chih, A Divided Conscience," in *1587: A Year of No Significance, the Ming Dynasty in Decline* (New Haven: Yale University Press, 1982) 189–222.

3. J.L. Faurot, "Hsu Wen-Ch'ang," An Archetypal Clever Rascal in Chinese Popular Culture," *Asian Folklore Studies* 36.2 (1977): 65.

4. In his preface to Wang Chang'an's 王長安 *Xu Wei sanbian* 徐渭三辨 (Beijing: Beijing zhongguo xiqu, 1995), the twentieth-century literary critic Chen Duo 陳多 describes Xu Wei as a man of arts and letters with talents spanning the fields of calligraphy, poetry, criticism, drama, and painting. He contrasts this with his childhood knowledge of "Xu Wenchang" as the archetypal trickster figure of popular legend, one who humiliates and fools others., which discusses apocrypha and legends about Xu Wei existing in folklore from different sources, such as Lin Lan's 1929 *Collected Stories About Xu Wenchang* (*Xu Wenchang gushi ji* 徐文長故事集) and his 1932 collection of regional versions of Xu Wenchang stories, *External Collection on Xu Wenchang* (*Xu Wenchang waiji*). Also see Nien-Hsu Sung, *Un Enfant Terrible. Siu Wen-Tch'ang (Traduit des récits populaires de Mme Lin Lan)* (Peking: Imprimerie de la Politique de Pékin, 1931); Howard Levy, *China's Dirtiest Trickster, Folklore About Hsü Wen-ch'ang (1521–1593)* (Arlington: Warm-Soft Village Press, 1974); Liao Ting 廖汀, *Xu Wenchang waizhuan* 徐文長外傳 (Hong Kong: Boyi chuban ji tu youxian gongsi, 1983); and Chang-tai Hung, *Going to the People: Chinese Intellectuals and Folk Literature* (Cambridge: Harvard University Press, 1986).

5. See note 20 in "Flawed Jade," Duncan Campbell's article on Zhang Dai's biographies. According to Campbell, Zhang Dai's great-grandfather, Zhang Yuanbian 張元忭 (1525–90), interceded in Xu Wei's release from prison after Xu Wei murdered his wife. Campbell also notes that Zhang Dai's friend Wu Xi once dreamt that Xu Wei had appeared to him in a dream to tell him that Zhang Dai was Xu Wei's reincarnation. Campbell, "Flawed Jade: Zhang Dai's Family Biographies," *Ming Studies* 62 (2010): 25–55. For a full-length English-language study of Zhang Dai, see Jonathan Spence, *Return to Dragon Mountain: Memories of a Late Ming Man* (New York: Viking, 2007).

6. On the late Ming championing of spontaneity, see Wai-yee Li, "The Rhetoric of Spontaneity in Late-Ming Literature," *Ming Studies* 35 (August 1995): 32–52.

7. Yang Ye, *Vignettes from the Late Ming. A Hsiao-P'in Anthology* (Seattle: University of Washington Press, 1999), 53–56. The original text may be found in "Xu Wenchang zhuan" 徐文長傳 in Yuan Hongdao, *Yuan Zhonglang xiaopin* 袁中郎小品 (Beijing: Wenhua yishu chubanshe, 1996), 226. For more on Yuan Hongdao's biography of Xu Wei, see Duncan Campbell, "Madman or Genius: Yuan Hongdao's 'Biography of Xu Wei,'" in *Asia 2000: Modern China in Transition*, ed. Dov Bing, S. Lim, and M. Lin (Hamilton: Outrigger Publishers, 1993), 196–220.

8. There are always dissenters, of course. Yoshikawa Kojiro summarily dismisses all of Xu Wei's poetry as "not as good as his painting and calligraphy," and supplies only one example for its historic interest, as it is about a Japanese pirate. See *Five Hundred Years of Chinese Poetry: 1150–1650*, trans. John Timothy Wixted (Princeton, NJ: Princeton University Press, 1989), 180.

9. *Xu Wei ji* (Beijing: Zhonghua shuju, 1983), 1:3 (hereafter *XWJ*).

10. Quoted in Mao Wenfang's "Looking at oneself: an analysis of portrait inscriptions of Ming figures" (Guankan ziwo: mingren shuxiang ziti xilun 觀看自我: 明人畫像自題析論), in *The Proceedings of the 2006 International Research Conference on Ming Dynasty Literature and Culture* 「2006年明代文學與文化國際學術研討會」發表論文 (Hangzhou: Zhejiang University, 2006), 99–158. http://www.hrc.ntu.edu.tw/attachments/9703/毛文芳.pdf (accessed August 10, 2011). This passage is translated and discussed in Duncan Campbell's "Madman or Genius," 206.

11. For an English-language translation of Xu Wei's autobiography, consult Jeannette Faurot, "*Four Cries of a Gibbon:* A *Tsa-chü* Cycle by the Ming Dramatist Hsu Wei (1521–1593)," Ph.D. diss., University of California at Berkeley, 1972, 150–62. Also see the biography in L.C. Goodrich, *Dictionary of Ming Biography* (New York: Columbia, 1976), 1182–85 and I-Cheng Liang, "Hsu Wei (1521–1593): His Life and Literary Works," Ph.D. diss., Ohio State University, 1973. Xu Lun's *Xu Wenchang* (Shanghai: Shanghai renmin chubanshe, 1962) is also a good source for details about Xu Wei's life. On his military activity, see Kathleen Ryor, "Regulating the *Qi* and the *Xin*: Xu Wei (1521–1593) and his Military Patrons," *Archives of Asian Art* LIV (2004): 23–33.

12. *XWJ*, 519–20.

13. Campbell writes in "Madman or Genius": "Yuan Hongdao removes all mention of drama. He is intent upon having Xu Wei understood within the context of the orthodox literary hierarchy—it is his prose and his poetry in particular that are to be highlighted" (205).

14. On the latter play, which shares the themes of misbehaving monks and courtroom trials with the plays in *Four Cries of a Gibbon*, see Kimberly Besio, "*Singing in Place of Screaming*: Subversion as Satire in Late Imperial China" in *Text, Performance, and Gender in Chinese Literature and Music: Essays in Honor of Wilt Idema* (Leiden: Brill, 2010), 153–74. Li-ling Hsiao notes the suggestion by scholars Luo Yuming and Dong Rulong that Lu Cai is the actual author of the *Nanci Xulu xulu* in note 73 of *The Eternal Present of the Past: Illustration, Theatre, and Reading in the Wan-li Period, 1573–1619* (Leiden: Brill, 2007), 110n73.

15. See Crump, *Chinese Theater in the Days of Kublai Khan* (Tucson: University of Arizona Press, 1980) for more on Yuan *zaju*.

16. William Dolby describes the different forms of drama in greater detail in *A History of Chinese Drama* (London: Elek, 1976).

17. Tina Lu, *Persons, Roles, and Minds: Identity in* Peony Pavilion *and* Peach Blossom Fan (Stanford: Stanford University Press, 2001), 11–12.

18. Craig Clunas describes how the Ming elite's cultivation of connoisseurship on "things" was a way of creating social distinctions in *Superfluous Things: Material Culture and Social Status in Early Modern China* (Honolulu: University of Hawaii, 1994).

19. For example, I-Cheng Liang traces *Zen Master Yu* to Xu Wei's time spent in Hangzhou, explaining that his unhappiness over the hypocritical behavior of the monks there was what compelled him to write the play. He also cites Xu Wei's participation in the campaigns against Japanese pirates as the inspiration for *Mulan*. See Liang, "Hsu Wei (1521–93): His Life and Literary Works," 28–32.

20. See Jeanette Faurot, "*Four Cries of a Gibbon*"; and Wilt Idema, "Female Talent and Female Virtue: Xu Wei's *Nü Zhuangyuan* and Meng Chengshun's *Zhenwen ji*," *Mingqing xiqu guoji yantaohui lunwen ji* 明清戲曲國際研討會論文集, ed. Hua Wei 華瑋 and Wang Ailing 王瑷玲 (Taibei: Zhongyang yanjiuyuan zhongguo wenzhe yanjiusuo choubeichu, 1998), 558.

21. Idema, "Female Talent and Female Virtue," 559–60.

22. *XWJ*, 1089. Wang Shifu's *The Story of the Western Wing* is translated in full with an excellent introduction by Wilt Idema and Stephen West (Berkeley: University of California Press, 1995).

23. John Hay, "The Body Invisible in Chinese Art?," *Body, Subject, & Power in China*, ed. Tani Barlow and Angela Zito (Chicago: University of Chicago, 1994), 51.

24. Although on the surface this might lead one to see a dichotomy between Chinese and Western representation, a closer look reveals some shared sensibilities. Anne Hollander convincingly argues, for example, that nudity in Western painting and sculpture is shaped more by the clothes that were in fashion at the time than actual body shapes. See Anne Hollander, *Seeing Through Clothes* (Berkeley: University of California Press, 1975).

25. Mark Elvin, "Tales of *Shen* and *Xin*: Body-Person and Heart-Mind in China During the Last 150 Years," *Fragments for a History of the Human Body*, ed. Michael Feher (New York: Urzone, 1989), 271.

26. Beginning with Song dynasty variety plays, role types such as *dan* (旦 female singing lead), *mo* (末 singing male lead), *wai* (外 secondary male non-singing), *jing* (淨 male villain), and *chou* (丑 clown) were later enriched with the addition, over the years, of roles such as *sheng* (生 young male lead) and more subdivisions within role type. Wang Jide's 王驥德 (d. 1623) *Song Rules* (*Qü lü* 曲律) presents the first thorough discussion of role types in drama up to his time, see William Nienhauser, *The Indiana Companion to Traditional Chinese Literature*, vol. 2 (Bloomington, University of Indiana Press), 1998, 19. This particular example of a *dan* made to dress up as a *chou* takes place in Kong Shangren's *Peach Blossom Fan*.

27. Eric Henry, "The Social Significance of Nudity in Early China," *Fashion Theory* 3.4 (1999): 485.

28. Charlotte Furth, "Androgynous Males and Deficient Females: Biology and Gender Boundaries in Sixteenth- and Seventeenth-Century China," *Late Imperial China* 9.2 (1989): 14.

Chapter 1

1. Luo Qiuzhao 羅秋昭, *Xu Wei "Sishengyuan" yanjiu* 徐渭四聲猿研究 (Taibei 台北: Qiye shuju youxian gongsi 啓業書局有限公司, 1979), 102.

2. It should be clarified that although the songs are limited to a single actor in *zaju*, that actor may well play different roles in different acts of the play, thus allowing for songs to be assigned different characters.

3. Yu-ming He, "Difficulties of Performance: The Musical Career of Xu Wei's *The Mad Drummer*," *Harvard Journal of Asiatic Studies* 68.2 (2008): 77–114.

4. This no doubt contributes to an autobiographical reading of the play, as Xu Wei confessed in his own obituary that he had feigned madness. See L.C. Goodrich and Chaoying Fang, eds., *Dictionary of Ming Biography, 1368–1644*, Vol. 2, 610.

5. Wilt Idema makes note of the unusual layers of Mi Heng's performance of madness in "Madness on the Yuan Stage," *Horin* 14 (2007): 80–81.

6. Xu Wei, *Sishengyuan Gedaixiao fu* 四聲猿歌代嘯附 (hereafter *SSY*), 2.

7. The host is Cao Cao, who has received Mi Heng in to his court as his guest.

8. Xu Wei, *SSY* 2.

9. David Knechtges, *Wen Xuan or Selections of Refined Literature, Volume 3* (Princeton: Princeton University Press, 1996), 49–57. For a study and translation of the parrot rhapsody (*fu* 賦), see William T. Graham, Jr., "Mi Heng's 'Rhapsody on a Parrot,'" *Harvard Journal of Asiatic Studies* 39, no. 1 (June 1979): 39–54.

10. Kong Rong 孔融 (153–208) served in Cao Cao's court in Xu 許 and was one of the very few men whom Mi Heng respected and considered worthy of his association.

11. *Hou Hanshu* (Beijing: Zhonghua shuju, 1965), 80b, 2652–59. Mi Heng is also similarly mentioned in the *New Account of Tales of the World* (*Shishuo xinyu* 世說新語) and *Romance of the Three Kingdoms* (*Sanguo yanyi* 三國演義).

12. Confucius, *The Analects*, trans. D.C. Lau (London: Penguin, 1979).

13. Confucius, *Analects* 10.6.

14. This attitude has caused scholars naturally to see Mi Heng as Xu Wei's alter-ego. Faurot, "*Four Cries of a Gibbon*," 53–54.

15. On assassins in *Shiji*, see Wai-yee Li, "The Idea of Authority in the Shih Chi (Records of the Historian)," *Harvard Journal of Asiatic Studies* 54.2 (1994): 372–77.

16. Interestingly, Wai-yee Li notes that this is the one place where Sima Qian embellishes the story, adding after the analogy of the woman making herself beautiful for her man, "Now [the Earl of Zhi] knew me. I must avenge him and die in the attempt to repay [him], so that my soul may be freed from shame." Li, "The Idea of Authority," 373.

17. Stephen Owen, *An Anthology of Chinese Literature: Beginnings to 1911* (New York: Norton, 1996), 82–83.

18. Dana Thomas, *Deluxe: How Luxury Lost Its Luster* (New York: Penguin, 2007).

19. Timothy Brook, *The Confusions of Pleasure: Commerce and Culture in Ming China* (Berkeley: University of California Press, 1998), 219.

20. Lin Liyue 林麗月, 衣裳與風教－晚明的服飾風尚與「服妖」議論 (*Yishang yu fengjiao—wan Ming de fushi fengshang yu 'fuyao' lilun* Costumes and customs: late Ming clothing trends and the discourse of "outrageousness"), *Xinshixue* 10.3 (September 1999): 111–57.

21. For more theories of drama and the audience, see Martin Meisel, *How Plays Work: Reading and Performance* (Oxford: Oxford University Press, 2007).

22. Erving Goffman, *The Presentation of Self in Everyday Life* (Garden City, NY: Doubleday, 1959).

23. Richard Bauman, *Verbal Art as Performance* (Prospect Heights, IL: Waveland Press, 1977), 11.

24. Bridget Escolme, *Talking to the Audience: Shakespeare, Performance, and Self* (London: Routledge, 2005).

25. Yu-ming He, "Difficulties of Performance," 85–86.

26. Xu Wei, *SSY* 2.

27. Xu Wei, *SSY* 2.

28. Xu Wei, *SSY* 3.

29. Xu Wei, *SSY* 2.

30. See Li-ling Hsiao, *The Eternal Present of the Past: Illustration, Theatre, and Reading in the Wanli Period, 1573–1619* (Leiden: Brill, 2007) for a broad discussion of this motif in late Ming theater and theater texts.

31. Xu Wei, *SSY* 5.

32. Hsiao, writing on the self-reflexivity of the play within the play, notes: "the highest achievement of the performers, then, is to transport the audience from the present to the past. The conflation of time as a dramatic ideal thus sets the highest demand on performers." *Eternal Present of the Past*, 199.

33. Xu Wei, *SSY* 2.

34. Xu Wei, *SSY* 6.

35. Xu Wei, *SSY* 2.

36. Xu Wei, *SSY* 2.

37. Xu Wei, *SSY* 4. The actual term for *jiechao* 解嘲, translated here as "silly excuses," is an allusion to Yang Xiong 揚雄 (53 BCE–18 CE), who wrote a reportedly autobiographical essay entitled "Dissolving Ridicule" (*Jiechao*) about the ridicule he suffered for his low status and failure in court life.

38. Xu Wei, *SSY* 2.

39. Xu Wei, *SSY* 9–10.

40. The play is also known by the titles "The Yuyang Triple Rolls" (*Yuyang sannong* 漁陽三弄), "The Yuyang Rolls" (*Yuyang nong* 漁陽弄), and "The Mad Officer" (*Kuangguli* 狂鼓吏). Luo Qiuzhao, *Xu Wei "Sisheng yuan" yanjiu*, 38.

41. Xu Wei, *SSY* 2.

42. Xu Wei, *SSY* 6.

43. Xu Wei, *SSY* 2.

44. Xu Wei, *SSY* 3–4.

45. Xu Wei, *SSY* 5.

Chapter 2

1. To reflect common English usage, I use the Japanese pronunciation and romanization Zen for the Chinese *chan* 禪 to describe this Buddhist sect.

2. Quoted in Faurot: "Master Xu [Wei's] *Four Cries of a Gibbon* is one of the most marvelous and unusual works of literature in the world. The northern style of Mulan, contrasting with the southern style of Huang Ch'ung-ku (in the play 'Girl Graduate') is a marvel among marvels. The master lived next door to me, and whenever he finished

writing a play, he would call me over to his studio and read it out to me in a clear voice, brim-full of self-satisfaction. I would select skillfully done passages for him to repeat, then raising his cup of Great White wine, he would drink it dry and say I was the only one who understood his music. Among the plays, 'The Moonlight Monk Saves Liu Tsui' was the earliest; 'Mulan' and 'Mi Heng' followed it. As for 'The Girl Graduate,' he asked me to search for a story to complete the number of 'Four Cries,' and I selected 'The Story of Spring Peach' 春桃記, which was praised by Yang Yung-hsiu (Yang Shen) 楊用修(慎)." Faurot, "*Four Cries of a Gibbon*," 32–33.

3. Ann-Marie Hsiung, "A Feminist Re-Vision of Xu Wei's *Ci Mulan* and *Nü Zhuangyuan*," in *China in a Polycentric World: Essays in Chinese Comparative Literature*, ed. Yingjin Zhang (Stanford: Stanford University Press, 1998), 73–89.

4. Wang Zhiyong 汪志勇, "*Du Liu Cui*" "*Cui Xiang Meng*" *yu* "*Honglian Zhai*" *sanju de bijiao yanjiu* 度柳翠翠鄉夢與紅蓮債三劇的比較研究 MA Thesis (Taibei: 1979).

5. An English translation of the play may be found in Yuan-shu Yen, trans., "Yellow Millet Dream," *Tamkang Review* 6 (1975): 205–39.

6. The *Supplementary Selections from the Yuan Dramas* (*Yuanqu xuan waibian* 元曲選外編), which was compiled by Sui Shusen and published by Beijing's Zhonghua shuju in 1961, includes sixty-two more plays. A full translation of the play is available in Wilt L. Idema and Stephen H. West, *Chinese Theater, 1100–1450: A Source Book* (Weisbaden: Franz Steiner, 1982), 313–40 and as *Zhongli of the Han Leads Lan Caihe to Enlightenment* in Stephen H. West and Wilt L. Idema's *Monks, Bandits, Lovers, and Immortals: Eleven Early Chinese Plays* (Indianapolis: Hackett), 283–313. For the original, see *Yuanqu xuan waibian*, 971–80.

7. Wilt L. Idema, *The Dramatic Oeuvre of Chu Yu-Tun, 1379–1439* (Leiden: Brill, 1997), 71.

8. Idema, *Dramatic Oeuvre*, 71.

9. For brief discussions of the play, see Idema, *Dramatic Oeuvre*, 71; and Luo Qiuzhao 羅秋昭, *Xu Wei Sishengyuan yanjiu* 徐渭四聲猿研究 (Taibei: Qiye shuju youxian gongsi, 1979). For a complete study of the antecedents, see Wang Zhiyong, "*Du Liu Cui*." The play is discussed here by its shortened name "Delivering Liu Cui" (Du Liu Cui) in an attempt to minimize confusion as it shares a title with a *huaben* that is also discussed in this chapter.

10. Idema, *Dramatic Oeuvre*, 67–69.

11. Michele Marra writes about this phenomenon in Buddhist plays about courtesans in medieval Japan in "The Buddhist Mythmaking of Defilement: Sacred Courtesans in Medieval Japan," *The Journal of Asian Studies* 52.1 (1993): 49–65.

12. Quotes from *Zen Master Yu* are taken from Xu Wei, *SSY* 21.

13. This is an "added" role type, as Hong Lian is a secondary female character. It highlights how she is distinct from a true female lead, which would be played by a *dan* role, as Liu Cui will be in the second act.

14. This is in contrast to the examples of righteous men who withstood similar temptations; the *Annals of Lü Buwei* 呂氏春秋, written during the late Warring States period, records the following story: "Yan Shuzi dwelled alone in his house. The widow next door also lived alone in her house. One night there was a violent storm that caused the widow's house to collapse. She fled to Yan Shuzi, who admitted her into his house and made her hold a lamp until dawn. When the wick was gone, he withdrew into his own room and stayed there. He himself thought that he had not been attentive enough to dispelling suspicion. One who is attentive ought to be like the man from Lu. There was a young

man in Lu who dwelled alone. The widow next door to him also lived alone. One night during a violent storm, her house collapsed, and the lady fled to him for shelter. The young man locked his gate and would not let her in. The woman said to him through the window, 'Why won't you let me in?' He replied, 'I have learned that, unless they are sixty, an unmarried man and woman may not be alone together in a room. Now, since you are young and so am I, I cannot let you in.' The lady said to him, 'Why not be like Liuxia Hui? He warmed with his body a woman who could not reach her gate, and his countrymen did not consider him unruly.' The young man replied, 'What was certainly proper for Liuxia Hui is certainly not proper for me. I would be using what is not proper for me to imitate what was proper for Liuxia Hui.' Confucius observed: 'Of those who desire to imitate Liuxia Hui, none equals this young man.'" In Lü Buwei 呂不韋, *The Annals of Lü Buwei* 呂氏春秋, trans. John Knoblock and Jeffrey K. Riegel (Stanford: Stanford University Press, 2000) 681–82.

15. A similar dumbshow on a Zen theme occurs in the *yuanben* entitled *Silent Zen* (*Da yachan* 打啞禪) by Li Kaixian 李開先 (1502–68), in which a Zen master rewards a butcher for understanding his mute finger-signed communications. It later turns out that the butcher had completely misinterpreted the supposed *koan* as a meat sale. This is discussed in Idema, "*Yüan-pen* as a Minor Form of Dramatic Literature in the Fifteenth and Sixteenth Centuries," *Chinese Literature: Essays, Articles, Reviews (CLEAR)* 6.1/2 (July 1984): 63–64.

16. Wang Zhiyong, "*Du Liu Cui*," 17–18.

17. Patrick Hanan, *The Chinese Story: Studies in Dating, Authorship, and Composition* (Cambridge: Harvard University Press, 1973), 56. This *huaben* is the thirteenth in the earliest-known collection of *huaben* entitled *Sixty Stories* (*Liushi jia xiaoshuo* 六十家小說), originally published by Hong Bian around the middle of the sixteenth century. The texts, discovered in the early twentieth century, are also more popularly known as the *Novellas Printed by the Qingping Mountain Pavilion* (*Qingping shantang huaben* 清平山堂話本, ca. 1550) after Hong Bian's 洪楩 (sixteenth c.) studio. The story is also reproduced as part of Story Number 30, "Abbot Mingwu Redeems Abbot Wujie" ("Mingwu chanshi gan wujie" 明悟禪師趕五戒, GJXS 30) in Feng Menglong's 馮夢龍 (1574–1645) seventeenth-century collection *Stories Old and New* (*Gujin xiaoshuo* 古今小說) with an added prologue and expanded ending. Hanan believes that the changes to Hong Bian's version were made by a later editor, possibly Feng Menglong. The *Qingping Mountain Pavilion* version, according to Patrick Hanan, predates *Zen Master Yu*. Although it does relate the story of a young girl named Red Lotus and her relationship with a monk, the plot of the story is significantly different from *Zen Master Yu*. Hanan discusses the dating extensively in Ch. 5, especially pp. 117 and 132. For more on Hong Bian and the "Sixty Stories," see Hanan, *The Chinese Vernacular Story* (Cambridge: Harvard University Press, 1981), 56–57.

18. The story is translated in full in French in *Contes de la montaigne sereine* (Paris: Gallimard, 1987), 419–33.

19. In Wu Changling's 吳昌齡 (fl. 1330) *zaju* "Four Girls in Su Dongpo's Dream" (*Huajian siyou Dongpo meng* 花間四友東坡夢), Su Shi attempts to undo the monk Foyin by sending a courtesan to seduce him. The tables are turned, and Su Shi and the courtesan are converted. The play is discussed in Anning Jing, *The Water God's Temple of the Guangsheng Monastery: Cosmic Function of Art, Ritual, and Theater* (Leiden: Brill, 2002), 169–71.

20. Besides the *huaben* "Abbot Mingwu Redeems Abbot Wujie" in *Stories Old and New* mentioned above, there is another *huaben* in the same collection, entitled "Moonlight Monk Delivers Liu Cui" (*Yueming heshang du Liu Cui* 月明和尚度柳翠, GJXS 29), that features characters and a plot that are almost identical to those of *Zen Master Yu*. However, the story's chronological relation to Xu Wei's play is less definite. It may well be based on Xu Wei's play rather than serving as its source. There is no evidence of an urtext combining the Liu Cui and Red Lotus text that served as a source for the story and *Zen Master Yu*. "Moonlight Monk Delivers Liu Cui" details Monk Yutong's seduction by Red Lotus. In the story, Yutong is then reborn as Liu Cui, and redeemed by the Moonlight Monk. Most of the elements in the play are also present in the *huaben*, with the exception of Moonlight Monk's elaborate pantomimes, which are replaced in the *huaben* with poems and more extensive dialogue between the Liu Cui and Moonlight Monk. There is certainly a relation between the two, as they share the poems that Yutong writes to Liu Xuanjiao as well as Liu Xuanjiao's poem to Yutong; the differences between the story and the play may be reasonably ascribed to differences in the genres of *huaben* and *zaju* rather than to differences in sources or dating. The only one of the discussed texts featuring Red Lotus that can be definitively thought to predate Xu Wei's play is the Song anecdote from Zhang Bangji, and it is likely that the Qingping Mountain Pavilion version also predates the play. Both stories "Abbot Mingwu Redeems Abbot Wujie" and "Moonlight Monk Delivers Liu Cui" are translated in full as "Abbot Mingwu Redeems Abbot Wujie" and "Monk Moonbright Redeems Willow Green," respectively, in the complete translation of the *Gujin xiaoshuo* in Feng Menglong, *Stories Old and New: A Ming Dynasty Collection*, trans. Shuhui Yang and Yunqin Yang (Seattle: University of Washington Press, 2000), 502–35.

21. See Idema, *Dramatic Oeuvre*, 69–71, where the YQX version of the play is discussed in the context of deliverance plays and a synopsis is given. For extensive discussion of the various titles of the play, see note 1 to the wedge in *Yuanqu xuan jiaozhu* 元曲選校注, ed. Wang Xueqi 王學奇, vol. 4a (Shijiazhuang: Hebei jiaoyu, 1994), 3372–73.

22. There is no documented connection until at earliest the early Ming dynasty, when the play is mentioned in Zhu Youdun's 朱有燉 (1379–1439) "Li Miaoqing huali wu Zhenru" 李妙清花裡悟眞如, but with no mention of Red Lotus. Luo, *Xu Wei "Sishengyuan" yanjiu*, 54.

23. His name, Niu 牛 (ox), references the Zen practice of using the ox as a metaphor to describe the process of finding enlightenment as being similar to seeking the ox while already riding on it, and that the state of enlightenment is like returning home on the back of an ox. In the twelfth century, monks began using pictures to accompany poems representing the path to enlightenment. See Scarlett Ju-Yu Jang, "Ox-Herding Painting in the Sung Dynasty," *Artibus Asiae* 52.1/2 (1992): 62–66, 70. In some of the examples of ox-herding paintings and illustrations in Jang's article, the ox disappears after enlightenment has been obtained. This underscores how concrete examples must be used on the path toward reaching enlightenment, and how, once enlightenment is reached, they become irrelevant.

24. Idema, *Dramatic Oeuvre*, 70.

25. *Yuanqu xuan jiaozhu*, ed. Wang Xueqi (Shijiazhuang: Hebei jiaoyu, 1994) 3371–72.

26. The story is quoted in Wang Zhiyong, "*Du Liu Cui*," 19–20, and reproduced in Luo Qiuzhao, *Xu Wei "Sishengyuan*," 55. It is translated in full in Faurot, "*Four Cries of a Gibbon*," 67–70.

27. The story's predominant function seems to be to explain the names of certain landmarks, such as a "Liu Cui bridge" and a "Liu Cui well." Named for the young woman's philanthropic efforts in public works, the landmarks betoken the kind of empowerment available to a woman of abased social status in combination with financial means and a convenient system of beliefs.

28. Faurot, "*Four Cries of a Gibbon*," 71.

29. Faurot remarks that this discrepancy is the strangest one, because Moonlight Monk is directly linked to Liu Cui's redemption in the source text for the Liu Cui story, the Yuan *zaju* bearing the same name as GJXS 29, "Moonlight Monk Delivers Liu Cui," and concludes that different stories developed around the basic plot structures of Red Lotus as seductress and Liu Cui as redeemed by monks. Ibid., 70.

30. I-Cheng Liang, "Hsu Wei (1521–1593): His Life and Literary Works," (Ph.D. diss., Ohio State University), 1973.

31. Luo Qiuzhao, *Xu Wei "Sishengyuan,"* 64.

32. Faurot, "*Four Cries of a Gibbon*," 73.

33. Tian Yuan Tan, on reading an earlier version of this chapter, pointed out, the potential for metatheatrical overlap created at the end of the play when the *dan* puts on male clothes, recalling to the audience the *sheng* from the first act.

34. Many Yuan *zaju* titles bear three attempts at conversion.

35. Xu Wei, *SSY* 20.

36. Xu Wei, *SSY* 25.

37. Xu Wei, *SSY* 35.

38. Xu Wei, *SSY* 33.

39. Xu Wei, *SSY* 33.

40. Judith Zeitlin writes about the reading of characters in dream interpretations in her chapter on dreams in *Historian of the Strange: Pu Songling and the Chinese Classical Tale* (Stanford: Stanford University Press, 1993), 140–54. Andrew Plaks discusses the Chinese tradition of riddles in "Riddles and Enigma in Chinese Civilization," in *Untying the Knot: On Riddles and Other Enigmatic Modes*, ed. Galit Hasan-Rokem and David Shulman (New York: Oxford University Press, 1996), 227–36. Xu Wei himself, as mentioned in the Introduction, had a breakdown of his name, Wei, as one of his sobriquets: Tianshuiyue (渭＝田水月).

41. Xu Wei, *SSY* 35.

42. Xu Wei, *SSY* 36.

43. Xu Wei, *SSY* 33.

Chapter 3

1. Shiamin Kwa and Wilt Idema, *Mulan: Five Versions of a Classic Chinese Tale* (Indianapolis: Hackett, 2010).

2. See Jeannette Faurot, "*Four Cries of a Gibbon*," 94.

3. Mark Elvin, "Tales of *Shen* and *Xin*," 285; and Matthew Sommer, "Dangerous Males, Vulnerable Males, and Polluted Males: The Regulation of Masculinity in Qing Dynasty Law," *Chinese Femininities/Chinese Masculinities* (Berkeley: University of California Press, 2002), 67.

4. Luo Qiuzhao, *Xu Wei "Sishengyuan,"* 76.

5. Xu Wei, *SSY* 57.

6. *Yuefu shiji* 樂府詩集 (Beijing: Zhonghua shuju, 1979), 373–75.

7. Feng Lan, "The Female Individual and the Empire: A Historicist Approach to Mulan and Kingston's *Woman Warrior*." *Comparative Literature* 55.3 (Summer 2003): 231.

8. Kwa and Idema, *Mulan*, 1–3.

9. Sufen Sophia Lai, "From Cross-Dressing Daughter to Lady Knight-Errant: The Origin and Evolution of Chinese Women Warriors," *Presence and Presentation: Women in the Chinese Literati Tradition*, ed. Sherry Mou (New York: St. Martin's, 1999), 86.

10. See Sufen Sophia Lai, "From Cross-Dressing Daughter to Lady Knight-Errant" and Feng Lan, "The Female Individual and the Empire," for these discussions of the differences between versions of the Mulan story.

11. For example, Luo Qiuzhao states that *Mulan* demonstrates that "women can do men's work just as well" as men. Luo Qiuzhao, *Xu Wei "Sishengyuan,"* 77.

12. Certainly, she would be used that way in later versions of the story. Siu Leung Li echoes the argument that Mulan is simply returning to her place in the Confucian order; see Siu Leung Li, *Cross-Dressing in Chinese Opera* (Hong Kong: Hong Kong University Press, 2003), 87. The most thorough critique of that view can be found in Ann-Marie Hsiung's "A Feminist Re-Vision of Xu Wei's *Ci Mulan* and *Nü zhuangyuan*," 73–89. This is echoed in Lan Dong's review of Hsiung's comparisons; see Lan Dong, *Mulan's Legend and Legacy in China and the United States* (Philadelphia: Temple University Press, 2011), 66–80. See also the Introduction to Kwa and Idema, *Mulan*, ii–xxxii.

13. Wai-yee Li, "Heroic Transformations: Women and National Trauma in Early Qing Literature," *Harvard Journal of Asiatic Studies* 59.2 (Dec. 1999): 363–443.

14. Judith Butler, *Gender Trouble: Feminism and the Subversion of Identity* (New York: Routledge, 1990) and Judith Butler, *Bodies That Matter: On the Discursive Limits of "Sex"* (New York: Routledge, 1993).

15. Judith Butler, "Performative Acts and Gender Constitution: An Essay in Phenomenology and Feminist Theory," *Performing Feminisms: Feminist Critical Theory and Theatre*, ed. Sue-Ellen Case (Baltimore: Johns Hopkins UP, 1990), 271.

16. Butler's impact in the field is widespread. We see it not only in works on cross-dressing, but in works that discuss the creation or reinforcement of gender distinctions as demonstrated in court cases and law codes, a direct descendant of Butler's use of Foucault and the power of language and cultural performance to create categories that are taken as natural or normal.

17. Butler, *Bodies That Matter*, 8.

18. Butler, *Bodies That Matter*, 231.

19. Butler, *Bodies That Matter*, 230.

20. Marjorie Garber, *Vested Interests: Cross-Dressing and Cultural Anxiety* (New York: Routledge, 1992).

21. Garber, *Vested Interests*, 9.

22. Garber, *Vested Interests*, 17.

23. Xu Wei, *Sishengyuan*, in *Guben xiqu congkan chuji* 古本戲曲叢刊初集 vol. 77 (Shanghai: Shanghai yinshuguan, 1954), 37a–b.

24. Wilt Idema notes that Mulan's verbal detailing of her military skills may follow a Yuan drama tradition of describing what is to come in a later act, as Li Kui and Yan Qing discuss in act 2 how they will act out their disguise in act 3. See Idema, *The Dramatic Oeuvre of Chu Yu-Tun*, 187–94.

25. To add another layer of complication to the acts of naming, Xu Wei gives the previously surnameless Mulan her surname of Hua and creates a genealogy for her.

26. Xu Wei, *SSY* 44.

27. Xu Wei, *SSY* 45.

28. We cannot account, apart from Xu Wei's stage direction, for how much time was actually spent in the removal of clothing or in the performance of other stage work.

29. Xu Wei, *SSY* 45.

30. Dorothy Ko, *Cinderella's Sisters: A Revisionist History* (Berkeley: University of California Press, 2005) 145–46.

31. Joseph Allen, "Dressing and Undressing the Chinese Woman Warrior," *Positions: East Asia Cultures Critique* 4.2 (1996): 355.

32. Xu Wei, *SSY* 45.

33. Xu Wei, *SSY* 45.

34. Xu Wei, *SSY* 46.

35. Xu Wei, *SSY* 44.

36. Xu Wei, *SSY* 47.

37. Xu Wei, *SSY* 45.

38. Ryor, "Regulating the *Qi* and the *Xin*," 23–33.

39. Xu Wei, *SSY* 48.

40. Xu Wei, *SSY* 48.

41. Xu Wei, *SSY* 55.

42. Xu Wei, *SSY* 45.

43. Xu Wei, *SSY* 46.

44. Meng Jiao 孟郊 (751–814) wrote: "The thread in the hand of a kind mother/ Is the coat on the wanderer's back./ Before he left she stitched it close/ In secret fear that he would be slow to return./ Who will say that the inch of grass in his heart/ Is gratitude enough for all the sunshine of spring?" (慈母手中線，遊子身上衣。臨行密密縫，意恐遲遲歸。誰言寸草心，報得三春暉。) In A.C. Graham, *Poems of the Late T'ang* (New York: NYRB Classics, 2008), 63.

45. Xu Wei, *SSY* 48.

46. Xu Wei, *SSY* 46.

47. Xu Wei, *SSY* 53.

48. Xu Wei, *SSY* 45.

49. Xu Wei, *SSY* 47.

50. Xu Wei, *SSY* 54.

51. Xu Wei, *SSY* 47.

52. This becomes an entire subplot in later versions, finding full expression in the romance between Mulan (dressed as a man, and even as a man dressed as a woman) and her officer Liu Yuandu in the 1939 film *Mulan Joins the Army*. See Kwa and Idema, *Mulan*, 53–102.

Chapter 4

1. The play is paired, by Wang Jide's own reporting in "Rules for Arias" (*Qu Lü* 曲律), with Wang's own play, *The Male Queen* (*Nan wanghou* 男王后), on the related theme of a boy dressed like a girl who is taken for a bride. Wang modestly states that he does not

presume to pair *The Male Queen* with his teacher's play, instead reporting that others in the know have drawn the comparison; he does claim to have suggested the topic as the finale for the quartet after having heard each play as Xu wrote it. It appears that this section of the "Rules for Arias" is used for dating purposes, as Wang Jide notes that *Zen Master Yu* preceded *Mulan* and *Mi Heng* and that *Girl Graduate* followed later. See Wilt Idema, "Female Talent and Female Virtue: Xu Wei's *Nü zhuangyuan* and Meng Chengshun's *Zhenwen ji*," *Ming-Qing xiqu guoji yantaohui lunwen ji* 明清戲曲國際, ed. Hua Wei 華瑋 and Wang Ailing 王瑷玲 (Taibei: Zhongyang yanjiuyuan zhongguo wenzhe yanjiusuo, 1998) 555–56n10. For more on Wang Jide's *The Male Queen* see Sophie Volpp, "Gender, Power, and Spectacle in Late-Imperial Chinese Theater," *Gender Reversals and Gender Cultures: Anthropological and Historical Perspectives*, ed. Sabrina Petra Ramet (London: Routledge, 1996), 138–47. The play is discussed and translated in full in Volpp, *Worldly Stage: Theatricality in Seventeenth-Century China* (Cambridge: Harvard University Press, 2011). Luo Qiuzhao implies that *Girl Graduate* only has significance for later readers because of Xu Wei's innovation of transplanting southern songs into the northern *zaju* format: "From the point of view of song-writing, *Girl Graduate* does not compare to *Mi Heng* and the other three earlier plays. But in terms of inserting southern songs into northern *zaju*'s form, it really is a pioneering work. Thus it is of value for later readers to take note of *Girl Graduate*." Luo Qiuzhao 羅秋昭, *Xu Wei "Sisheng yuan,"* 102.

2. Anne Waltner explores the Ming dynasty appetite for court cases, and the extreme similarities between legal casebooks and courtroom fiction, in "From Casebook to Fiction: Kung-An in Late Imperial China," *Journal of the American Oriental Society* 110.2 (April-June 1990): 281–89. She suggests that both types of texts use the same narrative devices to achieve resolution, even though one is fictional and the other purports to be a real legal document.

3. Judge Bao, or Bao Zheng 包拯 (999–1062), was a judge famous for his impartiality and intelligence in deciding cases during the Song dynasty. After his death, he became a legendary figure and the ideal standard of a fair judge. A tradition of vernacular fiction and especially drama was built around this figure. In opera, he is typically presented with a black face and a white crescent on his head. For more on courtroom drama of the period, see George A. Hayden, "The Courtroom Plays of the Yüan and Early Ming Periods," *Harvard Journal of Asiatic Studies* 34 (1974): 192–220.

4. Idema, "Female Talent and Female Virtue," 557.

5. Consult Wilt Idema, *The Butterfly Lovers: The Legend of Liang Shanbo and Zhu Yingtai, Four Versions with Related Texts* (Cambridge, MA: Hackett, 2010) for a thorough introduction to the legend and its ensuing literary tradition.

6. Roland Altenburger, "Is It Clothes That Make the Man? Cross-Dressing, Gender, and Sex in Pre-Twentieth Century Zhu Yingtai Lore," *Asian Folklore Studies* 64 (2005): 171–72.

7. Wilt Idema and Beata Grant, eds., *The Red Brush: Writing Women of Imperial China* (Cambridge: Harvard University Press), 679–85.

8. Zhang Xiaoyu and Luo Qiuzhao's readings of *Mulan* and *Girl Graduate* are discussed in the previous chapter on *Mulan*. Although Anne Marie Hsiung acknowledges the accomplishments of these women characters, she does not see their stories as a vindication of women's rights since they so quickly succumb to re-absorption into the typical patriarchal order. The most thorough study of the individual play is Zeng Xiba's Ph.D.

thesis, *Xu Wei "Nü zhuangyuan yanjiu"* 徐渭女狀元研究. Zeng's dissertation reads the play as evidence of Xu Wei's belief in women's power or as an evocation of Xu Wei's idea of utopia. He posits that Chonggu is Xu Wei's own dream substitute, achieving the academic success that Xu himself could not. Zeng's first reading interpolates a Freudian analysis of the idealized women in Xu Wei's life, beginning with his biological mother, and suggests that Huang Chonggu is the culmination of those ideals (77). Zeng offers the alternative, though complementary, reading that Chonggu is Xu Wei's alter-ego, succeeding in her quest to be the top graduate in a way that Xu Wei had not, thus vindicating his unrecognized skills (86). Zeng Xiba 曾西霸, *Xu Wei "Nü zhuangyuan" yanjiu* (Ph.D. diss., Taibei: Zhongguo wenhua xueyuan, 1978). The most thorough English language investigation of *Girl Graduate* is the previously cited article by Wilt Idema, "Female Talent and Female Virtue," which highlights the very visual and performative aspects of the play. Idema sums it up in this way: "Xu Wei probably wrote *Ci Mulan* and *Nü zhuangyuan* first of all as social criticism, venting his frustration over the general condition of society and his own lack of success. His choice of subject matter enticed him to consider matters of sex and gender, which he treated in a remarkably explicit manner. His dramatization of his sources placed the change of costume on stage, in full view of a select (male?) audience, and featured the conspicuous enactment of male behavior by a heroine in male attire. More than any literary qualities the texts may have, these aspects of the performance may well have ensured the early reputation of these plays." In "Female Talent and Female Virtue," 563.

9. Xu Wei, *SSY* 62.

10. Xu Wei, *SSY* 68.

11. Xu Wei, *SSY* 69.

12. Xu Wei, SSY 88.

13. Faurot, "*Four Cries of a Gibbon*," 101–3.

14. The *Taiping guangji* ("Extensive Records of the Taiping Era") story is found in the section on "Freaks" (*renyao* 人妖 or *renguai* 人怪). *Taiping guangji* 太平廣記, comp. Li Fang 李昉 (Beijing: Zhonghua shuju, 1961), 2924–25.

15. *Taiping Guangji*, 2925. The quotation is taken from the translation of the entire tale in Wilt Idema and Beata Grant, *The Red Brush*, 362–64. The translation is also included in Wilt L. Idema, "Female Talent and Female Virtue," 554–55.

16. Faurot, "*Four Cries of a Gibbon*," 104.

17. George Hayden, *Crime and Punishment in Medieval Chinese Drama: Three Judge Pao Plays* (Cambridge: Harvard University Press, 1978), 5.

18. Hayden, *Crime and Punishment*, 12.

19. Xu Wei, *SSY* 62. Of course the Chinese language, especially classical Chinese, allows the absence of pronouns and, certainly, of possessives, so that one should not make too much of these conventions as conscious acts of disguise or suppression. Nonetheless, it is not at all uncommon for a character to describe herself in the third person and identify herself as a young girl. Chuntao does not do this.

20. Xu Wei, *SSY* 62. This sentiment echoes the third line of another disgruntled female poet, Yu Xuanji 魚玄機 (844–69), who wrote a poem about how she could not take part in the civil exams. See her "Visiting the South Pavilion at Chongzhen Temple Where the Civil Service Exam Results Are Posted" (*You chongzhen guan nanlou du xin ji diti*

ming chu 遊崇眞觀南樓睹新及第題名處), which contains the line, "I only regret that my gauzy gown obscures my poetic lines" (*zi hen luoyi yan shiju* 自恨羅衣掩詩句).

21. Xu Wei, *SSY* 63.

22. Antonia Finnane notes the late Ming obsession with various fashionable hats: "It was an important signifier of social status, as well as, apparently, a convenient site of fashion experiment." See Finnane, *Changing Clothes in China: Fashion, History, Nation* (New York: Columbia University Press, 2008), 47. The hat may have been the most distinctive "male" signifier, as women did not wear hats as such, but rather head-dressings or certain decorative hairstyles. Male and female clothing, however, were becoming nearly indistinguishable in the late Ming. Finnane continues: "It was no doubt changes in the dimensions of the [*pifeng* 披風 gown] that occasioned some of the carping about women's clothing in the late Ming. Hems were descending and sleeves growing larger in the sixteenth century. With sleeves trailing well below the finger tips and descending hems threatening to cover skirts completely, the *pifeng* came perilously close to looking like a man's tunic. Hence the anxieties expressed by the distinguished official Huo Tao, who as Minister of Rites in Nanjing attempted in 1537 to reverse the trend: 'Men's and women's styles differ in length. A woman's upper garment is level with her waist, her lower garment meets with the top: earth supports heaven. A man's upper garment covers his lower garments: heaven embraces earth. When a woman's [upper] garment covers her lower garments, there is confusion between male and female'" (51).

23. Xu Wei, *SSY* 64.

24. Xu Wei, *SSY* 73. See note 37 in appendix 4.

25. Xu Wei, *SSY* 73.

26. Xu Wei, *SSY* 69.

27. Xu Wei, *SSY* 98.

28. Xu Wei, *SSY* 99.

29. Xu Wei, *SSY* 99–100.

30. Xu Wei, *SSY* 100.

31. Xu Wei, *SSY* 101.

32. Xu Wei, *SSY* 102.

33. Xu Wei, *SSY* 62.

34. Xu Wei, *SSY* 63.

35. Xu Wei, *SSY* 72.

36. Xu Wei, *SSY* 103.

37. Xu Wei, *SSY* 99.

38. Xu Wei, *SSY* 84–85.

39. Xu Wei, *SSY* 85.

40. Xu Wei, *SSY* 85.

41. Xu Wei, *SSY* 64.

42. Xu Wei, *SSY* 103.

43. Xu Wei, *SSY* 69.

44. Xu Wei, *SSY* 76.

45. Xu Wei, *SSY* 77. See note 48 in appendix 4 for a full explanation of the allusion.

46. Xu Wei, *SSY* 69.

47. Xu Wei, *SSY* 78.

Conclusion

1. Wai-yee Li, "The Representation of History in *The Peach Blossom Fan*," *Journal of the American Oriental Society* 115.3 (Jul–Sep 1995): 421.

2. Lynn Struve, "History and *The Peach Blossom Fan*," *Chinese Literature: Essays, Articles, Reviews (CLEAR)* 2.1 (Jan 1980): 57.

3. Wai-yee Li explains: 'Theatrical mediation is most obvious in the dense web of allusions to another famous example of historical drama, *The Singing Phoenix* (Ming-feng chi), attributed to Wang Shih-chen, a forceful indictment of Yen Sung's abuse of power. Through these allusions, characters in *The Peach Blossom Fan* perceive and define themselves and historical reality. Thus Hsiang-chün denounces Ma Shih-ying and Juan Ta-ch'eng as reincarnations of the villains Yen Sung and Chao Wen-hua (Yen's adopted son): 'Chao Wen-hua is by the side of Yen Sung; with his painted face he scurries to please in front of the banquest table. With clowning tune and revolting gestures, they perform the real *Singing Phoenix*. I will be the female Mi Heng, beating the Yü-yang drums. One denunciation will follow another: let's see if he understands or not?' The villains, however, seem totally blind to the comparison as they play the part of refined literati." Wai-yee Li, "The Representation of History," 426. Also see Stephen Owen, "'I Don't Want to Act as Emperor Any More': Finding the Genuine in 'Peach Blossom Fan,'" *Trauma and Transcendence in Early Qing Literature*, ed. Wilt L. Idema, Wai-yee Li, and Ellen Widmer (Cambridge: Harvard University Press, 2006), 488–512; and Tina Lu, *Persons, Roles, and Minds*.

4. The English translation of this passage is from K'ung Shang-jen, *The Peach Blossom Fan*, trans. Chen Shih-Hsiang and Harold Acton (Berkeley: University of California, 1976), 180. The original edition I used is Kong Shangren 孔尚任, *Taohua shan* 桃花扇 (Beijing: Renmin wenxue, 1997), 161.

5. Jonathan Spence, *The Search for Modern China* (New York: Norton, 1990), 241.

6. Images are reproduced in Antonia Finnane, *Changing Clothes in China: Fashion, History, Nation* (New York: Columbia University Press, 2008), 90.

7. Spence, *The Search for Modern China*, 240; Finnane, *Changing Clothes in China*, 89. Madame Roland, Anita Garibaldi, Sophia Perofskaya, Harriet Beecher Stowe, Joan of Arc, and Mulan are all named as significant predecessors in Qiu Jin's preface to her unfinished *tanci* poem *Stones of the Jingwei Bird*. A translation can be found in Amy D. Dooling and Kristina M. Torgeson, eds., *Writing Women in Modern China: An Anthology of Women's Literature from the Early Twentieth Century* (New York: Columbia University, 1998), 43–78.

8. A chronological biography of Qiu Jin is followed by selections of her writing in Kang-I Sun Chang and Haun Saussy, eds., *Women Writers of Traditional China: An Anthology of Poetry and Criticism* (Stanford: Stanford University Press, 1999), 632–66; and in Idema and Grant, *The Red Brush*, 765–809.

9. Chang, *Women Writers of Traditional China*, 634.

10. Finnane, *Changing Clothes in China*, 89, quoting Fan Hong; see also J.A. Mangan, "A Martyr for Modernity: Qiu Jin, Feminist, Warrior and Revolutionary," *International Journal of the History of Sport*, 18.1 (2001): 27–54.

Bibliography

List of Abbreviations

SSY Xu Wei, *Sishengyuan Gedaixiao fu*
XWJ Xu Wei, *Xu Wei ji*
SGZYY Luo Guanzhong, *Sanguo zhi yanyi* ("Mao" edition)
GJXS Feng Menglong, *Gujin xiaoshuo* [Stories old and new]
SSXY Liu I-ch'ing, *Shih-shuo Hsin-Yü*

Allen, Joseph. "Dressing and Undressing the Chinese Woman Warrior." *Positions: East Asia Cultures Critique* 4.2 (1996): 343–79.

_____. *In the Voice of Others: Chinese Music Bureau Poetry*. Ann Arbor: University of Michigan Press, 1992.

Altenburger, Roland. "Is It Clothes That Make the Man? Cross-Dressing, Gender, and Sex in Pre-Twentieth Century Zhu Yingtai Lore." *Asian Folklore Studies* 64 (2005): 165–205.

Bauman, Richard. *Verbal Art as Performance*. Prospect Heights, IL: Waveland Press, 1977.

Benn, James A. *Burning for the Buddha: Self-Immolation in Chinese Buddhism*. Honolulu: University of Hawaii Press, 2007.

_____. "Where Text Meets Flesh: Burning the Body as an Apocryphal Practice in Chinese Buddhism." *History of Religions* 37.4 (1998): 295–322.

Besio, Kimberly. "*Singing in Place of Screaming*: Subversion as Satire in Late Imperial China." In *Text, Performance, and Gender in Chinese Literature and Music: Essays in Honor of Wilt Idema,* edited by Maghiel van Crevel, Tian Yuan Tan, and Michel Hockx, 153–74. Leiden: Brill, 2010.

Besio, Kimberly, and Constantine Tung, eds. *Three Kingdoms and Chinese Culture*. Albany: State University of New York Press, 2007.

Birrell, Anne. "Mythmaking and Yüeh-fu: Popular Songs and Ballads of Early Imperial China." *Journal of the American Oriental Society* 109.2 (1989): 223–35.

Brook, Timothy. *The Confusions of Pleasure: Commerce and Culture in Ming China*. Berkeley: University of California Press, 1998.

Butler, Judith. *Bodies That Matter: On the Discursive Limits of "Sex."* New York: Routledge, 1993.

_____. *Gender Trouble: Feminism and the Subversion of Identity*. New York: Routledge, 1990.

_____. "Performative Acts and Gender Constitution: An Essay in Phenomenology and Feminist Theory." In *Performing Feminisms: Feminist Critical Theory and Theatre*, edited by Sue-Ellen Case, 270–82. Baltimore: Johns Hopkins University Press, 1990.

Cahill, James. *Parting at the Shore: Chinese Painting of the Early and Middle Ming Dynasty, 1368–1580*. New York: Weatherhill, 1978.

Campbell, Duncan. "Flawed Jade: Zhang Dai's Family Biographies." *Ming Studies* 62 (2010) 25–55.

_____. "Madman or Genius: Yuan Hongdao's 'Biography of Xu Wei.'" In *Asia 2000: Modern China in Transition*, ed. by Dov Bing, S. Lim, and M. Lin, 196–220. Hamilton, New Zealand: Outrigger Publishers, 1993.

Chang, Kang-I Sun and Haun Saussy, eds. *Women Writers of Traditional China: An Anthology of Poetry and Criticism*. Stanford: Stanford University Press, 1999.

Cheng, Liang I-Cheng. "Hsu Wei (1521–1593): His Life and Literary Works." Ph.D. diss., Ohio State University, 1973.

Chin, Frank. "Come All Ye Asian American Writers of the Real and the Fake." In *The Big Aiiieeeee! An Anthology of Chinese American and Japanese American Literature*, edited by Jeffrey Paul Chan et al., 1–92. New York: Meridian, 1991.

Chou, Chih-P'ing. *Yüan Hung-tao and the Kung-an School*. Cambridge, England: Cambridge University Press, 1988.

Chou, Hui-ling. "Striking Their Own Poses: The History of Cross-Dressing on the Chinese Stage." *The Drama Review* 41.2 (1997): 130–52.

Clunas, Craig. *Empire of Great Brightness: Visual And Material Cultures of Ming China, 1368–1644*. Honolulu: University of Hawaii, 2007.

_____. *Superfluous Things: Material Culture and Social Status in Early Modern China*. Honolulu: University of Hawaii, 1994.

Confucius. *The Analects*. Trans. D.C. Lau. London: Penguin, 1979.

Crump, J.I. *Chinese Theater in the Days of Kublai Khan*. Tucson: University of Arizona Press, 1980.

Dars, Jacques. *Contes de la montaigne sereine*. Paris: Gallimard, 1987.

Davis, Natalie Zemon. *The Return of Martin Guerre*. Cambridge: Harvard University Press, 1984.

Dolby, William. *A History of Chinese Drama*. New York: Barnes and Noble, 1976.

Dong, Lan. *Mulan's Legend and Legacy in China and the United States*. Philadelphia: Temple University Press, 2011.

_____. "Writing Chinese America into Words and Images: Storytelling and Retelling of *The Song of Mulan*." *Lion and the Unicorn: A Critical Journal of Children's Literature* 30.2 (April 2006): 218–33.

Dooling, Amy D., and Kristina M. Torgeson, eds. *Writing Women in Modern China: An Anthology of Women's Literature from the Early Twentieth Century*. New York: Columbia University Press, 1998.

Edwards, Louise. *Men and Women in Qing China: Gender in "The Red Chamber Dream."* Leiden: Brill, 1994.

_____. "Women Warriors and Amazons of the Mid Qing Texts *Jinghua Yuan* and *Honglou Meng*." *Modern Asian Studies* 29.2 (May, 1995): 225–55.

Elvin, Mark. "Tales of *Shen* and *Xin*: Body-Person and Heart-Mind in China During the Last 150 Years." In *Fragments for a History of the Human Body*, edited by Michael Feher, 267–349. New York: Urzone, 1989.

Epstein, Maram. *Competing Discourses: Orthodoxy, Authenticity, and Engendered Meanings in Late Imperial Chinese Fiction*. Cambridge: Harvard University Press, 2001.

_____. "Inscribing the Essentials: Culture and the Body in Ming-Qing Fiction." *Ming Studies* 41 (1999): 6–36.

Escolme, Bridget. *Talking to the Audience: Shakespeare, Performance, and Self*. London: Routledge, 2005.

Faurot, Jeannette Louise. "*Four Cries of a Gibbon*: A Tsa-Chü Cycle by the Ming Dramatist Hsu Wei (1521–1593)." Ph.D. diss., University of California at Berkeley, 1972.

_____. "Hsu Wen-Ch'ang: An Archetypal Clever Rascal in Chinese Popular Culture." *Asian Folklore Studies* 36.2 (1977): 65–77.

Feng Menglong. *Stories Old and New: A Ming Dynasty Collection*. Trans. Shuhui Yang and Yunqin Yang. Seattle: University of Washington Press, 2000.

Ferguson, Andrew. *Zen's Chinese Heritage: The Masters and Their Teachings*. Somerville, MA: Wisdom: 2000.

Finnane, Antonia. *Changing Clothes in China: Fashion, History, Nation*. New York: Columbia University Press, 2008.

Furth, Charlotte. "Androgynous Males and Deficient Females: Biology and Gender Boundaries in Sixteenth- and Seventeenth-Century China." *Late Imperial China* 9.2 (1989): 1–31.

_____. *A Flourishing Yin: Gender in China's Medical History, 960–1665*. Berkeley: University of California, 1999.

Garber, Marjorie. "The Occidental Tourist: *M. Butterfly* and the Scandal of Transvestism." In *Nationalisms and Sexualities*, edited by Andrew Parker, Mary Russo, Doris Sommer, and Patricia Yaeger, 121–46. New York: Routledge, 1992.

_____. *Vested Interests: Cross-Dressing & Cultural Anxiety*. New York: Routledge, 1992.

Goffman, Erving. *The Presentation of Self in Everyday Life*. Garden City, NY: Doubleday, 1959.

Goodrich, Luther Carrington, and Chaoying Fang, eds. *Dictionary of Ming Biography, 1368–1644, Vol. 2*. New York: Columbia University Press, 1976.

Graham, A.C. *Poems of the Late T'ang*. New York: New York Review Books Classics, 2008.

Graham, William T. (Jr.) "Mi Heng's 'Rhapsody on a Parrot.'" *Harvard Journal of Asiatic Studies* 39.1 (June 1979): 39–54.

Hanan, Patrick. *The Chinese Short Story: Studies in Dating, Authorship, and Composition*. Cambridge: Harvard University Press, 1973.

_____. *The Chinese Vernacular Story*. Cambridge: Harvard University Press, 1981.

_____. "Judge Bao's Hundred Cases Reconstructed." *Harvard Journal of Asiatic Studies* 40.2 (December 1980): 301–23.

Hanshu 漢書. Compiled by Ban Gu 班固. Beijing: Zhonghua shuju, 1963.

Hay, John. "The Body Invisible in Chinese Art?" In *Body, Subject, & Power in China*, edited by Tani Barlow and Angela Zito, 42–77. Chicago: University of Chicago, 1994.

Hayden, George A. "The Courtroom Plays of the Yüan and Early Ming Periods." *Harvard Journal of Asiatic Studies* 34 (1974): 192–220.

_____. *Crime and Punishment in Medieval Chinese Drama: Three Judge Pao Plays*. Cambridge: Harvard University Press, 1978.

He, Yu-Ming. "Difficulties of Performance: The Musical Career of Xu Wei's *The Mad Drummer*." *Harvard Journal of Asiatic Studies* 68.2 (2008): 77–114.

Henry, Eric. *Chinese Amusement: The Lively Plays of Li Yü*. Hamden. CT: Archon, 1980.

_____. "The Social Significance of Nudity in Early China." *Fashion Theory* 3.4 (1999): 475–86.

Hollander, Anne. *Seeing Through Clothes*. Berkeley: University of California, 1975.

Hou Hanshu. Beijing: Zhonghua shuju, 1985.

Hsiao, Li-ling. The Eternal Present of the Past: Illustration, Theatre, and Reading in the Wan-li Period, 1573–1619. Leiden: Brill, 2007.

Hsiung, Ann-Marie. "A Feminist Re-Vision of Xu Wei's *Ci Mulan* and *Nü zhuangyuan*." In *China in a Polycentric World: Essays in Chinese Comparative Literature*, edited by Yingjin Zhang, 73–89. Stanford: Stanford University Press, 1998.

_____. "Seeking Women in Pre-Modern Chinese Drama: A Feminist Re-Vision of Ming Drama (1368–1644)." Ph.D. diss., University of Hawaii, 1995.

Huang, Ray. *1587: A Year of No Significance, the Ming Dynasty in Decline*. New Haven: Yale University Press, 1982.

Hung, Chang-tai. *Going to the People: Chinese Intellectuals and Folk Literature*. Cambridge: Harvard University Press, 1986.

Hwang, David Henry. *M. Butterfly*. New York: Plume, 1988.

Idema, Wilt L. *The Butterfly Lovers: The Legend of Liang Shanbo and Zhu Yingtai, Four Versions with Related Texts*. Indiana: Hackett, 2010.

_____. *The Dramatic Oeuvre of Chu Yu-Tun, 1379–1439*. Leiden: Brill, 1997.

_____. "Female Talent and Female Virtue: Xu Wei's *Nü zhuangyuan* and Meng Chengshun's *Zhenwen ji*." *Ming-Qing xiqu guoji yantaohui lunwen ji* 明清戲曲國際, edited by Hua Wei 華瑋 and Wang Ailing 王璦玲, 551–71. Taibei: Zhongyang yanjiuyuan zhongguo wenzhe yanjiusuo, 1998.

_____. "Madness on the Yuan Stage." *Horin* 14 (2007): 65–85.

_____. "*Yuan-Pen* as a Minor Form of Dramatic Literature in the Fifteenth and Sixteenth Centuries." *Chinese Literature: Essays, Articles, Reviews* 6.1/2 (July 1984): 53–75.

Idema, Wilt L., and Beata Grant, ed. *The Red Brush: Writing Women of Imperial China*. Cambridge: Harvard University Press, 2004.

Idema, Wilt L., and Stephen H. West. *Chinese Theater, 1100–1450: A Sourcebook*. Wiesbaden: Franz Steiner, 1982.

Jang, Scarlett Ju-Yu. "Ox-Herding Painting in the Sung Dynasty." *Artibus Asiae* 52.1/2 (1992): 54–93.

Jing, Anning. *The Water God's Temple of the Guangsheng Monastery: Cosmic Function of Art, Ritual, and Theater*. Leiden: Brill, 2002.

Kingston, Maxine Hong. *The Woman Warrior.* New York: Knopf, 1976.

Knechtges, David, trans. *Wen Xuan or Selections of Refined Literature, Volume 3.* Princeton: Princeton University Press, 1996.

Ko, Dorothy. *Cinderella's Sisters: A Revisionist History.* Berkeley: University of California Press, 2005.

Kong Shangren 孔尚任 (K'ung Shang-jen). *Taohua shan* 桃花扇. Beijing: Renmin wenxue, 1997.

_____. *The Peach Blossom Fan.* Trans. Chen Shih-Hsiang and Harold Acton. Berkeley: University of California, 1976.

Kwa, Shiamin, and Wilt Idema. *Mulan: Five Versions of a Classic Chinese Tale.* Indianapolis: Hackett, 2010.

Lai, C.M. "Messenger of Spring and Morality: Cuckoo Lore in Chinese Sources." *Journal of the American Oriental Society* 118.4 (1998): 530–42.

Lai, Sufen Sophia. "From Cross-Dressing Daughter to Lady Knight-Errant: The Origin and Evolution of Chinese Women Warriors." In *Presence and Presentation: Women in the Chinese Literati Tradition*, edited by Sherry Mou, 77–107. New York: St. Martin's, 1999.

Lan, Feng. "The Female Individual and the Empire: A Historicist Approach to Mulan and Kingston's *Woman Warrior.*" *Comparative Literature* 55.3 (Summer 2003): 229–45.

Leung, K.C. *Hsü Wei as Drama Critic: An Annotated Translation of the Nan-Tz'u Hsü-Lu.* Eugene: University of Oregon Press, 1988.

Levy, Howard. *China's Dirtiest Trickster, Folklore About Hsü Wen-ch'ang (1521–1593).* Arlington: Warm-Soft Village Press, 1974.

Li Fang 李昉, comp. *Taiping guangji* 太平廣記. Beijing: Zhonghua shuju, 1961.

Li, Siu Leung. *Cross-Dressing in Chinese Opera.* Hong Kong: Hong Kong University Press, 2003.

Li, Wai-yee. "The Collector, the Connoisseur, and Late-Ming Sensibility." *T'oung Pao* LXXXI (1995): 269–302.

_____. *Enchantment and Disenchantment. Love and Illusion in Chinese Literature.* Princeton: Princeton University Press, 1993.

_____. "Heroic Transformations: Women and National Trauma in Early Qing Literature." *Harvard Journal of Asiatic Studies* 59.2 (December 1999): 363–443.

_____. "The Idea of Authority in the Shih Chi (Records of the Historian)." *Harvard Journal of Asiatic Studies* 54.2 (1994): 345–405.

_____. "The Representation of History in *The Peach Blossom Fan.*" *Journal of the American Oriental Society* 115.3 (July–September 1995): 421–33.

_____. "The Rhetoric of Spontaneity in Late-Ming Literature." *Ming Studies* 35 (August 1995): 32–52.

Li Yu 李漁. "Bimuyu" 比目魚 [Sole mates]. In *Li Yu Quanji* 李漁全集 [Complete collection of Li Yu's work]. Vol. 5, 105–211. Hangzhou: Zhejiang guji chubanshe, 1992.

Liang, I-Cheng. "Hsu Wei (1521–1593): His Life and Literary Works." Ph.D. diss., Ohio State University, 1973.

Liao Ting 廖汀. *Xu Wenchang waizhuan* 徐文長外傳. Hong Kong: Boyi chuban ji tu youxian gongsi, 1983.

Lin Lan 林蘭. *Xu Wenchang gushi* 徐文長故事集. Shanghai: Beixin shuju, 1929.

_____. *Xu Wenchang waiji* 徐文長外集. Shanghai: Beixin shuju, 1932.

Lin Liyue 林麗月. *Yishang yu fengjiao—wan Ming de fushi fengshang yu "fuyao" lilun* 衣裳與風教 - 晚明的服飾風尚與「服妖」議論 [Costumes and customs: Late Ming clothing trends and the discourse of "outrageousness"]. *Xinshixue* 10.3 (September 1999): 111–57.

Liu Dajie. *Zhongguo wenxue fazhanshi* 中國文學發展史. Taibei: Huazheng, 1988.

Liu I-ch'ing. *Shih-shuo Hsin-Yü.* Trans. Richard B. Mather. Ann Arbor: University of Michigan Press, 2002.

Lu, Tina. *Persons, Roles, and Minds. Identity in Peony Pavilion and Peach Blossom Fan.* Stanford: Stanford University Press, 2001.

Lü Buwei 呂不韋. *The Annals of Lü Buwei* 呂氏春秋. Trans. John Knoblock and Jeffrey K Riegel. Stanford: Stanford University Press, 2000.

Luo Guanzhong 羅貫中. *Sanguo zhi yanyi* 三國志演義. Hong Kong: Shangwu yinshuguan, 1962.

______. *Three Kingdoms: A Historical Novel, Complete and Unabridged.* Trans. Moss Roberts. Berkeley: University of California Press, 1991.

Luo Qiuzhao 羅秋昭. *Xu Wei "Sishengyuan" yanjiu* 徐渭四聲猿研究. Taibei: Qiye shuju youxian gongsi, 1979.

Ma, Y.W. "The Textual Tradition of Ming Kung-an Fiction: A Study of The Lung-t'u Kung-an." *Harvard Journal of Asiatic Studies* 35 (1975): 190–220.

Mao Wenfang 毛文芳. "Looking at Oneself: An Analysis of Portrait Inscriptions of Ming Figures" (*Guankan ziwo: mingren shuxiang ziti xilun*) 觀看自我: 明人畫像自題析論, in *The Proceedings of the 2006 International Research Conference on Ming Dynasty Literature and Culture* (2006 *nian mingdai wenxue yu wenhua guojixue shuyan taohui fabio lunwen*「2006 年明代文學與文化國際學術研討會」 發表論文), 99–158. Hangzhou: Zhejiang University, 2006.

Marra, Michele. "The Buddhist Mythmaking of Defilement: Sacred Courtesans in Medieval Japan." *The Journal of Asian Studies* 52.1 (1993): 49–65.

McMullen, David. "Recollection Without Tranquility: Du Fu, the Imperial Gardens, and the State." *Asia Major* 14.2 (2001): 189–252.

Meisel, Martin. *How Plays Work: Reading and Performance.* Oxford: Oxford University Press, 2007.

Mencius. Trans. D.C. Lau. London: Penguin, 1970.

Mikkelson, Douglas. "'Who Is Arguing About the Cat?' Moral Action and Enlightenment According to Dogen." *Philosophy East and West* 47.3 (1997): 383–97.

Minford, John, and Joseph S. M. Lau, eds. *Classical Chinese Literature.* New York: Columbia University Press, 2000.

Moore, Oliver. *Rituals of Recruitment in Tang China: Reading an Annual Programme in the Collected Statements by Wang Dingbao (870–940).* Leiden: Brill, 2004.

Mulan. Dir. Barry Cook and Tony Bancroft. Walt Disney Productions, 1998.

Nagel, Thomas. "What Is It Like to Be a Bat?" *The Philosophical Review* LXXXIII, 4 (October 1974): 435–50.

Nienhauser, William H. *The Indiana Companion to Traditional Chinese Literature.* Bloomington: University of Indiana Press, 1986–1998.

Orgel, Stephen. *Impersonations: The Performance of Gender in Shakespeare's England.* Cambridge: Cambridge University Press, 1996.

Owen, Stephen. *An Anthology of Chinese Literature: Beginnings to 1911.* New York: Norton, 1996.

_____. "'I Don't Want to Act as Emperor Any More': Finding the Genuine in 'Peach Blossom Fan.'" *Trauma and Transcendence in Early Qing Literature*, edited by Wilt L. Idema, Wai-yee Li, and Ellen Widmer, 488–512. Cambridge: Harvard University Press, 2006.

Peterson, Barbara Bennett, ed. *Notable Women of China: Shang Dynasty to the Early Twentieth Century.* New York: M.E. Sharpe, 2000.

Plaks, Andrew. "Riddles and Enigma in Chinese Civilization." In *Untying the Knot. On Riddles and Other Enigmatic Modes,* edited by Galit Hasan-Rokem and David Shulman, 227–236. New York: Oxford University Press, 1996.

Ruitenbeek, Klaas. *Carpentry and Building in Late Imperial China: A Study of the Fifteenth-Century Carpenter's Manual* Lu Ban Jing. Leiden: Brill, 1996.

Ryor, Kathleen. "Regulating the *Qi* and the *Xin*: Xu Wei (1521–1593) and His Military Patrons." *Archives of Asian Art* LIV (2004): 23–33.

Schmidt, Jerry Dean. *Harmony Garden: The Life, Literary Criticism, and Poetry of Yuan Mei (1716–1798).* New York: Routledge, 2003.

Shen, Guangren. *Elite Theatre in Ming China, 1368–1644.* New York: Routledge, 2005.

Shen, Jing. "Role Types in *The Paired Fish,* a Chuanqi Play." *Asian Theatre Journal* 20.2 (Autumn 2003): 226–36.

Sima Qian. *Records of the Grand Historian.* Trans. Burton Watson. Hong Kong: Chinese University of Hong Kong, 1993.

Sommer, Matthew. "Dangerous Males, Vulnerable Males, and Polluted Males: The Regulation of Masculinity in Qing Dynasty Law." In *Chinese Femininities/Chinese Masculinities*, edited by Susan Brownell and Jeffrey N. Wasserstrom. Berkeley: University of California Press, 2002, 67–89.

Soothill, Edward. *A Dictionary of Buddhist Terms: With Sanskrit and English Equivalents and a Sanskrit-Pali Index.* New York: Routledge, 2004.

Spence, Jonathan. *Return to Dragon Mountain: Memories of a Late Ming Man.* New York: Viking, 2007.

_____. *The Search for Modern China.* New York: Norton, 1990.

Strassberg, Richard, ed and trans. *A Chinese Bestiary: Strange Creatures from the Guideways Through Mountains and Seas (Shanhai jing).* Berkeley: University of California Press, 2002.

Struve, Lynn. "History and *The Peach Blossom Fan*." *Chinese Literature: Essays, Articles, Reviews (CLEAR)* 2.1 (January 1980): 55–72.

Sung, Nien-Hsu. *Un Enfant Terrible. Siu Wen-Tch'ang (Traduit des récits populaires de Mme Lin Lan).* Peking: Imprimerie de la Politique de Pékin, 1931.

Taiping Guangji 太平廣記. Beijing: Zhonghuashuju, 1961.

Tang shi sanbai shou xin zhu 唐詩三百首新注. Ann. Jin Xingyao 金性堯. Shanghai: Shanghai guji chubanshe, 1980.

Thomas, Dana. *Deluxe: How Luxury Lost Its Luster.* New York: Penguin, 2007.

Tian, Xiaofei. *Tao Yuanming and Manuscript Culture: The Record of a Dusty Table.* Seattle: University of Washington Press, 2005.

Tu, Ching-I. "Neo-Confucianism and Literary Criticism in Ming China: The Case of T'ang Shun-chih (1507–60)." *Tamkang Review* 15 (1984–85): 548–60.

Van Gulik, Robert. *The Gibbon in China, an Essay in Chinese Animal Lore.* Leiden: Brill, 1967.

Volpp, Sophie. "Gender, Power, and Spectacle in Late-Imperial Chinese Theater." In *Gender Reversals and Gender Cultures: Anthropological and Historical Perspectives*, edited by Sabrina Petra Ramet, 138–47. London: Routledge, 1996.

_____. *Worldly Stage: Theatricality in Seventeenth-Century China.* Cambridge: Harvard University Press, 2011.

Waltner, Anne. "From Casebook to Fiction: Kung-An in Late Imperial China." *Journal of the American Oriental Society* 110.2 (April–June 1990): 281–89.

Wang Chang'an 王長安. *Xu Wei sanbian* 徐渭三辨. Beijing: Zhongguo xiju chubanshe 中國戲劇出版社, 1995.

Wang Shifu. *The Story of the Western Wing.* Translated by Wilt Idema and Stephen West Berkeley: University of California Press, 1995.

Wang Zhiyong 汪志勇. *"Du Liu Cui" "Cuixiang meng" yu "Honglian zhai" sanju de bijiao yanjiu* 度柳翠翠鄉夢與紅蓮債三劇的比較研究. M.A. thesis. Taibei: 1979.

West. Stephen H., and Wilt L. Idema, eds. and trans. *Monks, Bandits, Lovers, and Immortals: Eleven Early Chinese Plays.* Indianapolis: Hackett, 2010.

Wixted, John Timothy. *Poems on Poetry: Literary Criticism by Yuan Hao-Wen (1190–1257).* Wiesbaden: Steiner, 1982.

_____, ed. and trans. *Five Hundred Years of Chinese Poetry: 1150–1650.* Princeton, NJ: Princeton University Press, 1989.

Xu Lun. *Xu Wenchang.* Shanghai: Shanghai renmin chubanshe, 1962.

Xu Wei 徐渭. *Sishengyuan. Guben xiqu congkan chuji* 古本戲曲叢刊初集. Vol. 77. Shanghai: Shanghai yinshuguan, 1954.

_____. *Sishengyuan Gedaixiao fu* 四聲猿歌代嘯附. Ed. Zhou Zhongming. Shanghai: Shanghai guji chubanshe, 1984.

_____. *Xu Wei Ji.* 4 vols. Beijing: Zhonghua shuju, 1983.

_____. *Xu Wenchang yigao.* Shanghai: Shanghai zazhi gongsi, 1936.

Yang Ye, ed. and trans. *Vignettes from the Late Ming. A Hsiao-P'in Anthology.* Seattle: University of Washington Press, 1999.

Yen, Yuan-shu, trans. "Yellow Millet Dream." *Tamkang Review* 6 (1975): 205–39.

Yuan Hongdao. *Yuan Zhonglang xiaopin* 袁中郎小品. Beijing: Wenhua yishu chubanshe, 1996.

Yuanqu xuan jiaozhu 元曲選校注. Ed. Wang Xueqi 王學奇. Shijiazhuang: Hebei jiaoyu, 1994.

Yuanqu xuan waibian 元曲選外編. Ed. Sui Shusen 隋樹森. Beijing: Zhonghua shuju, 1961.

Yuefu shiji 樂府詩集. Beijing: Zhonghua shuju, 1979.

Zeitlin, Judith. *Historian of the Strange. Pu Songling and the Chinese Classical Tale.* Stanford: Stanford University Press, 1993.

Zeng Xiba 曾西霸. *Xu Wei "Nü zhuangyuan" yanjiu.* Ph.D. diss. Taibei: Zhongguo wenhua xueyuan, 1978.

Zhang Dai 張岱. *Zhang Zongzi xiaopin* 張宗子小品. Beijing: Wenhua yishu chubanshe, 1996.

Zhang Xiaoyu 張孝裕. *Xu Wei yanjiu* 徐渭研究. Taibei: Xuehai chubanshe, 1978.

Index

acting, 26–27; actors, 5, 6, 12, 16, 42, 43, 59, 65, 103; as inhabiting, 4 (see also *Lan Caihe*); play-acting, 6, 9, 26, 39, 59, 71, 81–83, 95–99, 101, 103–4. *See also* *drama, roles, performance, theatricality*
Allen, Joseph, 77, 253
Annals of Lu Buwei, 248
audience, 16, 25, 27, 74–75, 107
authenticity, 9, 16, 80–81, 88–89; in drama, 10, 88–89
azaleas, 95–100, 219n

Ban Gu, 224n
Ban Zhao, 224n
"Bared Belly of the East." *See* Wang Xizhi
bense. See authenticity
Biographies of Eminent Women. See *Lienü zhuan*
Bodhidharma, 141n
body, 10, 11, 16, 35–36, 38, 43, 64–65; of actors, 5, 64–65
Brecht, Bertolt, 28
Butler, Judith, 72–73, 252
Brook, Timothy, 25, 246
Buddhism, 199n. *See also* Zen Buddhism

Cai Yong, 222n
Campbell, Duncan, 4–5, 243, 244
Cao Cao, 16, 17, 18–19, 28–36, 117n, 119n, 121n, 124n, 125n, 128n, 129n, 132n, 133n, 134n, 227n
Cao E, 222n
Cao Zhi, 119n
Chen Ping, 165n
Chen Zi'ang, 215n
chou, 11
chuanqi, 6, 86, 104
clothing, 7, 20–21, 25; costume, 37, 54, 59, 64–67, 69, 95–97; cross-dressing, 38, 72–83, 84–85, 105, 202n; in *Girl Graduate*, 85, 87, 95–99, 237n; in *Mulan*, 63–67, 69, 72–83, 253; disguise, 71, 95–97; improper dress, 19, 20–22, 24, 35; ornament, 96–97; relationship to language, 25, 54, 96–97; removal of, 7, 19, 25, 60–61, 85. *See also* foot-binding
Clunas, Craig, 245
Confucius, 20, 121n, 246
Consort Dong, 123n
Contes de la Montaigne sereine, 249
Copperbird Terrace, 119n, 134n
costume. *See* clothing
courtroom. *See* trials
cross-dressing. *See* clothing
cuckoo (*dujuan*), 219n

dan. See role types
Daoism, 40, 137n, 138n, 209n, 212n; Zhuangzi 156n
deliverance plays, 39–42, 47
Delivering Liu Cui, 39–41, 46, 247, 249
dharma, 140n
disguise. *See* clothing
Dong Cheng, 123n
Dongfang Shuo, 138n
drama 5–8, 12–14, 27, 28, 39, 65, 104, 108–109; *See also* chuanqi, zaju
dramatic irony, 10

dress. *See* clothing
drumming, 16–18, 130n; Yuyang triple rolls, 17, 33–34, 117n, 138n
Du Fu, 189n, 193n, 195n, 196n, 215n, 217n
Du Mu, 227n
Duke Mu of Qin, 221n, 235n

Elvin, Mark, 10, 245
Empress Fu, 125n
evidence, 57, 74–75, 87, 93–95, 99

falseness, 38
Faurot, Jeannette, 51, 243, 244, 251, 255
Female Mulan Joins the Army in Place of Her Father, The (*Ci Mulan tifu congjun*), 5, 7, 8, 12, 63–83, 85, 87, 254–55
Feng Menglong, 46, 199n, 250
Finnane, Antonia, 256, 257
foot-binding, 64, 76–78, 81, 172n, 173n
forgeries, 88, 102–4
Four Cries of a Gibbon (*Si sheng yuan*), 5, 7–9, 13, 113, 254–55. *See also individual listings by play title*
Furth, Charlotte, 12, 245

Garber, Marjorie, 73, 252
Ge dai xiao. See *Singing in Place of Screaming*
gender, 12, 63, 68–69, 70–71, 72–83, 96; gender performance, 72–75
gibbon, 156n
girl of Yue, 173n
Girl Graduate Rejects the Female Phoenix and Gains the Male Phoenix, The (*Nü zhuangyuan cihuang defeng*), 5, 7, 8, 12, 84–104, 254–55
Goffman, Erving, 26–27, 246
Guan Hanqing, 211n, 218n
Guanyin, 153n

Handan Dream. *See* Yellow Millet Dream
Han Wendi (Emperor Wen of the Han), 170n, 214n
Han Xin, 121n
Han Yu, 129n, 225n
Hanan, Patrick, 249
Hay, John, 11
Hayden, George, 93–94, 255
He, Yuming, 246
Henry, Eric, 245
hiding, 17, 72, 74–75
homophones, 161n, 200n
homonyms, 197n
Hsiao, Li-ling, 247
Hsiung, Ann-Marie, 248
Huan Tingjian, 216n
Huan Wen, 216n
Huang Chonggu, 85, 87–93, 96–104; literary antecedents, 92–93; for play of this title see *The Girl Graduate Rejects the Female Phoenix and Gains the Male Phoenix*
Huyang, Princess, 228n

Idema, Wilt, 41, 141n, 205n, 245, 246, 250, 254
identity, 39, 62, 63–65, 71, 80–82, 83, 88, 93–95, 95–98, 101, 103–4
imitation, 4, 5, 108–109
impermanence, 166n

Ji Junxiang, 61
Jin Wudi, 218n

Ko, Dorothy, 253
Kong Rong, 129n
Kong Shangren, 6, 105

Lai, Sufen, 252
Lan Caihe, 40, 42
Lan, Feng, 252
language, 13, 16, 53–54, 57, 102–103; ineffectiveness of, 56, 57; names for, 61, 64, 75; puns on, 56–57, 58–59; sound of, 57; written word, 55–57, 88–89; wordlessness, 49, 52, 60–61
Li Bo (Li Bai), 215n
Li He, 135n
Li Kaixian, 249
Li Shangyin, 135n, 232n
Li Shouqing, 46–48. See also *Delivering Liu Cui*
Li, Waiyee, 134n, 135n, 151n, 197n, 243, 246, 257

Li Zhi, 243
Liang, I-Cheng (Yi-cheng), 50–51, 251
Liang Shanbo and Zhu Yingtai, 87–88
Liang Wudi, 216n
Lienü zhuan, 221n
Liu Bang, 121n, 165n
Liu Bei (Xuande), 125n, 186n
Liu Biao, 125n
Liu Cong, 125n
Liu Cui, 37, 38, 46, 47, 59–62, 251
Liu Qi, 125n
Liu Xie (Xiandi), 122n, 123n, 125n
Liu Yong, 165n
Lu Ban, 215n
Lu, Tina, 6, 245
Luo Qiuzhao, 50, 245, 251

Mad Drummer Plays the Yuyang Triple Rolls, The (*Kuang guli yuyang sannong*), 5, 7, 12, 15–36, 85
madness, 16, 17, 20
Male Queen, The (*Nan wanghou*), 253
Mei Xiang, 237n
Mencius, 185n, 191n
Meng Jiao, 177n, 225n
Mi Heng, 18–19, 117n, 210n; "Rhapsody on a Parrot," 130n; for the play by this name see *The Mad Drummer Plays the Yuyang Triple Rolls*
Ming drama, 13
Mister Guo (Guo lang), 164n
Moonlight Monk (character), 37, 44, 47–50, 57–60; for plays that use the shortened title *Moonlight Monk* see *Zen Master Yu* or *The Moonlight Monk Delivers Liu Cui*; for *The Moonlight Monk Delivers Liu Cui* (*Yueming heshang du Liu Cui*) see *Delivering Liu Cui*
Mulan (*Mulan shi* ballad), 67–71
Mulan (character), 67–71; antecedents, 100, 254n
Mulan (play). See *The Female Mulan Joins the Army in Place of Her Father*

names. *See* language
Nanci xulu, 5
Nongyu, 186n, 212n. *See also* Xiaoshi
nudity, 12, 18, 73

Orphan of Zhao, The (*Zhaoshi guer*), 61

Peach Blossom Fan (*Taohua shan*), 6, 105–7, 257
Peach Blossom Spring, 149n
Peony Pavilion (*Mudan ting*), 6
performance, 8–9, 16, 27, 28, 30–32, 63, 70–71, 78; gender performance *See* gender; verbal performances, 27, 78; within a performance, 26, 29–30, 33;
play, 9; play within a play *See* performance
play-acting, *See* acting
puns. *See* language

qilin, 175n; Qilin study 217n
Qiao Zhou, 215n
Qin Xiu, 76, 79, 170n
Qingming, 144n, 146n, 219n
Qiu Jin, 107–8, 257

Raising the Beam, 222n
reading, 5, 9, 44
Records of the Grand Historian. See Sima Qian
Red Lotus, 43–44, 45, 47–52, 143n, 149n, 165n
reincarnation, 43, 44, 47, 52, 57, 159n
repetition, 17, 53
representation 3, 109
roles, 41, 94–95, 107–109, *chou* 11; *dan* 11, 51, 52, 61, 248; role-playing, *see* performance; role types, 11, 13, 51, 115, 245; *sheng*, 43, 51, 52; *tie*, 43, 51; *wai*, 44
Ruan Zhao, 154n

self, 10, 13, 64, 65, 80–82, 88, 102, 105, 107–9
self-introduction, 17, 28–29, 89
Shakespeare, William, 28, 55, 87
sheng. *See* roles
Shi Chong, 218n
Shiji. *See* Sima Qian
Shijing, 126n

Shishuo xinyu 171n, 216n
Sima Qian 21–24, 121n, 133n
Sima Xiangru, 195n, 215n, 219n. *See also* Zhuo Wenjun
sincerity, 4, 88
Singing in Place of Screaming (*Ge dai xiao*), 113
song, 15–17, 25, 28, 43; stage song, 16, 30–31, 34
Song Yu, 211n, 212n
Spence, Jonathan, 257
spontaneity, 9, 53
Story of the Western Wing (*Xixiang ji*) 9,
Su Shi (Su Dongpo), 46, 148n
subjectivity, 10
Sun Ce, 119n
Sun Chuo, 131n
Sun Quan, 125n, 186n, 227n

Taiping guangji, 209n, 255
Tan, Tianyuan, 251
Tang Shuyu, 209n
Tang Taizong (Emperor Taizong of the Tang), 174n, 178n,
Tang Xianzu, 6
Tao Qian (Tao Yuanming), 149n, 202n
theatricality 2, 9, 25, 27, 105
Three Kingdoms, 186n
Tiying, 76, 79, 169n
tie. See roles
trials, 16, 25–26, 29, 85; and *Girl Graduate* 86–88, 90–91, 93–95. *See also* evidence
Tuoba, 169n

Volpp, Sophie, 254

Waltner, Anne, 254
Wang Bao, 215n
Wang Can, 121n
Wang Changling, 233n
Wang Jide, 37, 39, 253
Wang Huizhi, 217n
Wang Xizhi, 171n, 217n, 239n
Wang Zhiyong, 248
Wei Dan, 217n
West, Stephen, 248
witness, 56
wordlessness. *See* language

Xianbei, 169n
Xiandi. *See* Liu Xie
Xiang of Chu, King (Xiang Yu), 133n, 165n, 211n, 212n
Xiang Ping, 212n
Xiao He, 217n
Xiao Shi, 186n, 212n, 234n. *See also* Nongyu
Xiao Ziyun, 216n
Xie An, 224n
Xie Daoyun, 224n
Xu Wei (Xu Wenchang), life, 1–4; poetry, 4, 244; prose, 3, 4, 9–10. See also *Four Cries of a Gibbon* (*Si sheng yuan*); *Nanci xulu*; *Singing in Place of Screaming* (*Ge dai xiao*)
Xuande. *See* Liu Bei
Xuanwudi, 209n
Xue Tao, 223n

Yang Xiong, 214n
Yang Xiu, 128n
Ye, Yang, 244
Yellow Millet Dream, 163n, 248
Yuan, 61, 86
Yuan Zheng, 154n
Yu Tong, 37, 43–44
Yu Xuanji, 255
Yuan Hongdao, 2, 5, 113, 244
Yurang, 21–25
Yutong, 43, 51–52, 55–62
Yuyang Triple Rolls. *See* drumming

Zaju, 5–6, 15, 39; Yuan 40–42, 61, 86, 248
Zeitlin, Judith, 251
Zen Buddhism, 45–46, 49–54, 142n, 247, 249; anecdotes, 139n; "Eyes of perception," 146n; koans, 142n
Zen Master Yu Has a Dream of Cuixiang (*Yü chanshi cuixiang yimeng*), 5, 7, 12, 37–62; antecedents, 45–50
Zeng Xiba, 255

Zhang Dai, 2, 4
Zhang Fengyi, 127n
Zhang Liang, 165n
Zhang Shizhi, 214n
Zhang Yuanbian, 4, 249
Zhou Yu, 119n, 227n
Zhou Zhongming, 114, 165n
Zhuge Liang, 119n, 131n, 214n
Zhuo Wenjun, 196n, 205n, 219n. *See also* Sima Xiangru

Harvard-Yenching Institute Monograph Series
(titles now in print)

24. *Population, Disease, and Land in Early Japan, 645–900*, by William Wayne Farris
25. *Shikitei Sanba and the Comic Tradition in Edo Fiction*, by Robert W. Leutner
26. *Washing Silk: The Life and Selected Poetry of Wei Chuang (834?–910)*, by Robin D. S. Yates
28. *Tang Transformation Texts: A Study of the Buddhist Contribution to the Rise of Vernacular Fiction and Drama in China*, by Victor H. Mair
30. *Readings in Chinese Literary Thought*, by Stephen Owen
31. *Remembering Paradise: Nativism and Nostalgia in Eighteenth-Century Japan*, by Peter Nosco
33. *Escape from the Wasteland: Romanticism and Realism in the Fiction of Mishima Yukio and Oe Kenzaburo*, by Susan Jolliffe Napier
34. *Inside a Service Trade: Studies in Contemporary Chinese Prose*, by Rudolf G. Wagner
35. *The Willow in Autumn: Ryutei Tanehiko, 1783–1842*, by Andrew Lawrence Markus
36. *The Confucian Transformation of Korea: A Study of Society and Ideology*, by Martina Deuchler
37. *The Korean Singer of Tales*, by Marshall R. Pihl
38. *Praying for Power: Buddhism and the Formation of Gentry Society in Late-Ming China*, by Timothy Brook
39. *Word, Image, and Deed in the Life of Su Shi*, by Ronald C. Egan
40. *The Chinese Virago: A Literary Theme*, by Yenna Wu
41. *Studies in the Comic Spirit in Modern Japanese Fiction*, by Joel R. Cohn
42. *Wind Against the Mountain: The Crisis of Politics and Culture in Thirteenth-Century China*, by Richard L. Davis
43. *Powerful Relations: Kinship, Status, and the State in Sung China (960–1279)*, by Beverly Bossler
44. *Limited Views: Essays on Ideas and Letters*, by Qian Zhongshu; selected and translated by Ronald Egan
45. *Sugar and Society in China: Peasants, Technology, and the World Market*, by Sucheta Mazumdar
49. *Precious Volumes: An Introduction to Chinese Sectarian Scriptures from the Sixteenth and Seventeenth Centuries*, by Daniel L. Overmyer
50. *Poetry and Painting in Song China: The Subtle Art of Dissent*, by Alfreda Murck
51. *Evil and/or/as the Good: Omnicentrism, Intersubjectivity, and Value Paradox in Tiantai Buddhist Thought*, by Brook Ziporyn

52. *Chinese History: A Manual, Revised and Enlarged Edition,* by Endymion Wilkinson
53. *Articulated Ladies: Gender and the Male Community in Early Chinese Texts*, by Paul Rouzer
54. *Politics and Prayer: Shrines to Local Former Worthies in Sung China*, by Ellen Neskar
55. *Allegories of Desire: Esoteric Literary Commentaries of Medieval Japan*, by Susan Blakeley Klein
56. *Printing for Profit: The Commercial Publishers of Jianyang, Fujian (11th–17th Centuries)*, by Lucille Chia
57. *To Become a God: Cosmology, Sacrifice, and Self-Divinization in Early China*, by Michael J. Puett
58. *Writing and Materiality in China: Essays in Honor of Patrick Hanan*, edited by Judith T. Zeitlin and Lydia H. Liu
59. *Rulin waishi and Cultural Transformation in Late Imperial China*, by Shang Wei
60. *Words Well Put: Visions of Poetic Competence in the Chinese Tradition*, by Graham Sanders
61. *Householders: The Reizei Family in Japanese History,* by Steven D. Carter
62. *The Divine Nature of Power: Chinese Ritual Architecture at the Sacred Site of Jinci*, by Tracy Miller
63. *Beacon Fire and Shooting Star: The Literary Culture of the Liang (502–557)*, by Xiaofei Tian
64. *Lost Soul: "Confucianism" in Contemporary Chinese Academic Discourse*, by John Makeham
65. *The Sage Learning of Liu Zhi: Islamic Thought in Confucian Terms*, by Sachiko Murata, William C. Chittick, and Tu Weiming
66. *Through a Forest of Chancellors: Fugitive Histories in Liu Yuan's* Lingyan ge*, an Illustrated Book from Seventeenth-Century Suzhou*, by Anne Burkus-Chasson
67. *Empire of Texts in Motion: Chinese, Korean, and Taiwanese Transculturations of Japanese Literature*, by Karen Laura Thornber
68. *Empire's Twilight: Northeast Asia Under the Mongols*, by David M. Robinson
69. *Ancestors, Virgins, and Friars: Christianity as a Local Religion in Late Imperial China*, by Eugenio Menegon
70. *Manifest in Words, Written on Paper: Producing and Circulating Poetry in Tang Dynasty China*, by Christopher M. B. Nugent
71. *The Poetics of Sovereignty: On Emperor Taizong of the Tang Dynasty*, by Jack W. Chen
72. *Ancestral Memory in Early China*, by K. E. Brashier
73. *'Dividing the Realm in Order to Govern': The Spatial Organization of the Song State,* by Ruth Mostern
74. *The Dynamics of Masters Literature: Early Chinese Thought from Confucius to Han Feizi*, by Wiebke Denecke
75. *Songs of Contentment and Transgression: Discharged Officials and Literati Communities in Sixteenth-Century North China*, by Tian Yuan Tan
76. *Ten Thousand Scrolls: Reading and Writing in the Poetics of Huang Tingjian and the Late Northern Song*, by Yugen Wang
77. *A Northern Alternative: Xue Xuan (1389–1464) and the Hedong School*, by Khee Heong Koh
78. *Visionary Journeys: Travel Writings from Early Medieval and Nineteenth-Century China*, by Xiaofei Tian
79. *Making Personas: Transnational Film Stardom in Modern Japan*, by Hideaki Fujiki
80. *Strange Eventful Histories: Identity, Performance, and Xu Wei's* Four Cries of a Gibbon, by Shiamin Kwa